Walking the Woods and the Water

Vivid and hard-won.

–Giles Foden, Condé Nast Traveller

Nick Hunt has written a glorious book, rich with insight and wit, about walking his way both across and into contemporary Europe. He set out in homage to Patrick Leigh Fermor's legendary tramp across Europe in the early 1930s, but his journey became – of course – an epic adventure in its own right.

What an achievement! Good writing about walking, even when the destination is not in doubt, can be weirdly compelling to the reader, and so it was with this brilliant book, which was – to me – a page-turner, and this was in large part due to the style and sharpness of eye and ear. So many memorable encounters with people and places! I shared your joys at the mist-swirled Danube, still wild despite the dams; at the ice-gripped German forests; and at the pleasures of being alone and in motion in the world. I think my favourite moment of all – and how PLF would have loved it – was when, exhausted and freezing, and in the beginnings of real trouble, you suddenly stumbled across the pilgrim-shack, with a made-up bed ready for you to sink into it! Magnificent. It stood, too, as an emblem for the hospitality you received along the way.

A book about gifts, modernity, endurance and landscape, it represents a fine addition to the literature of the leg.

–Robert MacFarlane, *author of* The Wild Places *and* The Old Ways: A Journey on Foot

In 2011 a rather older Nick Hunt, who as an eighteen-year-old had been inspired by A Time of Gifts, set out to follow in Paddy's footsteps. Walking the Woods and the Water is his account of the same journey seventy-eight years later, a narrative that ranks alongside Paddy's in its adventure, its observation of culture and nature, and in the quality of writing.

–**Peter Reason**, *author of* Spindrift: A Wilderness
Pilgrimage at Sea

This moving and profoundly honest book sometimes brings a sense of unlimited freedom, sometimes joy, sometimes an extraordinary, dream-like dislocation: always accompanied by a dazzling sharpness of hearing and vision. I see now how that youthful walk informed so much of Paddy's style. Before setting out Hunt was going to write to Paddy. The letter was never written, and by the time he set off, Paddy was dead. How touched and fascinated he would have been to read this book.

–**Artemis Cooper**, The Spectator, *author of* Patrick Leigh
Fermor: An Adventure, *co-editor* The Broken Road

In his 2,500-mile journey, which took him through eight countries, he nearly froze to death and he had innumerable encounters with the kindness of strangers. Hunt's narrative mixes description elegantly with reportage.

–**New Statesman**

The journalist's modern-day walk in a travel writing legend's footsteps reveal the heart of central Europe. ... Delightful, balanced and extremely well-written ... an impressive and timely effort. A worthy literary tribute to the classic of British travel writing.

–**Vitali Vitaliev**, E&T Magazine, *author of*
Passport to Enclavia

Walking the Woods and the Water

In Patrick Leigh Fermor's Footsteps
from the Hook of Holland to the Golden Horn

Nick Hunt

NICHOLAS BREALEY
PUBLISHING

London · Boston

For Caroline, who taught me to walk

First published by
Nicholas Brealey Publishing in 2014

Reprinted 2014

3–5 Spafield Street   20 Park Plaza
Clerkenwell, London   Boston
EC1R 4QB, UK   MA 02116, USA
Tel: +44 (0)20 7239 0360   Tel: (888) BREALEY
Fax: +44 (0)20 7239 0370   *Fax: (617) 523 3708*
www.nicholasbrealey.com
www.nickhuntscrutiny.com

ISBN: 978-1-85788-617-7
eISBN: 978-1-85788-953-6

British Library Cataloguing in Publication Data
A catalogue record for this book is available from the
British Library.

Printed in the UK by Clays Ltd, St Ives plc.

Contents

From Hook to Horn

*I would travel on foot, sleep in hayricks in summer, shelter
in barns when it was raining or snowing and only consort
with peasants and tramps. If I lived on bread and cheese
and apples, jogging along on fifty pounds a year ... there
would even be some cash left over for paper and pencils and
an occasional mug of beer. A new life! Freedom! Something
to write about!*

A Time of Gifts

IN DECEMBER 1933, EIGHTEEN-YEAR-OLD PATRICK LEIGH FERMOR
set out in a pair of hobnailed boots to chance and charm
his way across Europe, 'like a tramp, a pilgrim or a wandering scholar', on foot from the Hook of Holland to Istanbul.
The books he later wrote about this walk, *A Time of Gifts*
(1977), *Between the Woods and the Water* (1986) and the post-
humous *The Broken Road* (2013), are a half-remembered,
half-reimagined journey through cultures now extinct,
landscapes irrevocably altered by the traumas of the twentieth century. The brilliant bubble of his writing captures
a world of moccasin-shod peasants and castle-dwelling aristocrats, preserved in perfect clarity; at times his focus is so
sharp the effect is hallucinogenic. But war, political terror
and brutal social change lay on the horizon. That bubble
was about to burst, and the raw light of the modern world
would soon come flooding in.

I encountered these books when I too was eighteen, and
they had a deep impact on me. On the simplest level, the
narrative of a young man setting out to find his place in the
world was something I identified with, because that's what

1

I was trying to do; I admired his guts, his panache, his inexhaustible delight, even if some of his fascinations – High Baroque architecture and the bloodlines of Europe's noble families – were things I could hardly relate to. But the essential spirit of the books – the essential spirit of Paddy himself – sunk into my subconscious and never went away.

And that spirit had company there. The irresistible archetype of a wanderer in unknown lands first materialised in the figure of my great-uncle, mountaineer John Hunt, who led the first successful ascent of Everest in 1953. I had grown up on his tales, wondrously embellished over the years, of weird howls above the wind and yeti footprints in the snow around his tent. His house was crammed with souvenirs from a lifetime of adventures, and his antiquated climbing gear – cracked leather and polished wood, ludicrous-looking oxygen tanks, gloves the size of wellington boots – seemed like artefacts from an age of greater magic. As a child I accepted that he had been to the realm of gods, a pure and everlasting place far beyond man's ordinary reach; rare adventurers such as him might be permitted to visit a while, but when they left, the mountain would return to its timelessness. The knowledge that such places existed – as secure as fairytales, or my own imaginary worlds – was deeply comforting.

Paddy's vision of an older, wilder Europe hooked me in a similar fashion. Before I'd finished reading the books, I knew with absolute certainty that one day I would follow in his footsteps, retracing his route through Holland, Germany, Austria, Slovakia, Hungary, Romania, Bulgaria and Turkey, in search of whatever was left of wildness and adventure. One passage from A *Time of Gifts* – spoken by an old polymath in Austria in 1934 – particularly haunted me: 'Everything is going to vanish! They talk of building power-dams across the Danube and I tremble whenever I think of it! They'll make the wildest river in Europe as tame as a municipal waterworks. All those fish from the East – they would never come back. Never, never, never!'

Those words articulated my quest. Had Europe been tamed? Had everything vanished? One day, I would walk until I found the answer.

The idea lay dormant for twelve years. Perhaps if I'd lived in a different time I might have set off there and then, but I came of age in an era of untaxed aviation fuel and limitless opportunities for travel; Europe, diluted – so I imagined – by the homogenising forces of modernisation and globalisation, would have to wait. Who wanted to visit Germany, when India was a short flight away? Why bother with the Rhine, when I could see the Ganges?

After a decade of jetting off to distant corners of the world, however, the instant gratification of flying began to lose its magic. I no longer enjoyed the sensation of being ripped out of time and place, of distance divorced from effort. I'd been to places remote and strange and gorged myself on the unknown, but I hardly knew a thing about the continent I lived in. That half-forgotten fantasy of following in Paddy's footsteps swam back into focus, and as I reread the books, the impulse returned with urgency: I was almost in my thirties, and if I didn't do it now, I probably never would.

The simplicity of walking – the essential humanness of putting one foot in front of the other – made a deep kind of sense. The more I thought about taking that first step, and following it with another, and another, the more fundamental it felt. What better way to know Europe than to expose myself to it completely, to be aware of each splatter of rain, each stone beneath my feet? How better to understand the processes of loss and change than to travel in the shadow of Paddy's words? Above all, what better way to have an old-fashioned adventure?

Once I had set a date - 9 December 2011, exactly
seventy-eight years after Paddy started his walk - I prepared
as little as possible. I stubbornly refused to train: walking,
I decided, was an activity as natural as breathing, requir-
ing no special preparation (this romantic optimism caused
a lot of pain). It was important not to go as journalist,
but journeyer; in an age of total information, I preferred
to make my way in a spirit of wide-eyed discovery, to let
the continent surprise me. For this reason, beyond buying roadmaps and putting out calls for accommodation, I
deliberately did no research into where I was going. Paddy's
books, eight decades out of date, would be my only travel
guide. With his experience underlying my own, I would see
what remained of hospitality, kindness to strangers, freedom, wildness, adventure, the mysterious, the unknown,
the deeper currents of myth and story I believed - or longed
to believe - still flowed beneath Europe's surface.

Six months before I started, Patrick Leigh Fermor died,
at the age of ninety-six. For weeks, I'd been planning to
send a letter to his home in Kardamyli, Greece, where
generations of travel writers had gone to pay literary homage, to explain my reasons for following his road. I'd even
written 'Dear Paddy' at the top of a sheet of paper, but
hadn't known how to go on. He was an extraordinary man
- adventurer, war hero, bon viveur and raconteur - but
my interest wasn't biographical, and I wasn't trying to cast
myself as a modern-day version of him. It was his journey
itself I was after, the contrast between his walk and my
own; really, I'd simply wanted to tell him I was on my way.
Now it was too late. The walk would have to be my letter.
Through woods and water, wind and rain, fields, forests,
cities, suburbs, mountaintops and motorways, I hope he
would have approved.

WEST

A Time of Gifts

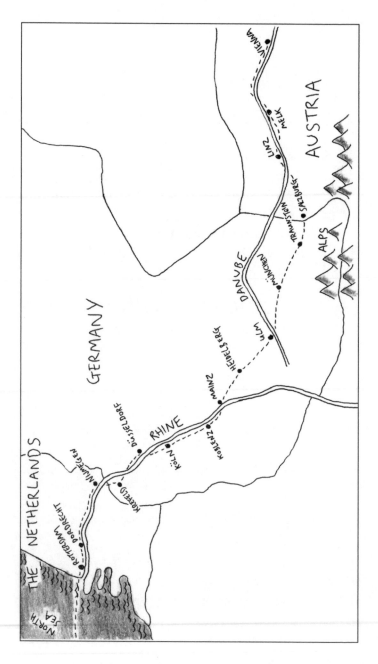

From the Hook of Holland to the Slovakian border

I

A Circuit Board of Fields and Water

The Low Countries

*Even before I looked at a map, two great rivers had already
plotted the itinerary in my mind's eye; the Rhine uncoiled
across it, the Alps rose up and then the wolf-harbouring
Carpathian watersheds and the cordilleras of the Balkans;
and there, at the end of the windings of the Danube, the
Black Sea was beginning to spread its mysterious and
lop-sided shape; and my chief destination was never in a
moment's doubt. The levitating skyline of Constantinople
pricked its sheaves of thin cylinders and its hemispheres out
of the sea-mist.*

A Time of Gifts

THERE WAS A RARE BLACK SKY OVER LONDON, A PERFECT MOON
above the streetlights; being able to see beyond the city,
even if only directly up, made it feel like the right night to
be starting. After posting my keys through the letterbox of
the flat I was leaving for good, I christened my boots on
Kingsland Road on the way to Hackney Wick, where my
girlfriend Anna and her car were waiting. It was a walk
I'd done countless times without ever needing to notice it,
but the importance of this departure suffused the familiar sights with borrowed significance, making everything
glow with a secret light. Past the steamed-up windows of
Vietnamese noodleries, past kebab shops with their revolving meats, past grubby clusters of street drinkers squatting
by cairns of empty cider cans, past smokers in skintight
jeans conversing loudly about nothing outside bars in

various stages of gentrification: the unremarkable sights of East London on a typical Friday night, which, as if through a stranger's eyes, became remarkable.

Paddy had left under torrents of rain from a different borough in a different age – 'a thousand glistening umbrellas were tilted over a thousand bowler hats in Piccadilly' – and three friends had accompanied him in a taxi to Tower Bridge, where a steamship called the *Stadthouder Willem* waited to depart. London's wharfs had long since emptied, and no ships rode at anchor now, so Anna sped me from her warehouse flat to Harwich International Port to catch the eleven o'clock ferry across the North Sea. My only perception of that road was orange lights strobing past and, as we neared the port, long-distance Netherlandish trucks looming hugely in the night, emblazoned with phlegmy strings of vowels. Both of us sat in the limbo state that exists before a long parting, in which the course of normal conversation runs suddenly up against shocked silence when you remember why it is you're actually in the car. Each silence was an overture to the physical distance ahead, notes of absence and longing filling the car with anticipatory sadness. A few hours later, Anna was no more than a tiny cone on matchstick legs, waving in a sodium-lit wasteland of parking lots and cranes. To her, I was just a smudge against the giant letter S of the *Stena Hollandica*, a ship so huge it may as well not have had a name.

The distance was too vast for shouting, so we said our goodbyes by mobile phone as the engines began to turn, churning the dock's greasy water like a stirred-up sink. Static roared as the wind picked up, and seagulls rose and plunged against the skyscraper-high steel walls. Anna's tiny form dissolved into the dirty grain of the quay, the frozen cranes and shipping containers rapidly became lost in darkness, and soon just a glow of light pollution was all that was left of England. Somewhere beyond the port, a fishing boat came bouncing over the water, the whoops of the lads on board carried on the wind: 'You crazy bastard! Stupid fucker! Crazy son of a bitch!'

I didn't take them personally, but it seemed these cries, and not my girlfriend's words of love, would be my parting shot.

From my hip flask I took a nip of the whisky I'd bought in the last Turkish corner shop, but the wind was soon too cold to write, and I went inside with crabbed pink hands. No one else had ventured outside. When Paddy embarked on his voyage, 28,489 days before, he'd been the only passenger. Now bald men sat listlessly in front of pints or fruit machines, and children played in plastic pens of brightly coloured toys. I wandered through a labyrinth of duty-free shops and safety signs, past casinos, internet stations and gleaming canteens. I found my way to the C-View Bar and sat under a flatscreen television advertising Sacher Torte for €3.75. Jazz seeped from hidden speakers. White plastic Christmas trees twinkled on their wires.

Cabin number 10303 lay in a long corridor of identical doors. I spread the contents of my rucksack over the bunk and across the floor – warm clothes, waterproof clothes, sleeping bag, tin cup, *A Time of Gifts* and *Between the Woods and the Water* swaddled in plastic bags – before packing them back in as jumbled as before. At one o'clock I fell asleep, breathing processed air. The porthole was designed not to open, so the sound and the smell of the sea lay far outside my dreams. I woke at intervals in the night and gazed through the reinforced glass; first to see the full moon silvering the waves, and later distant structures lying far out across the North Sea, gantries with blinking red lights, their purpose mysterious. Soon after dawn I was roused by the opening chords of the reggae song 'Don't Worry, Be Happy' coming from a speaker in the ceiling.

There were no immigration procedures to speak of. The sleepy-eyed passengers disembarked, a cavalcade of wheelie bags rumbling along the platform to board the Rotterdam train. I watched them go with a pleasantly abstracted feeling. I hadn't talked to a soul on board, out of some superstition I couldn't have explained, an instinct that told me a journey like this was best started quietly. The train pulled away, leaving me standing with a bitter wind stinging my face.

The sky above the Hook of Holland was massed with clouds, boiling banks of salmon and gold punctuated by luminous rays that poured down on the sea. Everything shone with a translucence that was indefinably different to any light that would fall on London. I took a few steps and then stopped, not knowing how to start. Standing at the edge of the car park, gazing at a green verge and watching the grasses shiver in the wind, I was filled with an unexpected reluctance to begin. All I had to do was walk. Surely it couldn't be that simple? I felt there must be a catch, something I hadn't considered.

I might have continued standing there, staring idiotically, if not for the appearance of an old man with a bushy white moustache on a bicycle. '*Goedemorgen,*' he nodded, 'good morning' – it may as well have been English – and clattered past me down a cycle path. It looked like vaguely the right direction, and after following for a minute I found a signpost to Rotterdam, 33 km, further than I'd expected. That arrow was all I required. It really was that simple. I put one foot in front of the other, and began to walk.

Almost at once rain started to fall: an oddly dry, sharp kind of rain it took me a moment to recognise as hail, tinkling musically in the beachgrass, rattling off my hat. That wintry shower swiftly passed, leaving the ground littered with ice that crunched pleasingly under my boots, and the sun reemerged. The cycle path led through a wood of leafless silver birch, twittering with unseen birds. Fields lay beyond the wood. The sky was as cold and blue as the sea. I scaled a bank of earth I realised must be a dyke, and suddenly, ridiculously, ahead of me was Holland. A latticework of canals lay between polytunnels that could only contain tulips; two windmills were silhouetted in the distance. Farmers were whistling and yelling, inefficiently chasing a flock of chocolate-coloured sheep around a sodden field, and on the horizon a bank of turbines – the industrialisation of windmills, which looked quaint in comparison – helicoptered in the wind against a forest of factory chimneys.

The cycle path followed the canal alongside a row of intensive greenhouses. A matted stench carried on the wind, and I turned to see three lamas galloping in pursuit of another flock of sheep, which bleated in terror as they rounded the corner and disappeared. I'd just finished being amused by this when I was almost mown down by a trio of middle-aged men on racing bikes, clad in matching bodysuits and wraparound sunglasses.

The Oranjekanaal led eastwards, into the rising sun. The world was laid out in parallel lines, a circuit board of fields and water, utterly functional. Cycle paths and canals insinuated themselves into the landscape; cargo ships bisected the fields, Maersk and Norfolk Line vessels stacked with shipping crates. The strangest thing about the flatness was the apparent lack of division between industry and agriculture. Farmland and petrochemical plants lay in the same field of vision, separated only by distance, or subdivided by waterways as subtle as ha-has on English country estates. It seemed less a landscape than a diagram of power and transport networks, an infrastructural blueprint. The 'geometric despotism of canal and polder and windmill' held as firm as it had when Paddy laid eyes on it.

By the time the sun was overhead I had reached the Nieuwe Waterweg, the New Waterway leading to Rotterdam and, although I didn't realise it then, from there to the River Waal, which itself swung south to become the Rhine. On an information board, a thoughtfully graffitied cock ejaculated over my location. The first residential streets were lined with modern redbrick houses, reassuring signs marking pedestrian lanes and safe zones for children. It was only two weeks until Christmas; candles flickered on windowsills, and small dogs peered through net curtains. It looked a trim, conventional place, but small things kept surprising me. In Rotterdam's suburbs I passed a shop advertising, in English, 'Real Brazilian Hair'. I thought it must be a reference to waxing until I saw clumps of glossy black hair dangling from the ceiling. The green church spire I'd been using as a landmark, trying to pinpoint the centre of town, turned out to be the minaret of a mosque.

I was fortunate enough to have a relative in Rotterdam: my cousin Adam, who I hadn't seen since I was too small to remember, was waiting in his red Ford Transit outside the station. A half-naturalised Dutchman after twenty years in the country, he made his living painting cranes in Rotterdam's vast docklands. Pleasantly scruffy, sandy-haired, with a slight social clumsiness that suited my end-of-day exhaustion, he rolled cigarettes behind the wheel as he piloted his van from the station and into heavy traffic.

Rotterdam gave me an intimation of how much Europe's urban landscapes had changed since the 1930s. 'The beetling storeys were nearly joining overhead; then the eaves drew away from each other and frozen canals threaded their way through a succession of hump-backed bridges,' Paddy wrote, but those words were all that were left of that city now. The winding alleyways were replaced by generic high streets, retail units and chain shops, steel and glass insurance buildings, a clone of every other post-war city in Western Europe. Squinting my eyes to blur the street signs, I might have crossed the North Sea and walked my first twenty miles to find myself in Coventry city centre.

Seven years after Paddy was here, one square mile of streets and houses was pancaked by German bombs, a single, sustained bombardment that left almost nothing standing but the fifteenth-century church and – an odd survival – a statue of Erasmus reading a book. Paddy had seen snow settling on the great humanist's bronze shoulders; there was no snow in my December, but there he stood all the same, leafing through the pages as if too absorbed to notice.

The glimpse I had of Rotterdam was almost as brief as Paddy's own – he walked on at once, pausing only for eggs and schnapps – but the continuity between our two cities was absolutely severed. The Rotterdam of the Middle Ages had been blasted into the realm of fairytales, and the new reality of McDonald's and Lush, Starbucks and Vodafone had rushed to fill the vacuum. The destruction seemed less an act of war than apocalyptic town planning, a Europe-wide sweep of medieval clutter to clear the way for the consumer age.

Luckily, the street Adam lived on was as unscathed as Erasmus. It lay just five hundred metres from the 'fire line', the point at which the bombs stopped falling. I could only picture a wave of fire rolling outwards from a white-hot core. The buildings looked so delicate it was incredible they had survived: orangey brick with plaster curlicues, peculiar gabled rooftops with pretty patterns of red and white tiles, resembling almonds set in a cake. My legs throbbed as I climbed the stairs into one of these gingerbread houses. Inside the flat, Adam clumped two beers on the table and produced a pot of steaming-hot lamb stew.

'I painted logos in Sliedrecht, looks like you'll be going that way. Cleaned windows in Hardinxveld-Giessendam. Painted a crane somewhere near here...' After the dishes were cleared, he traced the first part of my route on his laptop. The satellite image on Google Earth showed brown rivers ahead, their banks stubbled with little towns, squared blocks of green and grey; dragging and clicking, dragging and clicking, my journey unfolded before me in an abstraction of pixels. Planning my walk in this kind of detail was something I'd deliberately avoided – the element of surprise seemed important – but I had no map of Holland, so took this opportunity to scribble down a basic diagram of waterways and bridges.

I got to like my cousin more and more as the night progressed. He talked of the psychology of the Low Countries, a fatal dam collapse in Zeeland that people didn't speak about – 'things like that are never mentioned because we're all so vulnerable' – and the disappearance of the owls: 'I used to hear them on nights like this, but people messed about with the trees. Now the owls have gone from Kralingen.' The name of this neighbourhood was known in a local saying, '*Zo lang als de weg naar Kralingen*', which Adam translated for me. 'So if anyone asks how long your walk is, say "As long as the road to Kralingen". It's like "how long is a piece of string?" It might come in handy.'

We sat talking until I was so tired I could hardly focus. I dragged my aching limbs upstairs, where he'd laid out a bed in his workshop, which was scattered with woodworking tools and half-completed carvings. I went to sleep instantly and woke to the smell of sawdust. My thighs and calves were cramped from sleep, but outside was a clear sky, perfect for my second day on the great trudge. Adam accompanied me to the bridge over the River Maas, a double-humped frame of steel girders rumbling with morning traffic, and saw me off with a thermos of coffee and an almond-filled biscuit called a *speculaas staaf*. It would be the first of countless leavings.

The Maas was as broad as the Thames, and soon split into two. Turning my back on Rotterdam's skyline, I followed the road east, bicycles tearing past me, Lycra-clad riders puffing steam in the morning air. A man resembling a circus strongman spotted me looking confused beneath a tangle of flyovers and pointed me on my way. 'Walking?' he asked when I explained what I was doing. He seemed entertained by the idea.

From Rotterdam, Paddy had plunged into winter countryside, a landscape like a Brueghel painting, children skeetering down canals on fantastical ice-yachts. That reality was so distant it almost physically hurt. Now browns and greys seeped in from all sides and nothing shone or sparkled. Frequently the river disappeared behind smashed-out warehouses, piles of rusting machinery in decrepit dockyards. The map I'd drawn the night before was hopelessly inadequate; by lunchtime I realised I was lost, wandering in a patch of wetland fringed by tower blocks that shouldn't, according to my childish scrawl, have been there at all. The only other person in sight was an old man in a sailor's cap dragging a peculiar wagon, who pointed in two opposite directions when I asked for help. Eventually I found the road towards the satellite town of Ridderkerk.

The morning had left me blank. It was hard to derive an impression of this landscape, which lay in the uncomfortable zone between light industry and suburbs, never resolving itself into one thing or the other. Ugliness needs to be extreme in order to be interesting, and this territory was ugly only by virtue of its blandness. With ice-yachts as remote from this world as will-o'-the-wisps or unicorns, I was left despondent. But just as enervation washed through me, a car pulled up and a cheerful blonde woman waved from the window.

'We saw you walking, and thought you might like to come in for a cup of coffee and a rest!'

Her name was Hanneke van de Voorde, and within minutes I was sat on her sofa in an overheated house of children and chirruping budgerigars, while her husband Co, a stout, waistcoated man with ears like swollen mush-rooms, heaped my plate with biscuits.

'We always try to meet people. We are interested in everybody. We saw you walking and thought, "Why not?" We wanted to learn all about you.'

Hanneke and Co were Reformed Church Christians; Adam had said these congregations were scattered around this suburb. Co turned out to be a painter too. 'I'll paint anything! If you give me a banana and say you want it green, I'll paint it green.' He paused and thought about what he had said, looking slightly worried. 'Actually, no. I wouldn't do that. Come, you must see our *honk!*'

The honk turned out to be a garden shed fitted with a bar and gym equipment. 'A honk means just a cosy place. This is where we dance, sing and pray. Also, if I have a conflict with my wife...' He chuckled, but then looked trou-bled again. He kept going too far.

They invited me to sleep in the honk, but it was only afternoon; Dordrecht wasn't far away, and I was expected there. After giving me some hard-boiled eggs, they set me on my way. I walked on, marvelling at what had occurred. The promise of the day was restored, and Ridderkerk sud-denly didn't seem so dismal after all.

Crossing another humped steel bridge, barges rumbling under my feet, I saw the elegant steeples of Dordrecht through a latticework of girders. This river city wasn't bombed in the war and its roofs were still ornamented with turrets and ironwork flourishes, pinnacles of fish-scale tiles, while the lower floors of canal-side houses were covered in green slime from the water channelled through the narrow streets, crossed here and there by iron bridges. I sat on a bench by the Grote Kerk, the Great Church, and watched the jackdaws circling the belfry, trying to imagine the noise of clogs clop-clopping on cobblestones. Apart from this absent sound, and the lack of snow, the experience couldn't have been much different to when my predecessor rested here.

One thing that had certainly changed was the price of accommodation. In the early stages of his journey Paddy relied on cheap hostelries, lodgings of a kind that didn't exist any more. Economic growth and the tourist trade had destroyed Europe's dosshouses, and offers to stay in cosy honks weren't as frequent as that day's encounter might have suggested. But accommodation was waiting all the same. While I'd started my journey without a map and no information on where I was going apart from a record eight decades old, the internet had provided me with a string of occasional beds through the Couch Surfing website. The idea was beautifully simple: strangers offered a bed for the night and trusted that someone would offer the same to them in the future. It was a modern expression of something much profounder in Europe: an ancient tradition of hospitality, something Paddy encountered often, to which the internet had given new meaning. Between these open-hearted hosts, friends of friends I met on the way, occasional strangers and a bit of rough sleeping, I was only to pay for a single night's sleep between here and Vienna.

An MA student by the name of Remco was my man in Dordrecht. He regaled me with tales of previous vagabonds he'd given shelter to: one had been on his way to Jerusalem, relying on social media to find free beds and food. 'Queen Beatrix gave a speech last year about how social media can destroy relationships,' Remco said, leading me up to my room. 'Of course, she's on Twitter now, the old fart.'

We smoked cigarettes on the balcony overlooking the dark canal, the bridges underlit with green, while he talked in flawless English about the state of education in Holland. 'This is the last year I can graduate without running into massive debts. My professor says our generation is screwed. The baby boomers have taken the lot. For the first time since the war, we will grow up poorer than our parents.'

I hardly slept that night. Despite the physical exhaustion, my head was too crowded to rest. I left groggily the next morning, crossed a mechanical bridge that looked like an oiled black engine, and followed the river.

~~~~~

Gradually the industrial landscape gave way to the rural. It lost its grip begrudgingly, sprawling for miles of car showrooms, glass-fronted office complexes and ugly new-build homes. In Sliedrecht, where Adam painted logos, a giant petrochemical plant dominated the river. Two barges slid by, mountained high with coal, pushing against the river's flow towards Germany. It took another hour of walking before I was free of industry, and I stopped to eat yesterday's speculaas staaf on the bank of the Merwede. Tentative magic crept into the scene. Sunlight glittered on the water, a line of leafless trees rattled their twigs in the wind, and the spirit of a heron trembled on the opposite bank.

I hoped I'd be able to hug the river all the way to Gorinchem, but the A15 motorway had the same idea.

Although I'd picked up a cycle path again, traffic thundered behind a soundwall, drowning out the whisper of reeds from the wetlands. When at last I outmanoeuvred the motorway, industry returned, shipyards pumping out the sugary stench of heavy solvents. Somewhere during the past few hours various pains had appeared. They shifted from my knees to my toes, and back up again to my ankles and shins, as if trying to find a permanent place to settle. I observed them with a feeling of detachment, hoping they might go away; the foolishness of this strategy wouldn't become apparent until the next evening.

It was only just starting to occur to me that travelling this way was so much slower – indescribably slower – than other forms of transport. Bicycles passed me with speed and grace that I envied, but at least recognised as merely a faster version of what I was doing; cars travelled so incomprehensibly fast I'd already begun to see them as something quite alien, engaged in an activity entirely different to my own. The ludicrousness of walking pace could be deeply frustrating. The trick, as I would come to discover, was to ignore the destination and fill my mind with the journey – if I was in a hurry I wouldn't have been walking in the first place – but this lesson would be weeks in coming.

The pale steeple of Gorinchem stubbornly maintained its distance, appearing exactly the same size every time I looked, while the incomprehensible cars screamed past and the pain explored my legs. For the last few miles I found myself thinking of a half-remembered fairytale about a castle that never drew closer, no matter how long the traveller walked. The story might have been daydreamed up by an earlier version of me.

When at last I arrived, Gorinchem reminded me of a snobby town in the Cotswolds. Women in fur coats glanced suspiciously at the stick in my hand – I'd snapped it from a pile of branches, and it ended in a jagged spearpoint - and when I sank down on the steps of the church people glowered at my tin cup, which had fetched up between my feet like a begging bowl. I felt like a medieval pauper wandering in from the marshes.

In this town Paddy had slept as a guest in the local police station, which functioned as a lodging house when there was an empty cell. I didn't need to resort to this: a young couple called Joost and Mika put me up in their apartment, two more generous souls who had come to me over the ether. Joost immediately invited me to join them for a night out in Rotterdam, where he and his friends were getting drunk to celebrate someone's birthday. The thought of finding myself back in the city I'd spent two days walking from was violently unappealing. Besides, my shins hurt too much.

'Not to worry,' Joost assured me, 'you can stay here and play with the kittens. We have the best medicine for you - lots and lots of booze.' He indicated a shelf in the corner stocked with every conceivable brand of whisky, vodka, brandy, rum, schnapps, aperitif and liqueur. When the two of them had gone I medicated liberally, while the kittens amused themselves trying to topple the Christmas tree.

Next morning, I left Joost and Mika snoring. A blustery wind blew splatters of rain down the deserted streets. The town ended at a dyke, a windmill and a river, with church towers and further windmills scattered on the far bank.

I thought briefly about the warm flat, the kittens and twinkling lights on the tree, then cast these things from my mind. It was a day for staying inside, but I was glad I wasn't. I fastened the Velcro straps at my wrists, tugged up the hood of my raincoat, and started along the dyke above the pigeon-coloured river. Bloated clouds rolled in the heavens. Tiny waves lapped in the puddles at my feet.

Everything felt marvellously Dutch. The dyke curved ahead, looming protectively above cottages with thatched roofs and checkered shutters, defending these mild communities from the river. The wide open landscapes of the day before were gone and everything seemed to have shrunk – the buildings, the river, even the horizon – or it might have been the effect of being snugly wrapped up, my view of the world framed by dripping Goretex.

The rain drove horizontally across the fields, trickling down my sleeves and water-resistant trousers. Polders and vegetable plots swam past, farmhouses of stout stone, hay bales stacked under stilted roofs. The farmyards were as neat and tidy as model railway scenery. The rain slackened long enough for me to roll a cigarette, then came back in a drizzly blast that made pulp of the paper.

For a mile I was followed by an Alsatian that obviously thought I was going somewhere worthwhile. A car caught us up and screeched to a halt, the door flew open and a pair of strong arms hauled the dog inside; I had a glimpse of a woman's glaring face, as if I'd been caught kidnapping. 'I saw you yesterday,' cried another woman from another car – being accosted by women in cars was becoming a regular occurrence – 'you were walking to Gorinchem! And you are still walking now! When will you stop?'

'Istanbul,' I said. It was the first time I'd confessed it to a stranger.

These entertaining small encounters, and the meditative tunnel vision that plodding in the rain induced, had so far distracted me from thinking about my shins. It was late afternoon when I had to admit to myself that the pain wasn't going away and was now officially a problem. What had started as dull discomfort had grown to a steady, repetitive ache, and with nine miles to go it became a stabbing pain. The light was beginning to fade, folding away across the landscape. The dyke path ended and the new tarmac surface sent agonising jolts up my bones at every step.

I fumbled in my rucksack for bandages, winding them tightly from the ankles to the knees. It dulled the sharpest of the pain, but the muscle tissue throbbed. Pigheadedly I continued walking. I couldn't seem to stop. At a service station I bought Coca-Cola, mixing it up in my thermos with the rest of the hip-flask whisky. I thought perhaps it would numb the pain, as recommended by Dr Joost. The medicine didn't work; I was in as much pain as before, but now I was drunk as well.

Darkness rolled across the land. In the distance the lights of Tiel inched incrementally closer. The last few miles were like a bad dream, but I'd reached a state where somehow, perversely, it was harder to stop than to carry on. A stubborn inertia prevented me from flagging down a car.

In Tiel lay rows of darkened houses in empty, rain-washed streets. Searching for the address of the ally who had offered me shelter that night, all I could find was an enormous, institutional-looking mansion standing alone in an overgrown ornamental garden. It looked too grand to be possible. I hobbled to the front door and peered through the glass to a hallway with coat hooks on the walls. Barely visible in the gloom were what appeared to be two children dressed in Puritan-style clothing, standing absolutely still and staring at each other.

I didn't like the look of that at all. Retreating, I staggered up one side of the street and back down the other, gasping now with pain at every impact. At last, despairing, I returned to the door; it was the only possibility. And then lights blinked on in the hall and a figure waved from a high window, ushering me in.

The children turned out to be painted statues. The place used to be an orphanage – *weeshuis*, I learnt in Dutch – and two smaller statues flanked the door, crumbled effigies of a boy and a girl with distressed goblin features. After the orphans had gone the house became a home for the disabled, and later still was converted into accommodation for asylum seekers. Now it was rented cheap by a guitar teacher called Mark, who kept the squatters out.

None of this I learnt right away; I hobbled straight to an echoing bathroom to run my legs under freezing water to reduce the swelling. Perhaps with a few Ibuprofens my condition would improve. But merely walking to the next room sent pain shooting up my legs; it was clear I wouldn't be going anywhere the next day.

Of course I could stay another night, Mark said graciously when I asked. We were eating a bowl of Dutch *hutspot* - hotchpotch, it must have been - in a cavernous hall containing almost nothing but his bed, his computer, a spare mattress and a few guitars. A gentle man with a face like a smiling conquistador, he had quit a rock-and-roll lifestyle to reorient his life around reading and meditation; he had come to the weeshuis, I gathered, as a kind of sanctuary. It sounded like a story you'd hear from a drug-addled rocker in middle age, but Mark was only in his early twenties. He'd jumped ship decades early.

I spent the next day knocking back aspirin and holding frozen peas against my legs. My host went out to give guitar lessons, leaving me alone. It was a monastic place in which to rest and recover. Rain pattered against the windows, submerging the room in a murky twilight. Church bells tolled every quarter hour, but it felt like time had stopped and nothing in the world was moving. I made the mistake of browsing internet forums, which filled my head with unsettling phrases like 'shin splints' and 'peroneal tendon sprain', making my legs hurt even more. By evening I was anxious and miserable. Barely four days into the journey, I had lamed myself.

Of course I could stay another night, said Mark again. I couldn't express how grateful I was. There was nowhere else for me to go. The next day rolled past much the same, though in the middle of the afternoon I ventured carefully into town to find an *apotheek* – 'apothecary' sounded more powerful than 'pharmacist' – to buy elasticated bandages, heat rub and arnica gel. The only thing I remember of Tiel was a hideous piece of public art: three enormous plastic babies, one pink, one brown and one yellow, crawling clockwise round a tree, their faces covered by grotesque animal masks. Speakers mounted in the trees played 'Take My Breath Away'. It seemed like a weird town.

The arnica and the bandages helped. The heat rub, some fiendish Dutch concoction, seared the skin of my legs so badly I expected to see flesh blistering; it felt like they'd been doused in petrol and set ablaze. Who knows, maybe that helped too: by the next morning I was ready to attempt walking on. The shooting pains had diminished to a steady, pulsing ache, which could be dulled by keeping my shins bound tight. Essentially I had fashioned puttees, exactly the kind of bindings that Paddy had wrapped his legs in, and I understood their function now. Perhaps my initial lack of puttees was the reason I'd hobbled myself, or perhaps it had more to do with my disregard for training. Mostly, though, I blamed the millions of tonnes of tarmac and cement that had been laid across these landscapes since the 1930s.

A heightened awareness of terrain – of its capacity not merely for ugliness, but for causing physical harm – changed the way I walked from that point on. Instinctively I avoided the hard-impact surfaces that jolted every muscle and bone, sending shockwaves through my body; grassy verges, municipal flowerbeds or even rotten leaves were better than naked road. Navigating urban sprawl became a series of tactical decisions, marking me out as a different type of walker to the strollers in the streets. I wasn't walking in town, I was walking through town, and the tenuous threads of greenery, strips of soil and decomposing mulch became organic passageways threading back to the countryside.

The anxieties that had settled like flies during my nights in the orphanage lifted as I continued walking, borne away in the slipstream of new movement. The rain held off, and by afternoon I was crossing the railway bridge over the sluggish river Waal towards Nijmegen, my last town in Holland.

On the opposite bank lay streets of shops and tumbledown houses, festive lights blazing on the lampposts. Nijmegen was the site of Operation Market Garden in the war, a doomed Allied airborne operation to seize the occupied Netherlands; the waterfront dives where Paddy had slept were gone, destroyed by war or gentrification. Hoping to find some lingering spirit of sailors' bonhomie, I stepped into the nearest hostelry, a jauntily decorated place called the Café De Beurs. Half a dozen brawny men with faces like Mervyn Peake illustrations were clanking glasses at the bar, puffing out clouds of cigar smoke at the No Smoking signs. The interior was all dark wood, doily curtains and polished brass; some kind of god-awful fairground music was playing at high volume. I ordered a celebratory schnapps and lost myself in the hubbub of Dutch, some of it familiar sounding, the rest completely extraordinary. A phrase of Mark's had stuck in my mind: 'Dutch is an open, wide language. It's pale and white, like the landscape.'

I'd been invited to dinner that night by a man called Johan, one of the numerous aficionados of Patrick Leigh Fermor who materialised on my route, offering beds and meals, like literary spirit guides. He was one of a network of fans whose existence I'd known nothing about until I started planning this walk, but who now appeared to play a shadow role in my life. They had lent their encourage-ment, and I sensed a certain amount of vicarious pleas-ure in my journey. Sometimes, admittedly, I found their presence slightly overwhelming; their enthusiasm for my predecessor could be borderline obsessive, and there was a cult-like intensity to some of their exchanges. But they were unfailingly knowledgeable about history and about Paddy's work, and as generous with food and drink as they were with stories.

Johan took me to the oldest pub in town, a fourteenth-century inn called In De Blaauwe Hand, where we sat under heavy beams surrounded by scrolling iron-work. He bought two glasses of Rooie Tiep Top, a beer named after a local jester, and pronounced: 'We will start with the pea soup, and then eat our way through the menu until you're fat.'

The night ended incongruously in a hash-fragranced circus tent pitched in a nearby park. During the meal we'd been joined by a mustachioed student called Dick who offered to put me up for the night, and they both suggested we should visit the local Occupy camp. So by midnight the three of us were huddled around a wood-burning stove with groups of softly spoken anarchists discussing the Arab Spring, the impending collapse of the EU, alternatives to capitalism and a new type of engine that ran on water.

They had been there two months, and the liberal local government was happy to let them be. In the winter of 2011, as Europe lurched from one economic crisis to another, the Occupy movement was at its height and pro-tests had spread to hundreds of towns across the continent, popping up like mushrooms from the mycelium of the internet; in some extraordinary way, the Nijmegen camp was an outgrowth of the camps at St Paul's and Finsbury

Square I'd visited before leaving London. The protesters said they would stay indefinitely, camping on the hill to offer an alternative vision of the future.

'I've been waiting for this all my life,' said someone sitting nearby. 'I've always felt uncomfortable with the way the modern world looks, the cars, the buildings, the roads, the ugliness. This is something new.'

He was a ruminative man called Pepe, with a straggly beard and half-moon glasses, who could have been any age between twenty-five and forty. I talked with him for much of the night – his discomfort with cars and roads was something I identified with – while Johan chipped in now and then with a sceptical aside.

'Nijmegen is an interesting town,' Pepe said. 'The people here are Bataves, the same tribe who acted as auxiliary troops along Hadrian's Wall. Bataves have always been different – independent, radical. We are a revolutionary region.'

'I always find it strange,' said Johan, watching him roll a cigarette, 'that the left-wing youth in the Netherlands is also the biggest supporter of the smoking industry in the Netherlands.'

Pepe didn't rise to the bait. 'There are predictions about Nijmegen,' he said enigmatically, looking like a wise old gnome in the flickering firelight. 'They say that in 2012 everything will change. When humanity first began, some went west and some went east. The ones who went west gained the knowledge of the Incas, and the ones who went east gained the knowledge of Tibet. Some say these two movements will meet again in the middle, in Nijmegen, the oldest town in the Netherlands, to survive the changes 2012 will bring.'

'The Incas and Tibetans will meet here?' Johan asked incredulously.

'That's one theory...'

'Here? In *Nijmegen?*'

'Some people say this.' Pepe had a knack for utterances that were both completely assured and entirely vague. Most of it made no sense at all, but that didn't bother me; no one else, in this time of collapse, was making a lot of sense either.

Moving away from the dawn of a new age, he asked about why I was walking. I was learning to hone my explanation: 'I want to see how things have changed' seemed the simplest way to describe what I had set out to explore. 'I want to see what has vanished. Has all the mystery and wildness gone? What has Europe lost in the last eight decades?'

Pepe thought about this a long time. 'I think there will be no sky any more,' he said eventually, stroking the yellow wisps of his beard. Rain rattled on the canvas above, and logs spat in the stove. 'The sky is like a chessboard these days, full of chemical trails. One thing I think that has disappeared between 1933 and now is silence. On your road from here to Turkey, you will find very few places with true silence.'

During the coming months, these words would often return to me. They became part of the background mutter, the internal monologue of my walk, which would be added to phrase by phrase, thought by thought, as I travelled.

That small circus tent in the rain often returned as well. As a movement, Occupy had already lost momentum; the camps were soon to disappear, either abandoned out of choice or violently evicted. It was easy to write off their visionary psychobabble, but the candlelit faces that night were part of something broader and deeper, an undercurrent of dissatisfaction that would surface again and again from here to the Bosphorus. Pepe's claustrophobia underneath a crisscrossed sky was linked with the tarmac roads I walked, the autobahns and the advertising, the corporate remodelling of Rotterdam's new core. It was linked with the people I'd meet in half a dozen countries ahead who mourned the vanishing of the wild, yearning for an imagined past that was freer and less constricted.

Of course, none of this was in my mind as I set out the next morning, having woken on a fold-out bed in Dick's student flat, to make my way through nearby Groesbeeck, skirt the toadstool-studded woods and climb, at last, from the lowlands and into higher ground.

Already the country had a different feel: the gentle rise of hills, the shadow of pine trees on the horizon, the fungal outcrops that put me in mind of Brothers Grimm fairytales. Ice on the puddles, the first I had seen that winter, creaked under my boots. A deer froze in the middle of a field, turned and leapt away. Now and then came wooden discs elevated higher than telephone poles, as-yet-uninhabited platforms to provide nesting places for storks migrating from Africa, quite possibly the descendants of birds Paddy had seen; it was reassuring to think of their seasonal patterns unchanged.

Around the middle of the afternoon, leaving the bright fields behind me, I crossed a road and came to the edge of a forest. Ahead stretched rows of regularly spaced pine trees as far as I could see, and I plunged down a path running due east, with no deviations, like a trick of perspective.

After half an hour I passed a couple walking their dog. They nodded and smiled. '*Guten Tag!*'

Was it my imagination or were their features less knobbly, sandier, squarer-faced? Were their clothes very slightly different? Probably not, but immediately it felt like everything had changed. There had been no checkpoints, or even signs saying *Willkommen*. But this was the Reichswalde forest, and I was in Germany.

2

Rain on the River

The Rhineland

Fragmentary walls, pierced by old gateways, girdled most
of the little towns. I halted in many of them for a glass of
wine out of one of those goblets with coloured stems and a
slice of black bread and butter, sipping and munching by
the stove while, every few minutes, my dripping boots shed
another slab of hobnail-impacted snow several inches thick.

A Time of Gifts

THE PATH THROUGH THE FOREST RAN SO STRAIGHT IT MIGHT
have been scored with a ruler. The trees tracked identically
past, quadrants of managed pine interspersed with leafless
oak. It was a tame, regulated forest, but nonetheless thrill-
ing after the horizonless skies of the Low Countries. Now
and then came glimpses of other walkers far away, receding
down distant corridors at the right-angled junctions where
paths converged. There was something dreamlike about it,
a nowhere space where one country ended and the next
had yet to begin. Even after sixteen years of the border-
less Schengen zone, it felt unreal to leave one country and
enter another without so much as a fluttering flag to sug-
gest that anything had changed. Despite the exhilaration, I
felt oddly cheated.

When I'd left Gorinchem, Joost had given me a parting gift: three pre-rolled joints of hash, plastic-packaged
and barcoded, as legal in Holland as a pack of cigars. The
path showed no sign of ending and one of these helped
pass the time. The hash was simultaneously very mild and

very strong, and turned the forest into a conveyor belt of repeating trees, a zoetrope of identical images reeling past. Time collapsed, my feet went on, trudging mechanically in the leaves, and the dreaminess of the situation grew. As long as I kept plodding east, senses dulled, my thoughts wrapped around me, I guessed I'd emerge more or less where I wanted to be. There were no sounds apart from birdsong and the wind. I thought Pepe's prediction was already proved wrong until I heard the rumble of planes, so constant I hadn't noticed it, playing contrail chess games in the sky.

Suddenly, my nerves leapt in panic. Advancing squarely was a pair of men in uniform – blue trench coats and peaked caps – marching in perfect step, Alsatians tugging ahead on lengths of chain. The border patrol! How naïve to assume I could simply stroll across, from the drugs capital of the continent, without being searched. Those were clearly sniffer dogs, and carrying the pungent reek of hash I didn't stand a chance. Pretending to adjust my boots, I scooped a hole in the mulch and stamped the two remaining joints under wet leaves. My heart was pounding as I walked on, eyes down, trying to look as innocent as I could.

With the guards a few feet ahead, I glanced up to meet my fate. Instead of two uniformed brutes it was an elderly couple in anoraks, walking a pair of dumbly smiling Labradors. '*Guten Tag.*' '*Guten Tag.*' My relief was tinged with shame: the image had come straight out of a war film. The paranoia faded away, but the embarrassment lingered.

'The crunch of measured footfalls and the rhythm of a marching song sounded. Led by a standard bearer, a column of S.A. marched into the square ... Their shirts, with a red arm-band on the left sleeve, looked like brown paper, but as they listened to an address by their commander they had a menacing and purposeful look.' This, perhaps, might have explained my semi-hallucination back there. Paddy had seen his first Nazis in Goch, the town I reached beyond the woods, after the landscape had opened up into a spread of fields and farms, a steeple the shape of a witch's hat, mounds of rotting cabbages heaped beside the road. The streetlights were flickering on and the church bells had a jaunty clang, unlike the rather twee twinkles of the ones I'd heard in Holland. I wondered in which of the cosy shops Paddy had seen a window display of 'swastika arm-bands, daggers for the Hitler Youth, blouses for Hitler Maidens and brown shirts for grown-up S.A. men; swastika buttonholes were arranged in a pattern which read *Heil Hitler*'. My overriding impression of Goch was one of decency and dullness; fanaticism seemed improbable, as far from today's placidity as Alsatian sniffer dogs were from Labradors.

The next day's walk was only ten miles, by country roads between villages, through a wide and windswept land of copses and ploughed fields. The trees were the scattered remnants of the original Reichswalde, which, before agriculture spread, had covered a vaster terrain. Formations of geese passed overhead, iron filings drawn across the sky, and occasionally came the shriek of a hunting bird. My shins were playing up again. Frequently I had to stop to readjust my improvised puttees, developing a routine of binding them as tight as possible, walking until my calves swelled up, and then loosening them again; in this way, I managed to get half an hour's pain-free walk until the cycle started up once more. It was a ludicrous way to travel. I felt like a wandering leper.

Under a signpost to Kevelaer, three small boys asked if I was a *Pilger*. Assuming it was some childish insult I denied it and walked on; only later did I realise that they'd asked me if I was a pilgrim, and that I was on my way to one of the holiest pilgrimage sites in Catholic Germany. Soon enough, the spires of its churches were visible over the fields.

I wasn't a pilgrim – at least not in the way those boys assumed – but there was something fundamental about heading directly for the church, in Kevelaer and in the towns that followed. Settlements grew up around churches, as they did along rivers, and once I had reached a church or a river my feet stopped naturally. On my predecessor's journey, steeples would still have been the tallest things on most horizons, instinctive points of orientation, dominating the skyline. Now that dominance was broken– they had been outgrown by tower blocks, pylons, radio masts – but still I found myself navigating by them, like any medieval walker.

I arrived at Kevelaer's basilica ahead of a sloppy shower of rain, and sought sanctuary inside with a group of bratwurst-eating old folk. I had expected grey stone walls, but instead was plunged into colour: the walls and pillars were richly painted, hung with tapestries, oak-leaf borders and fleur de lis sparkling up to a vaulted ceiling spangled with gold stars. I sat in a post-ambulatory daze, watching rows of votive candles trembling behind their grates, and when I finally emerged winter had pounced on the town: snow was falling in wet clumps from a darkened sky.

Once a year, Kevelaer hosted a pilgrimage of Catholic bikers, who prayed for the dead of the biking fraternity before attending a rock concert. There was also, apparently, an annual pilgrimage of dogs. I learnt these things from Nonno, an aged hippy with a buccaneer's beard, who gave me a sofa for the night and reeled off story after story while sinking endless cups of black coffee; an ex-alcoholic, he kept his narrative fuelled on quarts of caffeine. He talked of his exploits on the Hippy Trail, of conscription in the

West German army and smoking opium from a rifle barrel, of an episode in which he knocked out a mugger's teeth in the Bronx. 'You go to sleep now,' he said at midnight, 'I will play chess on the computer and listen to hard rock music in my room.' He retired with a freshly brewed pot of coffee and a litre of Coca-Cola.

The snow was gone the next morning – I wouldn't see decent snow again until the Bavarian border – and that day's landscape was much the same as the one before. The names of villages I passed, Geldern and Winnekendonk, still had a hokey, Netherlandish feel, and the open fields reminded me I hadn't stepped far beyond Holland. The pale disc of the sun poured no heat on the land. Rooks rasped from leafless branches, and trees staggered into the horizon in receding shades of grey. Here and there, candle-lit shrines flickered by the roadside.

'Even the leaden sky and dull landscape round Krefeld became a region of mystery and enchantment,' Paddy wrote of his arrival in this grubby industrial city. The sky was still leaden, the landscape still dull, but enchantment came in the form of Michaela, another spirit of the internet, who whisked me away to the house she shared with her husband Tom. The table was piled with apple cake, almond biscuits and Ceylon tea, and elderly parents came and went, formulating sensible questions in a methodical German way, keeping to ordered lines of thought and conversation. We sat up late with a pile of maps, plotting my route down the Rhine. Krefeld lay on the edge of the Ruhr, and the map showed the city bleeding into conjoined blobs of grey, a conurbation larger than the area of Berlin. Anticipating the rhythmic shin jolts ahead, my heart sunk a little: an ugly map promises an ugly landscape.

Wet snow lay on the ground the next morning, and the air was blue and bitter. Tom drove me to Burg Linn,

a fortress of frosted battlements hulking behind a moat –
and, these days, islanded by highways – and from there to
the city's outskirts. He seemed reluctant to let me go, and
kept suggesting he drive a little bit further, a little bit further, until I insisted. He stopped the car and out I trudged,
towards a distant line of trees whose trunks turned out,
when I arrived, to be half-submerged by the swollen and
yellowish waters of the Rhine.

~~~~~

The river looked much the same as when I'd left it several
days before, in its Dutch incarnation as the Waal, shouldering its greasy way through dull-coloured countryside.
But the name change had given it power, invested it with a
sense of romance wider than itself. The Rhine, or Rhein,
conjured mystery in both English and German – it carried
weight, and sweetness too – and suddenly it felt as if a clear
path had opened up. All I had to do was follow this body of
water upstream, walking against its flow, and it would lead
me halfway across Germany, into the continent's heart.

The bank led south through slush-dripping woods, the
snow crisscrossed by rabbit tracks and here and there yellow stained to mark the pissing spots of deer. I sheltered
from sleet in a rotting bird hide at the edge of a field, sipping thermos coffee and stamping to keep out the cold.
There was no sign of the Ruhr's industry, and for this I was
glad; better grey skies over wet woods than grey skies over
concrete. Cargo barges flew downstream and agonisingly
crawled back up as they struggled against the force of the
river, which gave me the peculiar sensation of travelling the
wrong way; as if, even as a walker, I was also pushing against
a powerful current.

It wasn't far to Düsseldorf. Surprisingly quickly the
first of the city's suspension bridges to the *Altstadt*, the old

town, rose on the eastern bank. It was happy hour and the fake Irish pubs were spilling over with student drinkers; avoiding anywhere with green paint, I dived into a cavernous tavern with wood-panelled walls, where a waiter with a walrus moustache and a look of deep embitterment brought me a glass of the city's dark Altbier. The tavern was sonorous with murmured conversation, though occasionally a door flew open and a blast of drunken bawling carried through. Two tables with rival football colours flapped their scarves at each other in merry rivalry. Another waiter rushed through the room yelling something about warm figs, clicking his tongs like an angry crab.

Paddy had stayed in a workhouse here run by Franciscan monks, chopping wood in exchange for his bed, but I had an invitation to stay with a family friend. Actually, the chain of acquaintance that linked me to Kerstin Meyer was more convoluted than that – she was the sister of the girlfriend of the friend of my father's friend – but the connection would serve me well to Bavaria and beyond. The Meyers were a sprawling Catholic family with relatives scattered down the Rhine, and the Düsseldorf branch welcomed me in like a long-lost cousin.

Kerstin was an instantly likeable woman, with the easygoing energy that came from constantly being engaged in some compelling task or other, balancing a busy professional life with bringing up five children. The children – though there were only four here, the youngest having been sent ahead to Austria with the Christmas presents – ranged between the ages of five and fifteen, and, with their blond hair and blue eyes, confidence and perfect humour, were almost ridiculously beautiful. I joined them at the kitchen table while Kerstin fried up slabs of ham, and they asked me intelligent questions in estimable English. My admiration for this wonder brood grew when she showed me, later that night, all of them sharing one enormous bed in her and her husband's room: 'They all have beds of their own, but they prefer to share. They are such good friends, and no one likes to sleep alone.' In a couple of days they would decamp to spend Christmas in an Alpine chalet. I pictured all seven of them snoring happily, matching nightcaps on their heads, as snow drifted past the window.

Düsseldorf was a pleasant city and might have held me longer, but it was early days in my journey and the long road beckoned. Maybe because of a subconscious desire to linger, I made a series of clumsy decisions that took me a circuitous route back across the Rhine, the long way around the river bend and into industrial environs and acres of allotments. I lost the river entirely; by the time I found it again it was almost afternoon, and I still hadn't actually left the city. I went back across another bridge and the Rhine vanished once again in a maze of suburbs. For such an unmissable river, it had a knack of getting away.

By mid-afternoon I was in Dormagen, a town as dispiriting as its name, one of the blobs of grey on Michaela's map. The world was mud brown, lifeless green, pollution blooming into the sky from smokestacks bullying the road. Determined to relocate the Rhine, I force-marched through dismal suburbs along a roaring highway. Passing drivers craned their heads, shooting me baffled and suspicious glances, as if I was either lost or insane or doing something vaguely illegal.

The environment in which I walked determined to a large extent the way I was perceived. In the open countryside, with my boots and two-week beard, I was accepted as a walker; in a historical city centre, eating bread and cheese on the steps of a church, I passed for a tourist. But in a nowhere land like this, an in-between space, neither urban nor rural, there was no explanation for my presence, no category to which I belonged. This wasn't a walking-designated zone; I was out of place. Paddy's walk took place at a time when motorised traffic was a novelty, an entirely different technological and sociological era. Only in Romania, where horse-drawn traffic never went away, would I go for days on end with some intimation of the kinds of roads my predecessor tramped down.

Quietly and viciously brooding on the brutality of cars, cursing at drivers who rubbernecked too much, I made it through the greylands and back to the Rhine. The river-scape was Dutch again, the sky suffused with the yellowish, pinkish light I thought I'd left back in the Low Countries.

The daylight was preparing to die. At any moment, I kept thinking, the famous spires of Köln cathedral would rise across the countryside: the spires that, in Paddy's words, 'commanded the cloudy plain'. Maybe seventy-eight years before, that would have been the case. But Köln's industrial outskirts had spread and the cathedral commanded nothing. Now I mistook twin pylons for spires, and factory chimneys once again belched ahead of me.

The sunset sky glowed red above the gleaming architecture, an industrial belt of steam-spewing pipes and throbbing machines. Intestinal tram and train lines tangled down the centre of the road, and angular edifices rose either side with occasional lights in high steel turrets, like the laboratories of evil factory-wizards. There was not a soul in sight; the only sounds were electronic bleeps and the hiss of pressurised steam.

I'd been walking for almost ten hours, and as I finally approached what looked like a residential part of the city – a place in which real human beings, made of flesh and bone, might live – my shins experienced a resurgence of pain. I toyed with the thought of catching a tram, and waited at the nearest station with a line of burly Turkish workers. But when the tram actually came I baulked at the idea. Binding my shins double tight, I walked the last few miles fuelled by whisky from my hip flask and a sausage Kerstin had given me. This was the way, after all, that a city should be breached.

At last, exhausted, I reached the Dom, Köln's great twin-spired cathedral. Up close, its command was intact. The walls teemed with grubby saints and a forest of pillars soared to a vaulted ceiling. Gaggles of candle lighters huddled in waxy pools of light, and coins rattled in collection boxes like an inverse casino. In the thronging streets outside, commerce and Christmas continued much as it had in Paddy's time, though the scurrying shoppers were clutching Esprit and Lacoste carrier bags rather than armfuls of parcels.

A flight of steps led down to the quay. These days there were no tramp steamers moored beneath the spans of the bridge, and the rowdy sailors' bars were replaced by municipal architecture. This was becoming a theme: along Europe's waterways a sanitisation had taken place, the dives and dosshouses had gone, first softened up by enemy bombers and later swept clean by domestic town planners, as if the two waves of attack were designed with a single purpose. An out-of-season restaurant boat bobbed forlornly on the river. A lone skateboarder practised grinds on the concrete steps.

Christian Peters was another generous soul who had offered support for my journey, part of that shadowy network of travel literature geeks. In a brick-ceilinged cellar, over glasses of light, refreshing Kölsch – the diametric opposite to Düsseldorf's dark Altbier – he explained his research into social geography, with an emphasis on how skateboarding reclaims the public sphere. The Catholic authorities had recently banned skating in front of the

Dom, which he viewed as an assault on the concept of public space: 'Children are welcome in the city centre only as consumers. If they're not buying things, they're kicked out and moved on.' I thought of the shoppers clutching their bags, and the solitary skater, rumbling in the dark. This was all connected, somehow, to the lack of drunken sailors on the quays, and also to the suspicion on the faces of drivers who passed me. Public space was being squeezed, regulated, tidied. As the Kölsch washed down I found myself viewing Paddy's journey from the far side of a gulf, an alienating change so huge I couldn't make out its dimensions.

Next morning I was back on the streets with the sky still blue-dark. Neon lights puddled on the pavement as I navigated to the Dom, locating it by a clanging of bells like a ship lost at sea. Drizzle filled the air and the saint-encrusted walls were lit by a greenish light. With its twin spires looming in a halo of rain, it looked less like a cathedral than a barnacled wreck, drowned in a murky ocean; appropriate for a building moored to the banks of the Rhine, connected to the sea by that great river.

As the bells died, I descended to the quay. I was looking for a boat, hoping to follow Paddy's example of cadging a lift on a coal barge as far as Koblenz. But, as I'd established last night, there wasn't a friendly bargeman in sight; all I could find were tour boats full of elderly Americans on private holiday cruises, glimpsed through the tinted windows of cocktail lounges. '*Das Schiff nach Koblenz gehen?*' 'The ship goes to Koblenz?' I tried my atrocious German out on a few sailors fooling around with ropes on deck, but none appeared enthusiastic about having a muddy tramp accompany their paying clientele upriver. So I set off, as usual, on foot.

The drizzle didn't stop, even for a minute. The Rhine bled wetly into the sky with only a misty furze of trees to show where one ended and the other began. The path led through dripping woodland, and for hours the only sounds were the sad croak of birds, the slap of falling water, and the slosh of my boots through wet leaves. Later came smokestacks billowing out white smoke, a zone of petro-chemical factories where I took a shortcut through a rail yard, ignoring the *Verboten!* signs, and had to cross multiple train tracks and hop a fence to escape.

Chilled to the bone and dripping wet, I dragged myself into Bonn. Until the fall of the Berlin Wall this was the capital of West Germany – it still bore the honorary title of *Bundesstadt*, Federal City – but since those days it had apparently sunk into cosy provincialism. Prim little cafés with elegant cakes were not what I required now; instead, I wolfed down a plate of wurst and sought shelter in the nearest bar, enveloped in a humid fug among middle-aged women with booze-ravaged faces, artfully blowing nicotine into the roots of their dyed hair. This was still Kölsch ter-ritory, and the drink kept coming, glass after slender glass, until the barman was ordered to stop. Old regulars eyed me morosely over the smouldering tips of cigars; I'd probably occupied one of their seats, but I was too tired to care.

That night I stayed with a woman called Sarah who lived on the opposite side of the river. The highlight of that house was a friend called Wolfgang, who had come, ostensibly, to survey a door damaged in a break-in attempt the night before. A mauve-cheeked man with John Lennon glasses and a drooping grey moustache, he plumped him-self down at the table and embarked on an extraordinary monologue that lasted from the moment he arrived to the moment he left. 'Why are you walking all that way? Why do you not wear roller skates, hmm, and travel along the highway? *Scheiße!* The people in Bonn tell me I look like I live under a bridge and drink red wine all day. There are two sorts of people, the people who live under bridges and drink red wine all day, and the people who are stuck in a hamster wheel, going round and round. So I don't care what they say. *Scheiße!* Sarah, you must give this man a huge breakfast tomorrow, five eggs, sausages, black bread – not toast-bread like they serve in England, you eat ten slices of that and at one o'clock you are hungry again. Black bread, sausages, porridge – English people love to eat porridge. So you are leaving tomorrow, hmm? I will come with you on a motorbike. *Scheiße!*'

The trusting nature of people I stayed with constantly amazed me. Sarah left early for work the next day, and told me to help myself to breakfast and depart when I wanted. The buzz of the doorbell sliced through my dreams and, bleary-eyed with sleep, I opened the door to find Wolfgang seemingly dressed in police uniform. It took a moment to understand that it wasn't Wolfgang at all, but a policeman who looked exactly like him, inquiring about the break-in. Round glasses and a drooping moustache must have been a popular look on that stretch of the Rhine.

Patches of blue were visible over Bonn's steepled sky-line. After clicking Sarah's door shut I crossed the Kennedy Bridge – a nod to Cold War allegiances – and spent a long time reading the messages engraved on padlocks secured to the railing: Tanja + Martin 06.09.2008, Andrea ♥ Edgar, Nici ♥ Hati, Sobi & Claudi, Heinz & Angelika In Liebe. The keys of these love-locks lay rusting below, sunk on the bed of the river. I thought of Anna, and the other people I loved, receding behind me. It made me miss her terribly; but the exhilaration of aloneness, of wandering through unknown landscapes, was another form of love taking shape inside me.

Past Bonn the flatlands leached away, and the land on the eastern bank rose into wooded hills, steeper and more purple as the day progressed. The stumps of ruined fortresses started to appear on both sides of the Rhine, the beginning of the 'amazing procession' Paddy had viewed from his barge: the castle of Petersburg, and the nightmarishly named Burg Drachenfels, protruding from their crags like solitary fangs. The river began to lose the meandering, sluggish aspect that had characterised it before, quickening and intensifying as it pushed through the steepening valley. The last hint of Holland was gone; I was entering the realm of German Romanticism.

Despite the lack of snow on the turrets in this unseasonably mild December, and despite the B9 road, which rumbled the length of the valley, the sinister magic of leering ruins and pine-forested slopes was intact. Daydreams of murderous knights and dark enchantments came naturally, a by-product of walking itself, as they must have done to travellers on this path for centuries. Outside Rolandseck my delight was magnified by a metal plaque, zigzagged into the paving stones, engraved with English words: 'a 2838 kilometre coast to coast walking journey on roads pavements tracks and bicycle paths from bilbao to rotterdam starting at the river nervion continuing to an alpine origin of the river rhine and following its course to the north sea ending at the hook of holland spain france switzerland germany the netherlands.' It was like discovering a letter, dropped for me to find. Hamish Fulton was the name of the artist who had left this record behind, and I found the knowledge of another walker deeply reassuring. Paddy was just one of many wanderers on strange, lonely quests, striking out on mysterious missions, most of whom had left no traces.

That night I was welcomed into a home in the tiny village of Sinzig, a guest of the Weissenfeld family. 'We never thought anyone would want to visit!' said the daughter, Stephanie, leading me up creaking stairs to an attic bedroom. 'My friends in the village are so jealous! Nobody ever comes here.'

After my daily ritual of pain management with aspirin and magnesium powder, I joined them downstairs by the wood-burning stove. Mother, father, daughter and son were constructing cigarettes from a rolling machine, puffing smoke out happily around the kitchen table. They were a family of storytellers. Not far from the village, they said, was Barbarossa's infamous Lustschloss, the castle where he kept his concubines to 'make erotic things with'. Further upriver, I would pass the legendary Rock of Lorelei, home to the water-maiden who dragged sailors to their deaths. And the Drachenfels, Dragon's Rock, the sight of which had gripped me earlier, was associated with the mythical hero Siegfried, who showered himself in dragon's blood to gain immortality.

'But a leaf landed here, on his shoulder, so that spot was not protected. Later he was betrayed by a friend, who knew his weakness, and killed him with a spear. But maybe that is not correct,' said Stephanie's father, waving at his laptop. 'I forget how it happened exactly. Better you look it up on Wikipedia so you know the true story.'

The peculiarity of this suggestion took a while to process. Of course, establishing the historical veracity of a man bathing in dragon's blood was a strange notion in itself, but stranger still was the assumption that the story was made less enjoyable if it differed from an internet-sanctioned version. What I should have said to Stephanie's father – but by the time it occurred to me, several days' walk lay between us – was that the real story was whichever way he told it. Like species, stories evolve through a process of random mutation; a myth is whatever people remember, and if he happened to remember it differently, then his was the genuine, living version. Besides, the tale of Siegfried and the dragon was one I'd rather hear in a wood-smoke-smelling room, the rain beating down outside, than on any internet page.

Hearing stories through happenstance and chance encounter became increasingly vital to my journey's purpose. My intention had always been that Paddy's books would be my only guide, and apart from their outdated information, I had done no research into what lay ahead. I'd even received abuse for this: someone had sent me an email telling me no one wanted to read my ignorant, unresearched views on countries I knew nothing about. But after hearing Siegfried's story – one I could have read previously if I'd only Googled it – I understood that the delight of walking lay in the accidental finding of things, letting small wonders reveal themselves shyly, at the speed of travel. Research only spoiled the mystery of what lay around the corner.

The rain was still falling when I woke the next day. Stephanie offered to drive me down the Rhine, but I was adamant. Throughout my walk I would constantly have to fend off well-meaning offers of lifts, and sometimes it was hard to make even myself understand why I couldn't accept. But once I'd trudged for half an hour, unfathomable happiness seized me: the river, the rain, the rising hills, the mysterious forested opposite bank, all combined to produce a sense of nameless anticipation. The hills were briefly lost from sight behind a sizzling mist of hail, and when the clouds broke apart sunshine whitened the tips of seagulls drifting in the sky. I was glad my advances had been snubbed by the shipmen of Köln: it was incomparably better to see things unfolding step by step, in the wet air and the wind, than through the tinted windows of a cruise ship's cocktail bar.

By afternoon I was skirting the old walls of Andernach, stopping to buy a bottle of Amaretto, an offering for the evening to come, and whisky to refill my hip flask. But the whisky didn't all fit, and rather than pour the surplus away it didn't seem such a bad idea to pull forward cocktail hour. Walking slightly drunk that day acted as a weird charm: out of a squall of rain appeared a wild-eyed, grinning man with broken teeth and a demonic-looking grey dog.

'Come, come, you must stay dry here,' he cried, motioning me into the shelter of someone else's garage. He then embarked on a strange monologue: 'My name is Harry. Like your youngest prince! But I am not a royalist, never! I am free. I hate hierarchy! Do you know that this class system, this system of kings and counts, was brought here by the Romans? Before the Romans came to this land we Germans were free, we were all equal, no one was better or worse than any other. We must overthrow this Roman mentality, so we can be free again...'

He went on in this vein until the clouds dispersed. It was only later that I came across a sign – a centurion's helmet and the word *Limes* – and remembered I was inadvertently tracing the ancient limit of the Roman Empire, marking the border between civilisation and barbarian lands. Had I really just met a man babbling a memory of tribal freedoms versus imperial oppression on that exact frontier? Perhaps I'd hallucinated Harry. With his hound and his crooked teeth, he might have been the shade of one of those wild forest tribes.

Night had fallen, and I was sober, by the time I approached Koblenz, sneaking along the bank down a strip of darkened parkland. This was where Paddy's barge ride had ended, and the ancient port town lay at the confluence of two important rivers: ahead, the Mosel flowed seamlessly into the Rhine. The town lights trembled in the water and on the opposite embankment glowed a triumphal winged statue that looked peculiarly, from this distance, like a Hindu temple. It turned out to be a monument to Kaiser Wilhelm I, a replica of the original destroyed by Americans in the war. As I crossed the bridge to the Altstadt the cathedral's bells crashed and boomed chaotically over the organ's drone, as weird and mesmerising a sound as an Indian harmonium. Again there was something Hindu about it, but I was getting my religions mixed up. Over the course of the day I'd forgotten: it was Christmas Eve.

I'd originally envisaged a lonesome celebration, camped up somewhere in the woods with a cake and a bottle of wine. But the Meyer family had come to my aid, and Kerstin had phoned from Düsseldorf to arrange for me to stay with her parents, who couldn't join them in Austria and would be spending the holiday alone. It took an hour to find their flat, which lay at the top of a very tall building down the end of a very long road, and something went wrong with my knees on the way, so I practically crawled up the stairs.

It was an uncomfortable arrival in more ways than one. Irmgard, Kerstin's mother, was at church, and Rolf, her liver-spotted father, seemed to be in a bad mood. He motioned me towards a sofa in a heavily furnished room and spent a long time making coffee, for which I felt instantly guilty. He spoke no English and my German was embarrassingly poor. My faltering attempts at conversation were cut off with a swipe of his hand, indicating I should wait until his wife returned. Hoping to ingratiate myself, I presented the Amaretto. His reaction was a scowl of bemusement, and he promptly put it in a cupboard where he didn't have to look at it. Impenetrable silence followed. I felt wretchedly awkward. What on earth was I doing, limping up in filthy clothes to someone's elderly parents' flat the night before Christmas? And why, out of all the drinks, had I purchased Amaretto?

My discomfort mounted minute by minute until keys rattled in the door and Kerstin's mother swept in like a refreshing wind. The awkwardness vanished; she appeared thrilled that I had come and immediately lit the candle I had brought, on Kerstin's advice, from Köln cathedral. She ushered me towards the shower, and when I emerged she was laying the table with a feast of white asparagus covered in ham and horseradish sauce, smoked fish and toasted bread, washed down by chilled Mosel wine in elegant green-stemmed glasses.

Irmgard covered for her husband's cantankerous silence by telling me about the drama several weeks before. That November had seen the lowest rainfall ever recorded – a month ago you could almost walk across the Rhine – and forty-five thousand people had been evacuated when an unexploded bomb was discovered on the exposed riverbed. It had fallen from an Allied plane, probably around the same time they destroyed the statue of the Kaiser. 'One of yours,' she said. 'You could maybe take it with you.'

On Christmas morning I wandered the damp and deserted streets, stepping into a church with walls of delicate flowers. With the Christmas tree next to the altar, and pillars painted with leaves and vines, it felt like an abstracted forest, an internalised sacred grove. The old Germanic spirits of the woods had reasserted themselves in the church; even Jesus was nailed to two planks of wood.

In the afternoon, Irmgard took me on a drive up the winding Mosel Valley, through villages of Tudor-framed houses with turrets and lopsided walls, grapevines hanging over the streets, serifs of masonry. It was a glimpse of a southern, vale-dwelling, wine-drinking culture, altogether different to the beer-swilling lowlands. But the vineyards were cut back for winter and the slopes of the valley were brown; suddenly and intensely I found myself longing for summer.

I left Koblenz after dawn the next day, promising Irmgard I'd send a card from Istanbul. As I shook hands with Rolf banknotes rustled against my palm, and when I tried, genuinely, to protest, he closed my fingers around the money with draconian insistence. I felt instantly guilty again, but for different reasons.

Even in winter the Mosel had looked an airy and delightful river – 'the last stretch of a long valley of the utmost significance and beauty,' wrote Paddy – but my path continued up the darker, broodier Rhine. The purple hills glowed like plums and cloud bunched in the valleys. The town of Boppard swam past, its inhabitants pleasantly strange – an old woman who resembled a Quentin Blake illustration was fishing out leaves with a pink umbrella, while other old folk strolled the quayside in hats and coats, chortling – and then came innumerable river bends where castles blended chameleon-like into the crags they loomed from, the same 'gap-toothed and unfailing towers' my predecessor had seen; militarily ineffectual for centuries, the war had passed them by. By dusk, I had reached Sankt Goar.

No bed was waiting for me here. Paddy had walked almost to Hungary before it was warm enough to sleep outside, but that was before climate change had diminished Europe's winters. The air was mild, soft to the touch. It seemed as good a night as any to try my luck in the open.

Various options presented themselves. Nosing around for a suitable spot, somewhere sheltered, dry and discrete, I investigated and discounted railway arches, an abandoned woodshed, even under the tarpaulin of a boat moored in the marina. Then my eyes swung upwards to the ruin of Burg Rheinfels, a heap of rock hunkered on the hill, and almost involuntarily my legs started climbing. The main castle turned out to be impregnable – impregnability, after all, being a castle's primary function – and the less derelict part now housed the Romantik Hotel Schloss Rheinfels. But underneath this four-star hotel was a series of perfect human-length tunnels set into the wall. It was too romantik to resist.

The first three tunnels were running with slime, but the fourth was powder-dry. It was a short scramble up the ivy-strangled wall, and once I'd stowed my bag I took myself upstairs for an expensive glass of Riesling. At a table with a postcard view of Sankt Goar and the river, the lights of ferryboats bobbing midstream, I sipped my wine and endured the dubious stares of other diners, while waitresses dressed as Rhinemaidens fluttered between the tables. At nine o'clock I descended to crawl into my sleeping bag, burrowed snugly as a worm in the castle wall.

The effect was alchemical. When I stuck out my head in the light of dawn, having not only survived the night but slept soundly in my hole – waking at dreamy intervals to the clatter of trains and the whoops of owls – somehow I belonged in a way that I hadn't before. Sleeping out produced a sense of enhanced connection with the land, a feeling almost akin to ownership: the paradoxical entitlement of the rough sleeper, whose lack of rights somehow grants him a greater right than anyone else. After a proprietorial coffee I took the ferry to the eastern bank, the glow of this feeling still upon me, to climb the switchbacking stairway up the Rock of Lorelei.

Four hundred feet below, a twist of current marked the point at which the valley squeezed the Rhine into its narrowest channel, a river kink perilous to shipping. If Siegfried was the Teutonic Achilles, immortal but for a single spot, then this was the lair of the Teutonic Siren, the golden-haired water-maiden who lured sailors to drown. Over the years Romantic poets had rendered the legend thoroughly twee, but the Lorelei still claimed her victims: the year before, she'd capsized a barge carrying thousands of tonnes of sulphuric acid. I wondered how many wrecks lay below, rusting like the keys of the love-locks under the Kennedy Bridge at Bonn.

The castles started appearing now with almost frantic regularity. A later informant explained that as Germany wasn't unified until the late nineteenth century, private fiefdoms had abounded, unchecked by higher powers. With no government to exert control, there was nothing to stop any blue-blooded chancer with a mace and a suit of armour erecting his own fortified turret and using it as a base from which to tax and plunder. Like Somali pirate towns, these ruins were manifestations of a power vacuum.

Each of the villages I passed, with its half-ruined chunk of tower, muddled roofs and winding streets, was locked in stasis, development stunted, squeezed between river and rock walls. Kaub was so calcified that even its people moved slowly, as if about to freeze into the stones. Wandering through the archways, past shuttered restaurants and hotels boarded up for winter, I found my eyes drawn to the ruins of the old schloss: the stained and tumbledown pile of Burg Gutenfels, which seemed to offer the ideal combination of being derelict enough to be empty and intact enough to offer shelter. The experience of the previous night had given me a taste for castle-squatting.

After dark I picked my way between vineyards towards the very image of a haunted castle, glowing weirdly against a green sky, the regular stumps of the cut-back vines discomfortingly like gravestones. Its builders, for reasons known only to themselves, had neglected the construction of convenient tunnels for wayfarers to sleep in, but at the end of one terrace yawned a promising void. It turned out to be a disused gateway sheltered by an arch of stone, screened by vines and rusted chains. There was even a bench to lie on.

I stretched out in my sleeping bag, then leapt up as a horrible knocking came from the wooden doors. Instantly my mind filled with ghosts, but it was only the end of the bench banging when I moved. It took some time to settle, but I was too tired to stay awake long. If ghosts came – and they probably did – they accepted my right to remain.

After that, I perused each castle for the telltale dark spaces that suggested sleeping holes. It was both a private game and a new way of looking at a place, scouting around for somewhere to hide, slipping between the cracks of the landscape. The perfect ruin of Fürstenberg was only a few miles from Kaub and made me linger longingly. But I couldn't spend all my time squatting in abandoned castles, and I tore myself away.

Regretfully I saw the hills flatten, the river grow slower and wider. That magical valley was gone, and modernity reasserted itself with dreary inevitability. That afternoon came Bingen, where Paddy had spent a kindly Christmas, now a drab and uninspiring town sprawled along the bank. On an island offshore stood the Mauseturm, Mouse Tower, about which a signboard read: 'The famous and infamous Mauseturm of Bingen, built on a rock in the Rhine, was a customs tower and the last shelter from the mice for the evil bishop. However, it was of no use to him as he was eaten up alive by the grey nuisance.' I wished for a few grey nuisances to liven Bingen up a bit, but none was to be seen.

Things did get interesting on the arrival of Hubertus, a fevered-looking man in his forties who'd offered me a couch. He picked me up from the station for the short drive to his home, in a former manganese-mining colony in the hills. 'Are you Irish?' was the first thing he asked, and when I claimed vague Irish ancestry he exclaimed in a satisfied tone: 'I knew it. Red hair and green eyes!' As I have brown hair and blue eyes, this was my first clue to his eccentricity. He revealed he'd been awake for several nights in a row, and I supposed the sleep deprivation was affecting his colour perception.

The mining colony was an appropriate lair for Hubertus to inhabit: he was a collector of semi-precious stones, and the reason he hadn't slept was that he was ambitiously photographing his entire collection to sell online. His house was crammed with display cases, and when he switched on the lamps every surface glittered with quartz, agate, malachite, topaz, garnet, jet and chalcedony. How many minerals did he have? 'I don't know. Fifty thousand? A hundred thousand? I've no idea.' After a large and meaty dinner – he was almost delirious with hunger – I helped him carry some heavy boxes up the stairs to the attic, where another stash of his treasure was stored, thousands upon thousands of stones stacked to the raftered ceiling.

Hubertus was someone to whom collecting came as naturally as breathing. Before rocks it had been comic books – thirty thousand at the peak – and rock LPs. He'd stockpiled pornography too: 'As soon as the Berlin Wall came down I sold it all to the East Germans, all my old *Playboy* and *Hustler* collections. They bought them all, all that junk, even when they had nothing to eat.' He had an extensive library and became exercised on the subject of literature: 'Patrick Süskind is bullshit! It's not literature, it's bullshit. Read Anthony Burgess, read Nick Hornby, read anybody. Never read Süskind! Alan Moore is the greatest writer, comic book or otherwise. Better than James Joyce. Much better than Shakespeare.'

That night I lay under heavy blankets surrounded by sparkling jewels and read my way through a pile of graphic novels, perfectly preserved in plastic sleeves. When I entered the kitchen in the morning the sink contained a huge lump of calcite, and Hubertus still hadn't slept. The strain was clearly getting to him: his movements were erratic, and he asked me to do the washing-up because he kept dropping the plates. 'After two or three days of this, I get problems with my heart. In my next life I will collect stamps,' he said, seeing me off at the door. 'Or maybe not collect at all. All collectors are crazy.'

It took an hour to regain Bingen, and when I arrived the Rhine was lit by the first sunshine I'd seen for days. The town looked better in the sunshine, but not much. An old man and a young Japanese girl were skimming stones by the ruins of a bridge destroyed in the war. I rattled along at a fair old pace through birch woods pierced by sunbeams.

Mainz was ringed by the usual shit – McDonald's, Aldi and a Nescafé factory poking through the traffic lanes – fencing off the centre like a modern city wall. This was where Gutenberg printed his first Bibles, but the city was smashed to rubble by the Allies in the last days of the war. My river plod to Oppenheim was lit by bronze crepuscular rays pouring through the clouds. The road crept closer to the river and soon squeezed out my path altogether, leaving me to stumble along a forty-five-degree slope of loose rocks and impenetrable brambles. Eventually it became too much, forcing me along the road to be blared at by furious horns, and I finished my walk on the railway line, anxiously watching for trains. I arrived in Oppenheim fuming at the virtual impossibility of walking, as if the road's planners never considered that someone might one day happen to visit without a form of motorised transport. It was a regular grievance.

A red-brick cathedral stood in the centre of Oppenheim's Altstadt, and on a hill behind the town a ruined monastery gave a view over a satisfying sweep of the Rhine. The river glowed in the winter sun, and an icy wind made spheres of mistletoe bob in the trees like buoys. I considered borrowing a tarpaulin from a woodpile and building myself a nest in an archway, but the air was growing bitter and my body ached. The thought of sleeping in a soft bed overruled my desire for open skies; in a snug guesthouse called Gästhaus Schroeder I shelled out €30 for a room, luxuriating in the privilege of rented privacy. The sense of munificence was increased when a tap on the door revealed Herr Schroeder himself, bearing half a bottle of wine and a plate of stollen.

Next morning I was thankful I hadn't slept out: the clear skies of the previous night had been replaced by drizzle. After coffee, I struck south towards a water-soaked horizon. A sandy path led through woods beside the Rhine's wave-lapped beaches; there was something infinitely mysterious in the wet, murky light, and as the river faded into the indistinguishable sky it gave me the curious impression of heading for the sea. It felt like the path might go on, with nothing changing, for ever. Eventually I came to a village and sought directions from an old man in earmuffs and a floppy tweed hat. '*Engländer?*' he asked. When I nodded, he haltingly said: 'I learnt English in an English prison. I was there in the end of the war, March 1945 to April 1946. I was sixteen and a half, one of the last boys called up. Sixteen and a half in the war, seventeen in the prison, eighteen back home.' His blotched face creased as he frowned. 'It was not a good war. I am happy now there is no war between our countries.'

I bade him *Auf Wiedersehen*, and he wished me luck for the coming year. It was the last afternoon of 2011.

Signs of New Year festivities were evident in Worms, the streets littered with spent fireworks, gunpowder peppering the air. Back in Sinzig Stephanie's family had told me the legend here: somewhere beneath these streets was buried the treasure horde of the Nibelungs, who were either, depending on who told the story, the royal house of the Burgundians or a race of dwarves. I chose dwarves; it seemed no less unlikely. I had vague fantasies of stumbling across the riches – glinting, perhaps, at the bottom of a drain or at the border of a flowerbed – but the only evidence was a signpost reading 'Nibelungenring'. It was sad, but not surprising, that the best the modern world could do with the legend of a dwarfish treasure horde was to make it the name of a ring road and a pun on Wagner's opera.

'A hundred million euros will be blown on fireworks tonight. And they call this an economic crisis!' A man named Oliver had invited me to celebrate Silvester, New Year's Eve, at a party with friends. I assumed the party was in Worms, but soon after meeting we were bowling along at ninety miles an hour down the autobahn to Mannheim, my destination for the next day. This fast forwarding of my journey seemed more quirk of fate than cheat, but I was amazed at how unfamiliar, after only a few weeks of walking, car travel had become. In a blur of raindrops and headlights illuminated signs flashed by for Basel, Stuttgart, Frankfurt, Hanover, divorced from their distances and the directions of the compass. We crossed the Rhine in a flash; it looked no more than a stream. I tried to imagine seeing myself, through a driver's eyes, beside the road, how static I would appear. We stopped to collect two kegs of beer and were off again. I was just starting to formulate thoughts about whether the divorce of landscape from effort was responsible for a wider disconnection between people and their environment, when the car screeched to a halt. A whole day's walking had been compressed into half an hour.

By midnight, I was in a crowd of revellers watching explosives light the sky. Fireworks erupted from every garden, and blurred figures stumbled about in a fog of gunpowder smoke, lit by blinding red and green flashes, hurling bangers called China-Böllers merrily at one another. It seemed most un-German behaviour, especially when seven- and eight-year-olds were encouraged to fire rockets from their hands, leaping in and out of the explosions at their feet. 'Our neighbour is eighty-five and she hates us, I don't know why,' yelled Gerhard, our host, over the bombardment. I noticed that more than one China-Böller ended up under her car. The party ended at dawn with a nightcap of Laphroiag – 'It tastes like a moor,' someone was insisting, 'why would anyone want to taste a moor?' – and a circular, drunken argument about the integrity of the music of Nine Inch Nails, about which I had no opinion at all; but which was being conducted, for my benefit, entirely in English.

I awoke on a wooden floor and helped with the general clean-up. We had a late breakfast of leftovers, and in the middle of the afternoon I carried on my way. I said farewell to Oliver, Gerhard and his wife Tina, who walked me to the edge of Mannheim to locate the river. I felt quite weepy as I departed; the continual turnover of new friends could get quite exhausting.

That day too I said farewell to the Rhine, my steady companion for the past fortnight. The hangover stole the depth from the moment and I hardly noticed it go. Now I branched onto the Neckar, a smaller, faster-flowing river running laterally to the distant blue mountains of Odenwald. Cloud rolled up the slopes, as if the valleys were smoking. The people became more country-looking, with great overcoats, wide-brimmed hats and bulky leather boots.

In Heidelberg my safe house lay in the home of an Englishman named Paul Daniels – another Paddy aficionado – his Italian wife and their two children, whose speech flowed seamlessly between English, Italian and

German. Together we walked the Philosophenweg, the Philosophers' Way, through the forest into the heart of the city, the Oxbridge of the Rhine Valley, seat of theological learning for over six centuries. 'They call it *Brotlose Kunst*,' said Paul. 'Art that earns no bread.' Now much of the city was generic high street, the shoppers heading to New Year sales with the mindless quality of consumers everywhere, but the old centre, with its uniform rose-coloured stone, was the same city Paddy was enthralled by. Its castle was an Ozymandian collapse of tortured red rock, soaring walls worm-holed with tempting alcoves, archways and over-hangs, in which, if I hadn't been staying with Paul, I might have found a week's accommodation. This was the fortress that kickstarted the Romantic aesthetic of ruined glory; a century later, Nazi architects would inherit this tradition, envisaging how their works might look in states of magnif-icent decline.

Heidelberg was the home of the Roten Ochsen inn, the Red Ox, where Paddy had stayed on the last night of 1933. The place was still run by the same family, and its inte-rior had remained virtually unaltered since my predecessor thawed his boots beside the stove: 'a jungle of impedimenta encrusted the interior – mugs and bottles and glasses and antlers – the innocent accumulation of years, not stage props of forced conviviality.' The years had only added to the kleptomaniac clutter. Frau Spengel, the widow of the son of the very innkeeper Paddy had befriended, led me into a pub that looked more like a museum, a minimal-ist's worst dream, every inch of vertical space teeming with heraldic crests, armourial shields, oil paintings, crockery, hunting trophies, with tables scarred by hundreds of years of knife-work. These rooms were still the haunt of local student fraternities, and their drinking horns hung from a graffitied ceiling, along with the sabres their forerunners had duelled with. Framed photographs recorded the visits of Mrs Eisenhower and Mark Twain. There was a thank-you note from Otto von Bismarck.

History covered each surface like limescale, dense concretations of heraldry, memory, culture and anecdote, which perfectly reflected Paddy's elaborate writing style. Frau Spengel gave me tea in a room that may or may not have been the one he stayed in, in which I found myself expectantly waiting for some echo from the past, a feeling of proximity or connection. Being inside the Roten Ochsen was like being inside his brain, a museum of his fascinations.

Heidelberg was a nexus of other pathways too. My grandfather Taid studied German here in 1936, two years after Paddy walked through. Excerpts from his diary recount walking out of propagandist lectures after being quizzed on his views of Jews and Marxists, experiences that recalled Paddy's encounter with a schnapps-drunk Nazi sympathiser in this very inn: 'He suddenly rose with a stumble, came over, and said: "So? Ein Engländer?" with a sardonic smile. Then his face changed to a mask of hate. Why had we stolen Germany's colonies? Why shouldn't Germany have a fleet and a proper army? Did I think Germany was going to take orders from a country that was run by the Jews?' Perhaps they'd even argued with the same Nazis; I felt certain Taid would have come to the Roten Ochsen. Suddenly I was on the trails of two separate ghosts, whose invisible paths must have crossed with each other, as mine did with theirs.

And while I was still in the city, news arrived from home. My other grandfather, Herbie, had died the night before. Before leaving England I'd said goodbye, as he lay in his hospital bed, knowing that he was very old and probably wouldn't be around when I returned. Another ghost had crossed this tangled road.

My two grandfathers never met, as I had never met Paddy. They came from different societies, lived different lives, fought different wars: Taid was an intelligence officer – like Paddy – and Herbie was a bricklayer. But now, in a quirk of fate, both had joined me in Heidelberg. This pink city would forever be linked to them, to Paddy, and to me.

Walking south the next mild morning, past pines and fields of flowering rape, I knew I couldn't absorb the loss all at once. The news felt pale, far away from the reality I was walking through. Herbie's memory would follow me, another invisible trace in the air, as I left the Rhineland and passed into High Germany. Sometimes all you can do with loss is walk, and carry it with you.

3

A Great Cold Coming

High Germany and Bavaria

Looking down, I could see a scarlet banner with the swas-
tika on its white disc fluttering in one of the lanes, hinting
that there was still trouble ahead. Seeing it, someone skilled
in prophesy and the meaning of symbols could have fore-
told that three quarters of the old city below would go up
in explosion and flame a few years later; to rise again in
geometry of skyscraping concrete blocks.

A Time of Gifts

SOUTH OF HEIDELBERG, SUBTLE DIFFERENCES CREPT INTO THE
country. My journey towards the Austrian border was characterised by incremental shifts in landscape, dialect, wine
and beer, modulations that occurred so gradually I hardly
noticed where one characteristic ended and another began.
Perhaps the most perceptible change was in colour. Behind
me lay the browns of the riverlands, and the weeks ahead
would bring the whiteness of the winter south, but the
uplands in between revealed themselves in sky blues and
pearl greys, opalescent clouds looming over landscapes that
felt much larger than those of before. The hills were ener-
gising. Despite a dull and vaguely ominous ache in my left
foot, throbbing in time with each step, I pushed on south
as the light grew dim, arriving as darkness fell outside the
gates of Bruchsal's ornate and ludicrous schloss.

This palace was my first encounter with the German
High Baroque, an intimation of the Catholic south.

Paddy had slept in this rococo pile as the guest of the resident *Bürgermeister*, but since then the building had been destroyed by Allied bombs – these scrolling red and yellow walls were a perfect replica, built from plans discovered in the ruins. There was no bed for me here; the place was now a museum. Instead I stayed in a modern apartment with an engineer called Thomas, and my first act was to slip in his bathroom and snap his toilet seat into two perfect halves.

Despite this destructive arrival, he negotiated me into the palace in the morning before opening time. The halls and corridors were slathered in pink and grey marble; pillars dripped with vomits of gold, and ceilings writhed with fleshy cherubs and plump, rosy-nippled women. The feeling it produced in me was one of intense claustrophobia, a reaction altogether different from Paddy's, who found it enchanting. I could dimly imagine the 'sensation of wintery but glowing interior space', the sense of magic he had felt, but for me it was outweighed by the decor's sheer grossness. The war wasn't the only time an invading force had torched the place: peasants had previously sacked it during a revolt in 1502. At ten o'clock, as the lights came on and gold dazzled up every wall, it wasn't hard to imagine why.

The land beyond Schloss Bruchsal rolled upwards into the gentle humps of the Baden hills. The sky, massed with clouds lanced through with yellow sunbeams, resembled the ceiling frescos of the schloss, lacking only chubby babies dancing in the heavens. In the suburbs of Bretten, perhaps not far from where Paddy had been sheltered by dialect-speaking peasants – 'smoke had blackened the earthenware tureen and the light caught its pewter handle and stressed the furrowed faces, and the bricky cheeks of young and hemp-haired giants' – I stopped to eat in a kebab shop. When I mentioned I was walking to Turkey they gave me free lentil soup and bread, glass after glass of sugary tea; hospitable peasants these days, it seemed, were more likely to hail from Anatolia than Baden. The balding, bespectacled manager shook my hand as I left, and other Turks smiled kindly at me, as you might when a stranger says he wants to be an astronaut.

Regularly along that road appeared little tin signs showing the silhouette of a woman driving an antiquated vehicle, with the words 'Bertha Benz Memorial Route'. Innocuous as they seemed, these markers commemorated a journey of unimaginable significance. In 1888, Bertha, wife of engineer Karl Benz, test-drove her husband's prototype automobile on this road from Bruschal to Pforzheim. This seemingly unassuming jaunt was the maiden voyage of the world's first car. Even Karl was dubious about attempting the rough carriageway of the time, but by driving between the two cities, his wife proved that the automobile was a viable form of transport.

Just how viable, neither she nor Karl could have imagined. Less than fifty years later, in logical extrapolation, Germany would give that first car's descendants the world's first motorised highways. Hitler's road-building programme kickstarted a new era of transport infrastructure, speed and communication; before long, autobahns rolled across the continent. Every motorway, dual carriageway, flyover, overpass and underpass I'd been forced to navigate had sprung directly from the first drive of the Benz Patent Motorwagen Number 3.

This was emerging as the crucial difference between mine and Paddy's journeys. In the early 1930s there were cities and there were towns, and, at least in Germany, industrialisation had gone some way towards filling in the gaps. But between these urban areas were roads largely unadapted to cars, country lanes designed for horses rather than horsepower engines; there existed nothing like the networked tangle I was forced to navigate, laced by auto-bahns, landscapes that had been torn up and reconstituted for cars. When Paddy walked, around seventy miles of autobahn had been laid in Germany; as I followed eight decades later, there were seven thousand. The effect on the landscape was obvious, but considering the wider impacts – the collapse of distance, the shrinking of the map, the homogenisation of cultures, the rampant individualism, the urban expansion, the suburbs and exurbs, to say nothing of climate change – I felt this road should be marked by more than a few tin signs. A cenotaph might have been more suitable, a tomb to the Unknown Walker.

Appropriately, the ominous ache in my ankle grew harder to ignore. Each time my foot came down on the hard-impact surface – Frau Benz's indirect gift – pain pulsed in my heel. I resorted to the old trick of wrapping bandages around my feet, but this grew less effective every minute I travelled. Diverting to a forest path, I came upon a peculiar sight: in a clearing, miles from anywhere, an enormous pile of fresh bread, tomatoes, apples, bananas and pears lay apparently abandoned. There was nobody in sight, and after deliberating for a while I ate some of it. Walkers can get as superstitious as sailors: over the next few weeks, when everything seemed to have gone so wrong, I sometimes melodramatically wondered if I hadn't stolen something cursed.

Beyond the forest lay luminous meadows, and a wind-blown descent into Pforzheim. In an *Apotheke* I sought some miraculous cure for my pain; the apothecary told me I could only rest, but as I left she threw me a packet of Ibuprofen. It was a day of unlikely gifts: first lentil soup, then pain pills.

In Pforzheim a young and rather nervous tattoo artist put me up in her flat. The walls were covered in designs of mustachioed men and eyeless madonnas weeping drops of blood, sabres and muskets and cannon smoke like nineteenth-century woodcuts. She said she would sleep until the next afternoon and I could let myself out in the morning, but when I awoke it was clear I was in no state to travel. I loitered guiltily in the flat, hoping she wouldn't mind.

The day went by. A storm hit the town, apocalyptic sleet and lightning zinging past the windows, and when it cleared the streets outside smelt of metal and ionised air. I felt uncomfortable asking to stay longer, and left in the darkness early the next morning, trying to convince myself my foot was better. If anything, it was worse. My priority now was finding somewhere to shelter me until I recovered – I needed another orphanage – but Stuttgart, my next destination, was a long day's walk away. Unless, I thought, I compromised: I would take the train halfway.

This seemed a momentous decision, and I didn't know if it was right or wrong. Even the thought of resorting to transport could be the start of a slippery slope, and everything about it felt bad; but the facts remained that it hurt to walk, Pforzheim was a dismal hole, and I needed shelter. As my train pulled out of the station, I despaired at the betrayal. The landscape flying past was meaningless scenery and the weather was only colours in the sky, not experience or sensation. I disembarked in Ludwigsberg, a small town to the north, determined to hoof it the rest of the way, regardless of the pain.

Before long I was limping again, practically dragging my foot. On Stuttgart's outskirts, in a peculiar interzone of woodlands, barns and pastel-coloured tower blocks, with a mixture of grief and relief I gave up for the second time. I hopped on a streetcar to the station and waited for a train to Ulm.

The defeat was total now. My Stuttgart bed had fallen through, and a couple called Dierk and Dora had invited me to stay in Ulm, fifty miles further on, for as long as I needed. The plan made sense from every point of view but the purity of my walk. It meant compressing two days' journey into fifty-seven minutes, and it felt like treachery. I hobbled round and round the station, compulsively eating Milka chocolate bars in a pathetic attempt to cheer myself up.

The only thing I saw of Stuttgart, the high-tech powerhouse of Germany's south, was a field of rubble. Outside the station, a demolition zone was enclosed by a chain-link fence covered in thousands of placards, political cartoons, Dalai Lama portraits, plastic flowers, teddy bears, laminated photographs of police blasting people with water cannons, and yellow stickers with the words 'Stuttgart 21'. It turned out to be a protest about – of all humdrum-sounding provocations – the proposed redevelopment of Stuttgart railway station. At an information booth a grey-haired lady explained to me that the project was deeply controversial, involving the felling of three hundred trees. Her anger clearly went beyond plans for redesigned transport infrastructure. The local politicians were corrupt, she said. The police had cracked down brutally on protest, even blinding a man in one attack. Just as the Occupy movement wasn't really about the banks but about a wider discontent – Pepe's words came back to me, 'the cars, the buildings, the roads, the ugliness' – the banners on that fence sprung from deeper grievances.

She asked if I would come to the protest the next day. I said I'd be in Ulm. '*Ach*, the Ulmer people,' she muttered. 'They would like to see this plan succeed. But not us. Not in Stuttgart.'

This was a distraction from my own woes, but it didn't last. Minutes later, another train jerked me out of time and place again, a dislocation from the hills and forests streaming past. The state of Baden-Württemberg flashed by in a series of broken images, a postcard book of Swabian Scenes, and before I'd had time to adjust I was on the Bavarian border.

Dierk was waiting at the station. Stocky, short, with jugged ears and a wide, laugh-lined face, he bounded enthusiastically to his car in a pair of rubber shoes with individual toes, which made him look distinctly like a goblin. The house he shared with Dora was an electric grotto of lights that speckled the ceiling like stars, pulsing from red to green to pink to purple in a slow hallucinatory loop; stuffed seagulls dangled above a table of some rare hardwood. Viking helmets crowned the mantelpiece, and when I turned on the shower the shower-head glowed with pink LEDs. Amid this kitsch I would begin my recovery.

Dierk and Dora's first act of healing was to take me to their regular Friday-night tavern, where I was introduced to a table of boozy faces. We had crossed the Danube from Baden-Württemberg to Bavaria – the city of Ulm straddled both – and gone were the dainty 0.2 litre glasses of Düsseldorf and Köln, gone the elegant green-stemmed goblets of the Rhine: this was a land of hefty mugs, clumped boisterously together to roars of '*Prost!*' Sauerkraut was delivered, and a hog's leg the shape and size of a charred log, and the barman regularly appeared – 'he is the one who killed the pig you ate' – to dole out complimentary drinks. My welcome was a homemade 'hot bear', liquor distilled from beer, topped with cream and nutmeg. It was fantastically strong, and absolutely delicious.

In the morning Dierk took me to visit the urbane Dr Prinzing, who diagnosed Achilles tendon sprain and proscribed a week's rest. 'You shouldn't be walking on roads,' he scolded, 'this is what has harmed you.' There wasn't much choice, I tried to explain: Germany was covered in them. It was the fault of Bertha Benz... but I didn't want to sound like a fanatic. Proof of EU residency got me free ultrasound therapy and even a course of acupuncture; the doctor went further, fixing me up with an ankle support and orthopaedic soles. I praised European integration.

Outside rose the famous Ulmer Münster, the tallest church spire in the world, needling over the city like forgotten technology from an alien civilisation. 'Many people say it was a miracle it wasn't bombed,' said Dierk as we left the surgery. 'Everything else was smashed flat, the whole medieval city. But my father was a navigator in the war and he said it was no miracle. The RAF kept it standing to use as a landmark.'

Dierk was an Ulmer born and bred, a repository of anecdotes. 'This guy knows all about local politics,' he said as we passed a tattoo parlour. 'He's an old friend of mine. The politicians come here because he is an expert in intimate piercings.'

'Your politicians have intimate piercings?' I tried to imagine the sober-looking leaders of Germany jangling under their suits.

'Not just the ones in Ulm. They come from München, from all over Bavaria. Tattoos too. He organises parties with prostitutes also. Here, we are on the border between South Sweden and North Italy.'

'South Sweden and North Italy?'

He grinned; it was clearly a favourite joke. 'Baden-Württemberg is South Sweden, because that's where northern Europe ends. Bavaria is North Italy. It's a different culture.'

I asked where he fitted in: was he South Swedish or North Italian?

'Neither. I'm from Ulm. We are Swabians.'

Swabia was taking shape in my mind as a kind of German Somerset; its dialect was famously gnarled, rooted in deep peasant culture, and Swabians had a certain rustic look about them, a roughness and readiness that Dierk seemed to encapsulate. It was something I understood better when, on Prinzing-loaned crutches, I was able to hobble around the Münster several days later.

The church had been constructed not on the order of pope or king, but by the people of the city themselves, an act of pride and passion. Generations of stone carvers had continued their parents' work, crowding the gutters with *Wasserspeier*, water spitters, in the form of griffins, lions, elephants, dragons, monkeys, fishes, hounds and boars, and the joyous irreverence of the carvings gave a sense of the cockeyed humour that must have thrived in the region. Murals depicted not only thieves and prostitutes being flung into hell but priests and kings as well, and in the Last Supper, the artist had included himself as a thirteenth disciple, angrily demanding more money for his work. One gargoyle was an ostrich that shot rainwater out of its arse, in the direction of the house belonging to a woman who had spurned the carver's advances. I wondered how the carver would have felt to know that house would later be obliterated by incendiary bombs.

'Scarlet-cheeked women from a score of villages were coifed in head-dresses of starch and black ribbon that must have been terrible snow-traps,' wrote Paddy. 'They gathered around the braziers and stamped in extraordinary bucket-boots whose like I never saw before or since ... A late medieval atmosphere filled the famous town.' But only a fragment of ancient Ulm had survived the firestorm, saved by a network of canals that stopped the flames from spreading. The Allied raid was as devastating as the Nazi bombardment of Rotterdam, and achieved an architecturally similar homogeneity. The few remaining timber-framed buildings looked like listing arks, ready to keel over at any moment. From the quays below, Swabian traders had once embarked down the Danube in box-shaped boats to the Black Sea. I would catch up with the 'Ulmer boxes' later, on the Hungarian border, but incapacitated as I now was I found it hard to believe I would get much further.

My ankle's condition barely improved, the pain ballooning morning and night. Without the crutches, it was an effort to cross to the other side of the room. Dora advised folk remedies, bandaging cottage-cheese poultices to draw out the swelling. I thought of Siegfried, the Achilles of the Rhine, and wished I could have smeared my heel with dragon's blood rather than cheese.

As the week crawled by, I fought down depression. Prinzing couldn't say when I'd be fit to walk again; injuries like this could take months to heal. This idea drove me into a state of near-total anxiety and I was overcome with bleak thoughts of simply giving up. I upped my Ibuprofen dose, taking 800 mg a pop, which gave me a full, fuzzy head and slight euphoria. Blizzards occurred outside the double glazing and I longed to be out in the snow, to feel the cold and the wind.

Dierk and Dora flew away on holiday after a week. They arranged for me to stay with friends, a young couple called Michi and Waldi, who, in the same open-hearted spirit, offered me their spare room for as long as I needed. Being in their company was a cure for my dismal moods, and one painstaking day at a time things started to improve. The throbbing diminished every morning; tentatively I discovered I could put weight on my foot, ascend stairs without pain, take myself out for cautious limps around the block. My first small triumph was climbing the hill that rose above their flat; at its summit lay the fortress of Kuhberg, a Nazi detention camp, but I associated that grim place only with relief.

Prinzing delivered his prognosis as the fortnight drew to a close. The tendon wouldn't fully heal for weeks, but if I started slowly, with hiking poles to take the strain off my foot, I might risk walking on. The best thing would be to cycle for the first few days, which would circulate blood to the foot without giving too much strain.

'You can borrow my bike,' said Michi. 'Ride it as long as you need, then leave it somewhere where I can come and pick it up in the summer.'

I asked if there was any limit to her generosity.

'The limit is Vienna,' she said.

So it was settled: I would leave on Monday. My joy was overwhelming. Cycling was a compromise, but at last I'd be moving again; it was a modern variation of Paddy's journey on borrowed horse over the plains of Hungary. To celebrate, Michi and Waldi took me to a *Ritteressen*, a fake medieval feasting hall, where we drank tankards of mead and ate pure fat off wooden platters while the host, a portly man dressed as a monk, encouraged tables of wildly excited students to drink themselves silly. We watched in horrified fascination as he fitted a chastity belt to a giggling student nurse, and forced her to down a stein of beer before giving her the key. Then he locked another student's head into an iron pig mask, into which he poured bottles of beer while the other diners pounded the tables to a chant of '*schluck, du Sau!*' Michi translated this, with some reluctance, as 'swig, you sow!'

A woman sitting at our bench turned to me with a concerned expression. 'Have you been in a German restaurant before? It is not always like this.'

Monday came, and I tethered my rucksack, with my brand-new hiking poles, to the rack of Michi's mountain bike. We hugged one another goodbye and I freewheeled down the hill.

There was a ritual to observe before I left the city. I couldn't go without climbing the seven hundred and sixty-eight spiral steps of Ulmer Münster, my own small victory parade. The staircase corkscrewed upwards like the calcified intestine of a dragon, a greater and grosser relative of the gargoyles teeming its walls. There below me was the city, obliterated and resurrected – an altogether different roofscape from the one Paddy had seen, but, blurred by height, 'the foreshortened roofs of the town shrank to a grovelling maze' much the same – while distantly, behind the winter haze, lurked the invisible Alps. Great heights have simplicity: behind me was how far I'd come, and ahead how far I had to go. I traced the green-brown ribbon of the Danube until it twisted out of sight; and then I descended, mounted my steed, and chased after it.

~~~~~

Within minutes the Münster was behind me, a rapidly shrinking needle of stone, and the city was whisked away into the folds of the river. It felt magnificent to be moving, whipping past hydroelectric plants squatting over the water they had quelled, disturbing waterbirds so white they looked like gaps in an unfinished painting. In Günzburg the streets were festooned with bunting for Carnival season. This was Bavaria and the dialect had shifted: the bread rolls in the bakery were not *Brötchen* but *Semmel*, and rather than *Guten Tag* the greeting was *Grüß Gott*, 'God greet you'. After those stationary days, speed was exhilarating and addictive. The only way to overcome any lingering reservations about replacing my feet with wheels was to throw myself into it, to enjoy it to the fullest extent. It was an absolute pleasure, therefore, to rush down the last green hill into Burgau, where I had shelter that night.

In the morning the landscape was white. After so many mild weeks, winter had come at last.

Snowploughs were out on the roads, piloted by identically chubby men who nodded solemnly as I passed. A leering car-park attendant was putting the finishing touches to a well-endowed snow-woman, smoothing the breasts with a mittened hand. On either side spread furrowed fields, the bordering pine woods etched in white as if dry-brushed. My tyres scored interweaving tracks of slush, shattered thin puddles. I ventured onto smaller lanes, out of the snowploughs' jurisdiction, churning through inches of powder that snowballed around the brakes and had to be frequently cleared. Soon I was beyond all roads, cutting a virgin path through forest, and when I stopped for thermos coffee the only sound was the soft collapse of snow from sagging branches.

Cupping my coffee in gloved hands, steam curling in the air, I felt a happiness so immense it almost couldn't be contained. The world was reduced to its simplest parts: things revealed themselves as they were, not what I expected them to be. Germany resolved itself in my mind, announced itself as real and whole, and perhaps for the first time on my walk I understood that I was actually there.

Revelations such as this would arrive infrequently, always sudden, always startling. I would realise that days had passed and I had been plodding along, letting one thing lead to the next, grown comfortable in certain rhythms of motion and of thought; then abruptly, the skin of the world would peel away without the slightest warning. I stared in astonishment, assembling the facts: I was in Bavaria, in a pine forest under snow, winter had begun at last, and I was alone. Each of these recognitions brought its own thrill, and when I pedalled on again I felt as if I had stepped through a hidden door.

The forest ended at a village where I bought fresh semmel and a pretzel, the staple of Germany's south. Dierk had said its three holes represented the Trinity, but the twisted shape looked older than that, a symbolic love-knot or entwined tree roots, something pre-Christian. Bavaria was Catholic country again – the roadsides scattered, as around Kevelaer, with candlelit crucifixions – but an earlier, more pagan sense underlay the religiosity. There was a feeling of deeper tradition, a stauncher conservative culture. In every village rose a tall wooden pole, painted with blue and white diamonds or stripes, topped with fir trees or sacred hearts and adorned with crests that depicted aspects of village life: blacksmiths, butchers, firemen and farmers were all represented. These were maypoles, annually renewed. And what was a maypole but a totem pole, the symbol of a tribe?

In the baroque city of Augsburg I stayed with Alexander, a combined hair stylist, ayurvedic chef and opera producer; his next production was *Der Ring des Nibelungen*, Wagner's fantasy of the legends I had heard on the Rhine. He fed me ethical super-foods and I spent a day poling round the streets with my aluminium sticks, acutely aware of how many other people seemed to have crutches, canes and other walking aids; we exchanged gloomy, understanding glances, as if members of a secret fraternity. The city was a resplendent hive of arches, pillars and balconies; its cobbled streets were laced with canals and gave off an aura of affluence and self-satisfaction. 'This is an obstructive city,' Alexander said dismissively. 'All its energy and creativity is drawn away by München. In the sixteenth century Augsburg was thriving and München was a backwater. Then something changed. München boomed, while Augsburg stagnated.

This stagnating energy remains. Augsburg thinks it's rich and proud but it has an inferiority complex, a jealousy of success.'

After another day on wheels I sighted München the next afternoon, a mass of towers bristling on a grey horizon. Having broken through its defensive rings of railways, roads and infrastructural sprawl, I came to a halt in a quiet square walled in neoclassical stonework. The last pool of sunlight drained and a chill rushed through the streets, a blue blast of frozen air spreading from the shadows. I pushed my steed through snowbound parks and boulevards of severe façades, feeling very small between the buildings. 'The draughtiest city in the world,' wrote Paddy, and I was inclined to agree: there was nothing colder than a stone city on a cloudless winter's night.

München was the birthplace of Nazism and its spiritual home. When Paddy was here Brownshirts were carousing in the beer halls, and the first concentration camp had recently opened in a village called Dachau ten miles to the north. 'The proportion of Storm Troopers and S.S. in the streets was unusually high,' he wrote, 'and the Nazi salute flickered about the pavement like a *tic douloureux* ... sentries with fixed bayonets and black helmets mounted guard like figures of cast-iron and the right arms of all passers-by shot up as though in reflex to an electric beam.'

Now I meandered past yuppies and punks, hipsters and tramps, immigrants and students, a pair of elderly Arabs in keffiyehs daintily lifting the hems of their robes over slushy puddles. But the week before, the police had fought to separate a hundred neo-Nazis from three hundred anti-fascist protestors in one of these same squares. Kettled behind police lines, the skinheads had provocatively blasted out the theme tune to the *Pink Panther*, the unlikely anthem of a racist group who had murdered Turkish kebab-shop workers over the past decade.

For two nights I stayed with the affable Holger, whose taste in interior decoration revolved almost exclusively around kitsch and vintage erotica. His flat was like a porno-graphic version of Heidelberg's Roten Ochsen inn: every surface was covered in a lifetime's collection of cheerful smut, ranging from Orientalist harems to lusty sci-fi alien vixens, statuettes of coy nymphettes, Hindu goddesses, African queens, round-breasted Indonesian dancing girls, plastic comic book figurines, 1960s nudey magazines, min-iature Priapi, Victorian porn, even an assortment of antique dildos posing as art objects. In a city so tainted by fascism, there was something glorious about it. It was the height of degenerate art; the Nazis would have burnt the lot.

Leaving this steamy den the next morning, I explored on foot. I'd heard much about Bavarians from Germans in other parts of the country, an antipathy perhaps analogous to how many Americans feel about Texans. 'Bavarians are... special,' Michi had said, while Michaela in Krefeld had given a revolted account of how they consumed white sau-sages: 'They squeeze them out of their skins like toothpaste. They eat them for breakfast. It's disgusting!' With this in mind, I made straight for a tavern to order *Weißwurst* and *Weißbier*, white sausage and wheat beer, on the traditional side of midday. The Weißwurst were served in a lion-headed tureen, floating in parsley-infused water, resembling waxed specimens from a medical museum. I didn't squeeze them out of their skins but ate them quickly, washed down with beer, and tried not to think about it too much. The interior of Sankt Kajetan church, which I visited afterwards, looked distressingly similar: fatty white columns twisting and bulg-ing like contorted sausages, angels and cherubs sculpted from pure fat.

My real destination that day was the famous Hofbräuhaus, where Paddy had drunk himself senseless in 1934. This cavernous beer hall was a nexus of converging stereotypes – lederhosen and oompah bands, woodcock-feathered Alpine hats, buxom barmaids and foaming beer steins – a temple to Bavarian gastronomic excess. Paddy had gone to town on the place: 'Hands like bundles of sausages flew nimbly, packing in forkload on forkload of ham, salami, frankfurter, krenwurst and bratwurst and stone tankards were lifted for long swallows of liquid which leapt out again instantaneously on cheek and brow ... features dripped and glittered like faces at an ogre's banquet.' Now the 'feasting burghers' had been replaced by American exchange students, Japanese tourists sipping coffee rather nervously and smiling politely at the drunks. The Hofbräuhaus seemed about as authentic as the mock-medieval feasting hall with the chastity belt-wielding monk; a theme park, a pastiche of Bavarian culture. There was even a gift shop selling branded baseball caps.

Not getting drunk wasn't an option, however. The very atmosphere brought on a feeling of instant intoxication. The drinkers were seated at trestle tables running the length of the hall, served by blondes with bulging breasts and pretzel girls posing for the cameras; one of these professional wenches delivered a glass as long as my forearm, and my table filled up with boozers who trammelled me to the furthest end, with no possibility of escape.

It was only four o'clock in the afternoon. I became sunk in boozy gloom that peaked around the middle of my second giant glass, and by the time I'd started the third it was lessening with every gulp. The alcohol flipped a switch, and Paddy's description sprung to life as if a ghost-train ride had commenced: suddenly my table-mates were shovelling down dripping lumps of knödel, sawing through Bible-sized slabs of meat, and the tubas and trombones kicked up a plodding, ponderous tune, intestinal tract music, geared less towards dancing than digestion. An abortive attempt to leave was thwarted by a sinister black-bearded character who motioned me back to my seat with a steak knife – '*Bier*, Nick, *Bier!*' he growled and I wondered vaguely how he knew my name – and inebriated songs started up at adjacent tables. This wasn't a cultural experience that could be comprehended sober, much less enjoyed: the beer made sense of the oompah band, and the oompah band made sense of the wider Hofbräuhaus, the clunk of the weighty mugs and the bellowed conversation, while the tourist tat was a diminishing smudge on my peripheral vision.

I had only seen a portion of the vast emporium. As I wandered from room to room the space unpacked itself, passageways segmenting into passageways, stairways expanding to other floors with warrens of smaller chambers. In these narrow ulterior rooms, time slipped backwards. These tables were lined not with tourists, but with elderly men cramming their cheeks with meats and pickles from greasy plastic tubs, playing cards with unfamiliar decks of acorns, leaves, hearts and bells. Extravagantly mustachioed and bearded, they were dressed in extraordinary costumes of lederhosen and leaf-green waistcoats adorned with gleaming brass medallions, rope-banded felt hats bristling with the feathers of forest birds, an abstract visual code like the symbols of sylvan freemasons. Blue eyes rolled grumpily as I passed between the rows; I wasn't sure I was welcome here. These clothes weren't worn for my benefit, or that of any other spectator; there was strength in their absurdity, and their almost deliberate ridiculousness felt like a mark of cultural pride, an emblem of apartness. When I woke the next day – rottenly hungover, surrounded by vintage porn – it felt like I'd blundered on the secret rites of a tribe.

I'd fared better than Paddy, at least, whose 'hoggish cat-alepsy' had resulted in the loss of his notebook, stolen by a pimply youth while its author drank himself unconscious. After splashing water on my face I loaded up the mountain bike and, my own book safely stowed, left Holger's and headed out into driving snow. More had fallen in the night and it was still falling. Cars groped their way down the streets in furrows of filthy slush. Across a bridge guarded by snow-shouldered statues, on the far bank of the river Isar, I was immediately out of the city.

Cold air and movement were excellent remedies for my *Katzenjammer*, the thumping in my head. I pedalled precariously through a white forest, snow drifting in small flakes and settling in my beard. Parents were dragging chubby children on toboggans like sacks of potatoes. Very black crows circled the Isar, and very white swans floated on it. A deep impression of silence had fallen over the land.

Riding a bicycle in these conditions was like being on a very unsteady, unpredictable animal that bucked at the slightest tremble of the handlebars; even moving my head at the wrong time was enough to throw me off. The snow changed everything, imposing its own terms on the world, and I skidded and lurched haphazardly through morning and afternoon. This would be my last day on wheels: after another night's freeze these roads would be impassable. Michi's bike was a hindrance now and would have to be abandoned. All I could do was hope that these four days had been enough and my ankle was strong enough to walk.

Half a day southeast of München came an architectural shift. The houses resembled Alpine chalets, barn-like buildings with carved gables dripping like wooden icicles, the eaves piled with blue-shadowed drifts. The villages smelt of wood smoke and horses. Sturdily wrapped men and women knocked ice off their boots outside yellow-lit bakeries; there was a cosseted, gossipy, provincial air. Above the villages misty forests rose into higher ground, the texture of pines like a wolf's matted fur in a picture book. Dimly recollected images of the previous night – those jaunty woodcock hats and brass-festooned jerkins – fell into place like the pieces of a jigsaw puzzle. This was the spirit those lederhosen-clad old men were channelling, never mind the Hofbräuhaus. This white, wolfish land was Bavaria's *genius loci*.

In a village called Holzolling a woman named Luisa had offered me a bed. She was a friend of Francesca, the girl-friend of Claudia, Kerstin's sister – I needed a mnemonic to remember all this – the last of the Meyer family connec-tions that had served me so well on the Rhine. She lived on a horse farm in the Mangfall Valley, and by the time I found the place the snow was indigo with night, and even with my winter gloves my hands were frozen to the curve of the handlebars.

Luisa was in the yard hefting sacks of horse food. I pitched in and was rewarded with slabs of black bread and cheese, and a mug of Earl Grey so good it almost made me cry. A rangy woman with strong blue eyes and a face nipped by wind, she had abandoned graphic design to move out here to follow her dream of breeding Trakehner horses. Once the horses of the Prussian nobility, one of the most popular breeds in the German Empire, Trakehners had almost been wiped out in the Second World War: req-uisitioned, machine gunned, eaten by starving refugees or frozen to death on the long flight west as Russian troops advanced. Now Luisa was trying to save the breed from dec-ades of decline.

'When I came here, at first the locals thought I was a silly rich girl, coming from the big city,' she told me. 'They learnt to respect me when they saw how serious I was. But farmers don't like horse people. What can I say? I don't like farmers much either. They don't like us because, since the war, horses have not been necessary. They are only used for carriage rides, or pulling beer barrels in Oktoberfest. They are seen as a luxury, and farmers resent the good way we treat them.' The grooms she employed weren't German, but Hungarian and Romanian. 'Eastern Europeans still understand horses, especially Romanians. Horses are part of life for them. I've tried hiring locally, but the boys round here aren't interested. They are looking for office jobs in the city.'

My bedroom smelt of hay and fresh bread; I opened my eyes to roosters crowing, horses stamping in the stalls. After breakfast I wheeled the bicycle to the barn, its duty done, to wait for Michi to collect it when the weather was warm. Luisa waved me off from the stables as I took my first tentative steps, learning the rhythm of the hiking poles, walking now with my hands as much as my feet. The poles took pressure off my weakened ankle, and although the tendon would still throb at the end of each day, like an insistent memory – it would continue aching for weeks – this felt like a new start.

Now began the misty uplands that crept towards the Austrian border, hazing in and out of forest and snatched-away horizons. These were my last days in High Germany, and my happiness at walking again was magnified by the knowledge of approaching a new country; a hushed, slightly breathless sense accompanied those miles. I followed the Mangfall, a noisy blue river bubbling with yellow pools, past riverside houses with no sign of life, their occupants apparently in hibernation, snuggled up like Moomintrolls in darkened rooms.

Rosenheim was a small, smug city with aspirations of being Italian, with pastel buildings and archways and coffee shops in cobbled squares. On clear days, I was told, there was a fine view to the Alps - a mountain called the Wildkaiser, the Wild Emperor, to the east - but, as on the days before, the range was hidden by the murk. Past Rosenheim I got lost in a mess of lakes, frozen ponds, heathlands and anonymous villages, locating myself at the Inn, a river famed for its green water, flowing like a stream of arsenic down towards the south.

A lengthy tramp uphill brought me to tiny Söllhaben, where Paddy had slept a night. It was a place of rather dull houses with woodsheds stacked with an intricacy that hinted at neat, obsessive minds; but once past those, a silent and secretive landscape spread away. Using my poles to steady myself in unexpected drifts, I practically waded into a valley of grey pines dusted white, the faintest intimation of mountains glowing under a golden sky. The snow played tricks on my senses. I kept hearing soft explosions that sounded like someone walking behind me hitting a barrel with a hammer, which turned out to be the rhythm of my trousers brushing together. The uniform whiteness was dizzying; I was unprepared for the visual relentlessness of winter. At one point the road ahead turned an unearthly green, and cars that passed irregularly did not seem to get further away, but shrank to a rapid vanishing point in nothingness.

On the frozen shores of the Chiemsee lake, I'd hoped to get a ferry to the other side - I still felt I was owed a boat ride after my snubbing on the Rhine - but no ferries ran that route in the depths of winter. Instead I stayed a night in Prien in a chalet buried under snow, and in the morning I continued south, skirting the lake, east past Röttau, through woodlands shimmering with ice. The temperature was plunging now and there were rumours of a great cold coming in the days ahead; people spoke of it in hushed, respectful tones, as if it was an important guest whose visit must be endured. The only sounds in those white forests were far-off axes chopping wood and the shuddering reverberations of woodpeckers, engaged in similar winter work. My breath poured out like steam from a ventilation shaft, and when I thought of the approaching cold a feeling of sheer lonely delight almost overwhelmed me.

'Vague speculation thrives in weather like this,' wrote Paddy. 'The world is muffled in white, motor-roads and telegraph-poles vanish, a few castles appear in the middle distance; everything slips back hundreds of years.' So it did for me. In the sinisterly named village of Marwang I stopped for Helles beer, and put away a sizzling mass of dumplings, potatoes, pork and cheese swimming in hot oil. Around the bar sat a group of farmers with faces as knobbled and gnarled as the gargoyles of Ulmer Münster, staring with a mixture of sorrow and shyness, unsure what to make of me. Their conversation sounded like a blend of German, Italian and Welsh, a peasant accent unlike anything I'd heard before. Every home had the cryptic sigil 20*C+M+B*12 chalked over the door. Caspar, Melchior, Balthazar 2012, I decoded: a salutation for the Three Wise Men.

The Alps lay tantalisingly close. Whenever there was a break in the trees I squinted south, hoping to see them, but the horizon stayed sullenly sunk in the same white gloom. My route lay along their northern flank, and it was possible I'd skirt them by miles without ever seeing them appear. But as my mind formed that thought – as I reconciled myself to their absence – I looked up and there they were. One peak then another gathered shape before my eyes, sharpening into perfect focus and then trembling out of existence, as if trying to make up its mind whether or not to establish itself in solid form. It felt inconceivable that things so huge could come and go so quietly. I stopped walking, determined to concentrate every part of my energy on them. Like shy animals they froze, then rapidly merged back into the sky. I waited, but they never returned. The whole vision couldn't have lasted more than five minutes, but when I walked on, my journey felt immeasurably greater for it.

'They come and go like that all the time. Sometimes we feel the mountains decide to go somewhere else for a day, as if they have a secret meeting place, and we are not invited.' Adrian and Helga, my hosts in Traunstein, had spent years living in the Alps before returning to the lower world, and they understood my sentiments. In Romania and Bulgaria, I would hear other mountain people talking in similar ways.

We drank wheat beer after dinner, and they taught me that in Bavaria glasses were clinked at the bottom, not the top. '*Weißbier und Frauen stößt man unten an*' went the phrase, roughly translated as 'wheat beer and women one bangs below'. Thus lubricated, the conversation swung to the subject of Bavarian uniqueness. Even though Bavaria combined every stereotype of Germany, as demonstrated by the Hofbräuhaus, Bavarians had more in common, culturally and spiritually, with their neighbours across the Alps than their compatriots on the Rhine. There was even a secessionist movement for an independent Alpenrepublik of Upper Bavaria, Alpine Austria and Tyrol, the mountain people united in a single Catholic state. This was a fantasy, a conservative utopia, but the thought experiment was intriguing. Despite the EU's unhappy convulsions the German federation seemed strong, although maybe it was only money that glued its cultures together. If the federation ever dissolved and an Alpine Republic seceded, what would be more natural than for the states to assume their ancient forms, rallying for protection and comfort around local dialects? Might there be another Bardische

Revolution, a Swabian revolt? I envisaged the Rhineland castles springing back to life as the strongholds of modern robber barons, stretching chains across the river once more to tax the shipping. It was an enjoyable fantasy for my last night in Germany.

The great cold had arrived, as predicted. After half an hour's walk the next morning, leaving the last friendly houses below, the water in my flask had frozen into a solid block. My beard and moustache had hardened into knotted clumps of ice that were too painful to remove, icicles of snot-water dangling from my nose, and the ink ran sluggish in my pen when I stopped to write. I passed through forests so deep in snow that the trees looked like melted candles; even the barbs on barbed-wire fences wore tiny caps of white. Growths of icicles hung from the roadside crucifixions, and frosted pine branches had been placed at the bleeding feet of the Christs like offerings to a forest god.

The snow was less in evidence on the leeward side of the hills. Disappointment filtered in when its perfect whiteness was broken up; something in me longed for it to get more and more extreme, to build towards a winter without end.

Yet the dreary-looking town of Ainring carried its own excitement. The smoky twilit land beyond – I could hardly tell if the grey squared blocks were fields or segments of a city – was the third country of my walk. Austria lay down a nondescript road that looked like it could only end at a suburban cul-de-sac, but brought me instead to the green Saalach river, where nothing stirred but a ginger cat picking its way along the bank. Over the footbridge, a battered tin sign informed me I was entering an *Atomkraftwerkfrei*, nuclear-free, Republic of Austria. Immediately over the river, the outskirts of Salzburg began.

There was little sense of transition. Bavaria and Salzburgerland formed the intersection of a cultural Venn diagram, and the gathering darkness masked their differences. It took two hours of tramping the streets, huffing clouds of frozen air, to find the house I was looking for; Alexander from Augsburg had given me the address of a friend, and by the time I arrived cold had seeped into my very core. Gudrun lived near the Salzach river – the Saalach was its tributary – and entering her warm apartment was like sinking into a restorative bath. She fed me pumpkin soup and black bread, and it seemed that no combination of pleasures could have been more perfect.

I stepped outside the next morning to a bright, bone-freezing day, the wind so cold it was like a slow fire burning at the ears. A curious herd of snow-covered mountains nuzzled the streets. The Salzburgers were natty dressers, the women in fur-trimmed coats and mufflers, the men in elegant leather gloves and black trilbies or Alpine hats, tapping along in polished shoes under the arches of grand stone buildings, trailing plumes of cigarette smoke. I got the impression they dressed that way in order to impress the city itself. It was a place of domes and stairways, ironwork and elaborate façades, architecture so proud of itself that even the McDonald's 'M' was displayed in a heraldic crest held aloft by a rampant lion. Mozart, Salzburg's most famous son, was referenced everywhere, mostly in the form of truffles displaying his smirking face; in a few hundred years, perhaps, the great composer would be misremembered as a long-ago chocolatier.

Gudrun set me on my way with a bag of these truffles the following day, and I left the white-stoned city along a suburban road heaving with morning traffic. The nearby hamlet that Paddy had stayed in, 'too small for any map', was on the map now and much the worse off for it, absorbed into the Salzburg commuter belt that I escaped by half sliding, half falling down a long hill into the snow-scape below.

At that temperature there was no soft ground. Tarmac was my friend again, hard and flat being preferable to hard and bumpy. Ploughed fields and frozen molehills were par-ticular perils for the ankles, and snow, I was finding out, was never a uniform surface. It looked simple enough to traverse, but my body had to work twice as hard to a rhythm of step-sink, step-sink, with the steady schoosh-schoosh of powder flying off my boots. A shortcut plunged me into a gulley surfaced with a frozen crust that collapsed when I took too heavy a stride, sinking me thigh deep. I could only proceed with tiny bird steps, concentrating on keeping my body as light as possible, but whenever my mind began to wander – even starting to hum an old tune – I would crash back through the surface.

After several hours of this my strength gave out and I threw myself down, too frustrated to go on, gnawing despairingly at a half-frozen sandwich. Sometimes giving up was the best strategy. I heard a snort, saw steam in the air, and out of nowhere appeared two riders on horses as hairy as dogs. I leapt up from my hole in the snow, brushing the crumbs from my ice-beard, gesticulating like a desperate goblin. The two purple-faced, fur-hatted men expressed no surprise when I asked for directions – I think if they had, I would have despaired entirely – merely pointing me on my way as if I was doing nothing unusual. Somehow this brief visitation gave me the strength to continue.

The next few days were a tug-of-war between wilderness and cosiness, the hardships of subzero walking interspersed delightfully with bouts of homely *Gemütlichkeit* – a quality translated as 'snugness, warmth, the feeling that you are accepted' – an evolutionary survival strategy in winters such as this. In the village of Windbichl, which truly was a hamlet too small for any map, another friendly house opened its doors and the ice in my moustache dissolved in a scalding shower. After schnitzel and sauerkraut the Starlinger family took me out to watch an *Eisstock* tournament. The game resembled curling, played on a pitch of ice down which the players slid *Stocks*, heavy wooden pucks banded with dented iron, to hit the *Taube*, 'dove', at the far end. Something about it felt familiar and I realised where I'd seen it before: exactly the same activity is taking place in the background of Breughel's 'Hunters in the Snow', a painting used, oddly enough, on the cover of one edition of *A Time of Gifts*. Apart from the fluorescent tubes lighting the scene, nothing about the picture had changed in four hundred years.

The tournament was competitive, but they charitably interrupted play to let me have a go. Much was made of showing me exactly how to grip the handle, how to bend my knees just so, and on my first attempt I sent the stock winging down the middle to hit the dove square on: a perfect shot. I expected hearty congratulations, but everyone looked a bit upset at my beginner's luck. The next stock was taken away from me and I wasn't allowed another turn.

Beyond Windbichl, I was back in wilderness again. Forest stretched to the next town and after a village called Unterfeitzing – even the names growing wilder now – the road I'd been following simply ended. I entered the woods up a track of ice that must have been a stream in the summer, and once that had petered out, for the first time on my journey, no path of any description lay ahead.

Following the shivering compass needle, I tried to maintain a straight line northwards through the trees. It was less navigation than an act of faith. My eyes kept inventing imaginary tracks, which led me in all kinds of wrong directions, and my feet automatically took me along the contours that suited them best, no matter how dogmatically my brain tried to keep them straight.

This brief encounter with pathlessness was a fantasy of freedom. But there was something else there too, and I was surprised to identify it as an undercurrent of fear that surfaced as soon as I sensed what genuine aloneness might be like. There was no one to help me find my way, no manmade things to guide me out. All I could do was keep going and trust that I reached the end of the forest before darkness fell.

The trees thinned. Ahead was a clearing and telephone poles, half a dozen farmhouses scattered down a white hillside. The sight of inhabitation brought a rush of relief, but at the same time, with equal force, regret and disappointment. Suddenly the adventure had ended. Now I couldn't go wrong if I tried. The freedom had been an illusion; it seemed absurd that I'd felt anything remotely like fear, with civilisation just over the next rise.

This was a feeling that would return again and again on my journey. Perhaps all adventures are like this: flirting with the wilderness but knowing we can't truly enter it, wanting to lose ourselves in imaginary realms like we once did in childhood stories, in the part-remembered, part-confabulated landscapes of Paddy's books, but being afraid to go too far in, so far we might not come back.

But walking brought freedom closer. And in that winter, walking alone through a snow-covered landscape seemed like the greatest happiness I could know.

4

White Winter

Austria to Vienna

I felt I had been let loose among a prodigality of marvels, and the thought was made more exhilarating still by the illusion of privacy. This landscape might have been an enormous and unending park, scattered with woods and temples and pavilions, for often the only footprints in the snow were mine.

A Time of Gifts

Austria introduced itself in disconnected episodes, images that didn't yet fit my understanding of the country. The towns and villages through which I passed had an incho-ate, dreamlike feel, as if they lay on the threshold between one thing and another; it was something to do with being in the no-man's-land between two geographical landmarks, the Alps towering at my back and the Danube unspooling ahead. There were miles of dappled pastureland, pleasantly dilapidated barns, ramshackle cottages with wood-shingled walls. In Ried im Innkreis I shared dinner with two skinny Italians, refugees from the fiscal collapse south of the bor-der. They had come to this small, chilly town to work in an aeronautical factory, and looked homesick in the subzero temperature, gazing unhappily at the inscrutable whiteness of the sky.

There was a chateau called Schloss Feldegg, on the door of which I knocked, vaguely hoping for an invitation to spend the night. Paddy had stayed in an unnamed schloss somewhere in these parts. This one looked almost French in its elegance, with red and white striped shutters and a pointed tower knotted with ivy; the door was opened by a woman who resembled an elf. The schloss was owned by her husband's family, but they didn't know anything about an Englishman who might have visited in 1934. Two walking poles of enormous height were propped in the porch; I imagined the resident giant stretching his long legs by the fire, while his elf-wife smiled sweetly on the step. A little girl pigged her nose at me from a window as I left, and that was the only contact I had with the remnants of Austria's gentry.

In Großstroheim the news was of Babsi, a miraculous two-headed calf born in the next village. Snow fell thick and fast outside while I warmed myself by a roaring china stove – a *Kachelofen* it was called, of a design I would see in houses from here to Transylvania – eating liver-dumpling soup while my hosts showed me newspaper cuttings of the mournful beast. The pictures showed two teddybear-like faces staring from one head. It had died several days before, otherwise I could have paid my respects; the creature had four eyes, four ears, two brains, but only one heart, which hadn't been enough to bear the strain.

Eferding came first thing the next morning in the softest powder snow. The fall had already claimed casualties: a van and a car had collided, and a policeman was mediating a scrupulously polite argument between the affected parties. In the distance a lone jogger was floundering into the white landscape, like an asylum escapee. I followed the road out of town, through ice-snagged woods and frozen marsh, and out of the zone of indistinction, the space between mountains and river. Austria was about to make sense, to assume what felt like its proper form: I was about to have my second meeting with the Danube.

When I'd last encountered it on the border of Bavaria, I hadn't given Europe's second-longest river much thought. Preoccupied with my injury – and perhaps a little in thrall to Paddy's own descriptions – I hadn't granted it the imagination it deserved. But what I saw now, as I cleared the trees and padded up the frosted bank, was so astonishing it literally stopped me in my tracks.

Since I had last laid eyes on it, the Danube had undergone a transformation so total it was almost a different category of thing. It wasn't a river any more but an open vein of ice, a whistling, heaving volume of slush shouldering its way eastwards. It was wider than any river should be, urging its way through the land. Broken rafts and bergs of ice lumbered in the current, turning each other like cogs, and along the bank the ice had been forced into ridges of diagonal scales, serried crystalline formations caused by frequent cracking and refreezing. Icy spindrift hung in the air, a frozen mist that dipped and swooped with the action of the wind. In the middle stood a solitary heron, like the ghost of a flamingo.

It was hard to tell which was more unreal, the sight or the sound. The constant nudging and barging of drift ice produced an extraordinary music: shuffling, creaking, clicking, hissing, punctuated by pops of air and occasionally a quick shushing sigh as something in the structure gave way and a larger drift pushed through. It sounded like hundreds of people murmuring, rubbing their hands together, engaged in a whispered negotiation. The thought occurred that what I was seeing – what I was watching and listening to – wasn't a geographical feature, something that might be marked on a map. It was a mechanism of winter; not an object, but a process.

The crunching of my boots in the snow muted the conversation of the river. The Donau, Dunaj, Duna, Dunărea would be my intermittent companion through the next four countries. The feeling of awe remained intact even when, several miles downriver, I reached a prosaic realisation: this ice flow wasn't natural at all, but essentially man-made. Ahead lay the first of the hydroelectric dams that would punctuate my journey to Vienna: a horizontal concrete block, like a piece of brutalist architecture, holding back the river's heave and slowing it until it flowed sluggishly enough to freeze. Nuclear-free Austria generated over half its power from these monolithic *Wasserkraftwerken*, and the Danube's power dams – which only existed in engineers' dreams in Paddy's time – were to become a recurrent theme. Beyond this dam the water flowed clear, sparkling blue in the sun. For a moment it felt like stepping into summer, but soon it was winter again.

Towards afternoon higher ground rose on either side of the river, which narrowed and darkened, flowing faster on the approach to Linz. The B129 intimidated me down the bank to follow a lip of frozen beach, stumbling on wreckage and rocks, until the sight of dark bridges and buildings, a monstrous traffic tunnel gouged through the rock, heralded my arrival in Austria's third-largest city. After the primitive awe of the river, it was a dull shock. One of the first sights was a custard-coloured brothel displaying photographs of middle-aged prostitutes, which slightly confounded my perceptions of Austrian society. In contrast lay the old centre, the faded façades of the Hauptplatz, sorbet-shaded townhouses ornamented with cherubim; a twisting column topped by a sunburst hinted at Hapsburg glory. Trams rumbled over the river, and on the pavements shoes slapped in corrupted snow. In a promising café-bar I ordered Marillenbrand, apricot schnapps to take the bite from the cold, served in a glass like something from an alchemist's workshop.

I followed Paddy in taking a bus to the monastery of Sankt Florian. Dedicated to the patron saint of firemen and chimney sweeps, the edifice rose above a pretty village of shining roofs and orchards like a rococo tenement block, staggering in its size. Domed ceiling frescos depicted plump pink bodies being tortured and mauled, while angels tooted golden horns above plasterwork so elaborate it looked like it had been spewed from the nozzle of a foam gun. My predecessor was enthralled by this place, but I preferred the simpler corridors of the adjoining wings. Far more resonant than the baroque hysteria of the architecture was a black and white photograph in one of those clean, quiet halls: Adolf Hitler examining manuscripts in the monastery library, surrounded by black-clad SS officers.

Linz was the Führer's home town – he had overseen its industrialisation and envisaged it as the future cultural showpiece of the Third Reich – and the visit documented here was in tribute to the composer Anton Bruckner, whom the Nazis admired. More of Hitler's handiwork was to appear the next afternoon, after I'd followed the Danube east under heavy snow. Ahead lay a village called Mauthausen, a name that didn't mean much to me until I came to it. But since Paddy had walked this way, tracing the northern bank of the great glassy river – perhaps in the same Gangetic light, with the same patches of ice revolving like lily pads in the current – horror had occurred here on an incomprehensible scale. On the hill above that village, a hundred thousand people had been murdered.

A road led through scenic woodland towards the memorial site. The uniform wooden bunkhouses were about the same design as holiday-camp accommodation, laid out in functional rows inside the fortress wall. Displays showed the familiar photographs of piles of emaciated corpses, grown men with the hips of children, inmates staring at the camera through eyes like empty holes, pathetically covering their genitals; but what disturbed me most was the banality of those bunkhouses, their straight lines and perfect right angles, their sheer practicality. It wasn't the site of a mas-sacre or even a place of execution, but a decommissioned factory for the processing of human body parts.

The factory opened in 1938, four years after Paddy was here; around the same time, I imagined, as Hitler was perusing old books in Sankt Florian's library. Inmates were transported here from overcrowded Dachau and occupied Poland, to die by gas or be beaten, lethally injected or fro-zen to death in 'death-baths'. Half were killed in the four months before the camp was liberated, as the factory's over-seers hurried to clear the backlog.

In the memorial garden, statues donated from each of the nations whose citizens had perished here loomed on granite blocks. Snow hurtled down in fist-sized clumps, reducing everything to black and white, burying the land. I stood there shuffling my feet for warmth, flexing and bunching my gloved hands, as if waiting for something to arrive: a sense of comprehension. It never came. The biting cold disturbed me more than the quantity of the dead. The most troubling thing about Mauthausen was how little it made me feel.

That night I slept rough again, despite the blizzarding snow. Something in me was averse to seeking comfort in that place; perhaps it was a further attempt to force myself to a point of understanding. With the air turning blue I made my way across a white hill, the snow falling so thickly now it blurred my footprints as I walked, towards what looked like possible shelter: a solitary hunting hide, a wooden box on stilted legs high above the ground. There was no padlock on the door. It was dry and carpeted. After I'd swept out the dust of wasps, trapped from warmer weather, it was habitable enough.

The concentration camp glowed to my left, and the headlights of cars flowed up and down the hill until closing time. On that same road, tens of thousands had been cattle-trucked to their deaths. It wasn't possible to know what that meant, not in the same way it was possible to know the snow piling down, the two deer crossing the field, the way they froze and swivelled their heads when I moved to see them better. Darkness came at half-past five. It was the longest night I could imagine. Wrapped up in all my clothes, two hats and a sleeping bag, with only my nose exposed to the air, I spent the next twelve hours plunging in and out of consciousness, the cold flooding first one then another region of my body.

When morning arrived, intricate patterns of ice crystals had bloomed inside the windows. Cautiously I stretched my limbs, feeling life return. The two deer crossed the field again, and on the hill the camp opened up for another day. I carried this odd thought with me going stiffly down the road, and it was only looking back that I realised that from this angle my sleeping place resembled a guard tower.

The village itself, the other Mauthausen, lay half an hour's walk downhill. Impossibly pretty cottages snuggled in the snowy streets, their walls painted with romantic murals of flaxen-haired maidens and handsome knights in swirls of summer flowers. Somehow this was more disturbing than the camp itself. I wondered if the inhabitants had carried on like this, living their cosy folksy lives, raising their hats to each other in the streets and sweeping the snow off their doorsteps, while industrial-scale butchery took place on the hill.

The same pinkish-orange haze lay on the river as the morning before, the drifting slush making its slow negotiation towards the sea. I exchanged *Grüß Gotts* with a grandmother on cross-country skis, and followed the creaking river east. The overhanging poplars were infested with mistletoe, perfect spheres like black fireworks frozen in mid-burst. At one point I was almost buried in a horizontal flurry of snow, a plough bearing down with blazing headlights, and had to leap from its path. Fresh flakes had already filled its wake.

The snow buried Mauthausen too. Before I had rounded the next bend, whatever halting insight I'd felt about the camp's horror had faded. It was a memory of a memory, something I'd once heard a story about, impossible to reconcile with the world I walked in. As the magic of that valley increased – the falling flakes of snow now perfect crystals, like children's paper cutouts – the camp receded into dark folklore, one of the Brothers Grimm's bloodier, nastier tales. That unimaginable inhumanity lay between Paddy's walk and mine, one more fathomless gulf separating our journeys; death on such an epic scale was as remote as the scenes of holy slaughter on Sankt Florian's walls. A sense of numb guilt followed me as the winter's beauty grew.

Nearing Grein, the valley changed. 'Old perils haunt these defiles. The name itself is thought to be onomatopoeia for the cry of a sailor drowning in one of the whirlpools, for the rapids and reefs of this stretch of the Danube smashed up shipping for centuries,' wrote Paddy, and the mood hadn't lightened. Precipitous cliffs flanked the river, and the friendly coniferous trees were replaced by forbidding slopes of pine, an altogether more savage-looking prospect: the fairytale lurching into dark subconscious realms. The turreted town nestled in a crook of the river, a few icebound barges lying at anchor on the approach. Again I was without a sleeping place and scouted around the edge of town until met by a suspicious farmer with dark stubble and a lumberjack shirt, who scowled until I retreated.

'I can find you somewhere cheap,' promised a carpenter called Andreas, who had become matey after I'd admired the carved horn buttons of his waistcoat in the bar. He launched into a series of phone calls and then disappeared for a long time, but came back with nothing. 'Off-season,' he said and, by way of further explanation: 'I am very drunken. Jägermeister and schnapps.' He insisted on giving me ten euros towards a hotel I couldn't afford, but I used the money to pay for the beer we'd drunk together, and returned to the edge of town as the light grew dim. The scowling farmer was not to be seen. On the fringes of the forest was another hunting hide.

This one was flimsier than the previous night's, with no glass on the windows and gaps between its boards so wide I could slip my fingers through. I struggled into down vest, ski mask and over-trousers and stuffed myself into my sleeping bag to wait for unconsciousness.

When I awoke, it was still pitch black. Cold was rushing through the floor like an invasive force. Cramp had gripped my legs, and exposing my face to the air was like plunging it into iced water. Outside, the moon was still struggling to clear the pines. When I checked the time, it was only nine o'clock.

From that point I woke every half hour, moaning profanities. My toes were nubs of ice, tingling to their own rhythm. The last hour before dawn was almost unendurable. With the moon still high above the mountains, the snow turning pink in the sunrise, I couldn't take it any more. I descended and hobbled into town, desperate to find warmth.

My boots had frozen solid in the night, and I thawed them on a radiator while I brought myself back to life with coffee. The little bakery had opened for me when they saw me staring in, and I repaid their hospitality by eating as much butter-bread as I could. Surviving those nights felt like a victory, and by midday, I had always forgotten quite how awful it had been.

The single-track road on the river's south bank had frozen over completely. Now and then a pool of sunlight filtered through the trees and I'd stop and bask for a moment, drawing on its warmth. The rocky slope was fanged with icicles longer than my body, stalactites of yellowish ice and frozen waterfalls in jellyfish-like formations of domes and tentacles. Some were as clear as glass, others opaque, oozing like cascades of fat that spilled across the road and froze into the river. All morning the hills rose and fell, ruins jutting out here and there, and along the banks were shuttered cabins and bound-up picnic umbrellas, abandoned for the winter.

An accretion of welded drifts announced the approach of Persenbeug. This unassuming town loomed disproportionately large in the imaginative landscape of my journey, and as the river choked with ice my anticipation grew. It was here, in a riverside inn, that Paddy had met the character he simply named 'the polymath', whose monologue encompassed everything from the wanderings of Germanic tribes to the decline of aristocracy and the creeping blandness of industrial civilisation. Artemis Cooper's biography suggests the loquacious old gentleman may never have actually existed – his character was a composite of several others Paddy had met – but the fact of his existence was curiously unimportant. He was a mouthpiece for a prediction that spoke a more fundamental truth: 'Everything is going to vanish! They talk of building power-dams across the Danube and I tremble whenever I think of it! They'll make the wildest river in Europe as tame as a municipal waterworks. All those fish from the east, they would never come back. Never, never, never!'

These words, real or imagined, carried a deeper meaning than the vanishing of certain species of fish, a meaning that went to the heart of what I'd set out to discover. Their totemic importance to my journey had given me a clear mental image of what Persenbeug would look like; I should have known better than to arrive with expectations. I'd always pictured the polymath's inn perched on a rock against a backdrop of vine-covered cliffs, water raging in a chasm far below. But there were no vines, no cliffs, no chasm. The river was as smooth as a retention pond, and the town was dwarfed by the monumental berm of the Ybbs-Persenbeug Donaukraftwerk, the hydroelectric power dam that bestrode the river.

Gazing at the immutable bulk of the reinforced concrete wall, I was struck by the retrospective inevitability of such a structure. Completed in 1959, this was the first of Austria's *Wasserkraftwerken*, the Bertha Benz Memorial Route of the Danube's industrialisation. It was as impossible to imagine a time when it hadn't been there – when the river was unencumbered by ice, and freshwater salmon, those fish from the east, had swum in these waters – as it was to imagine a time before traffic lights existed. Not only had the dam risen here, a concrete realisation of the polymath's prophecy, it had even been christened after the town itself.

There was a kind of grim satisfaction to the completeness of this discovery. It made me feel very much like mid-afternoon alcoholic consolation, and I made my way through the huddled streets in search of a match for the inn where, perhaps, a vestigial trace of the polymath might linger. My only clues were that it had overlooked the Danube, and was owned by an innkeeper whose daughter was called Maria. There was no inn within view of the river – another of Paddy's confabulations? – and the only bar

I could find had an interior vaguely resembling a 1950s diner. On attempting to explain to the waitress what I was looking for, I was ushered to the table of an elderly man with a liver-spotted face, immaculate in a light blue suit, sipping a glass of white wine. He looked like an aged mafia don, but turned out to be the town's former bürgermeister.

The aged ex-mayor was no polymath, but his monologue took as many rambling twists and turns, translated for me by two pierced teenagers smoking in the corner. He related tales of previous floods that had devastated the town, indicating the high-water marks with his wrinkled hands, telling me how, in 2002, the water had reached this or that shelf, that a certain mantelpiece was drowned. Presently we were joined by the cook, an enormously breasted woman clutching a book called the *Chronik von Persenbeug*, a chronicle of local life, from which she teased out a complex history of vanished taverns that may or may not have been owned by people with daughters called Maria. But the detail seemed irrelevant now; against the vastness of the dam, its importance was microscopic. The polymath's world had gone the way of the salmon. The prophecy had come to pass: the river had indeed been tamed, and everything had vanished.

Had I walked all this way just to find that out? The Danube had other ideas. When I set out down the bank at dawn, the river appeared to be on fire. Tendrils of mist groped and meandered, gliding with an eerie motion independent of wind. The Ybbs-Persenbeug Donaukraftwerk had lost all solidity, its totalitarian presence diffused behind a freezing veil that slid like smoke on the water. In that sulphurous, violent light the river became extraordinary again, a burning, freezing, powerful thing that jolted me into a sudden understanding of why it had once been worshipped as a living entity, a supernatural presence.

'Sailors who fell overboard were allowed to drown: they were looked on as propitiatory offerings to some Celtic or Teutonic god still surviving in secret from both pre-Roman and pre-Christian times. The Romans ... threw coins into the stream to placate the river-god Danubius; and later travellers took the sacrament before making the passage,' wrote Paddy. The dam, for all its bland functionality, was drawing off the same life force as ancient people had attempted to do with offerings, sacrifices, prayers. In tapping the energy of the river, it was another temple to the Danube's potency.

A series of concrete flood defences lined the bank beyond Ybbs, barriers guarding against the river's unpredictable moods. The ex-mayor's tales of infamous floods took on deeper connotations. The Danube's apparent domestication was only surface deep; its strength was still actively feared, and its beauty, in these swirling mists, still inspired a savage sensation of awe.

My sense of wonder had been restored. It would happen time and again on my journey: a loss of faith, followed abruptly by a reconversion.

~~~~

Renewed enchantment carried me to the monastery at Melk, a baroque cruise ship looming above the roofs of its little town. As in Sankt Florian, the interior decoration writhed into a crazed spaghetti mess I had no language to describe, and I preferred the space and silence of the icy courtyards. I plied myself with strudel and schnapps in a *Gasthof* down the hill, dining and drinking like a king before resorting, once again, to sleep in the woods like a tramp. Another hunting hide hid me at dusk, in a fringe of woodland next to Melk's own hydroelectric temple-dam – another cramped and frozen night, as intolerable as before – where I kept getting woken by a noise somewhere between a bark and a cry of rage, moving rapidly back and forth in the trees behind me. It gave me the horrors, but only because I couldn't imagine what it was; I was later to recognise it as the rasp of rutting deer.

Melk was the last outpost of civilisation before the wilds. The mountains closed upon the river as I entered the Wachau, a valley of astonishing beauty; over the next few days the polymath's prediction was challenged even further. Pines clustered blackly on the slopes, and the river's ice was meshed with islets of smashed wood, the work of unseen beavers. In the hamlet of Aggsbach Dorf the wind whipped bone-dry powder off the eaves to create ice-tornadoes, showering me in fine white dust. I wanted a bed, but there was no shelter; the houses were shuttered and deserted, their inhabitants having fled before the power of the winter. Under thickly falling snow I struggled up the forest track to the ruins of Burg Aggstein.

My intention of finding a cosy hole was dashed when I reached the top: that broken, black-stoned tower was the least hospitable dwelling imaginable. Snow surged in all directions, swooping vertically on the updrafts, cutting the castle off completely from the world below. Who had lived behind those cold walls, peering from his mean little windows, in such misanthropic isolation? It looked like a place of unnameable deeds, of gougings in the black of night, and the stories I later learnt – of overlords who taxed the shipping and hurled their prisoners off cliffs – confirmed the fairytale cruelty that ran alongside beauty in this valley; the nightmare link to Mauthausen suddenly resurfaced.

My shoulders and arms were covered in snow. I had stayed up there too long, transfixed by sinister thoughts. The chill was spreading through my body, and as the light drained away I dragged my feet downhill. But after several minutes' descent I realised I was no longer following the tracks I had made on the journey up; a different path had taken me, leading me along the side of the hill instead of down. Backtracking meant climbing steeply to Burg Aggstein again, not an appealing thought; I hoped this path would do the honourable thing and carry me clear of the woods before night. But even if it did, the villages were locked up and abandoned. It was too cold for hunting hides; this night would plunge to minus fifteen, and I needed shelter. My anxiety grew when the path tilted uphill, drawing me deeper into the woods. The familiar thrill of wildness tipped towards real fear.

And then came a moment of magic so pure I was back in the realm of legends. In the middle of the darkening forest appeared a little wooden hut; no hunting hide this, but a miniature house with curtains behind glass windows. The snow on its stoop was undisturbed and the door unlocked. I lifted the latch and peered inside, half expecting to see three bowls of porridge with three wooden spoons.

What lay within was just as good. There was a bed covered in duvets, piled high with pillows. The walls and ceiling were carpeted, and on the windowsill lay a first-aid kit, a few nibbled biscuits and a bottle of frozen lemonade. There was even a pair of slippers waiting by the door. I hesitated only a moment before pulling off my boots and burrowing beneath the mousey blankets, unable to believe my luck. The next day, I was to learn that the forest path was part of the Jakobsweg, the pilgrimage route that winds through Europe to Spain's Santiago de Compostela, and this perfect little house had been built to give shelter to wanderers like me, lost in the woods on snowy nights. The world felt impossibly kind.

Owls called searchingly in the woods, and later an animal screamed its last, less fortunate than me. After that, there was only the silence of the snow.

It was late morning when I woke, and I would have stayed in bed all day if it weren't for my hunger. Half an hour's walk downhill brought me back to the riverside road and I followed the Danube in search of food, slaking my thirst with mouthfuls of snow; my water bottle had been frozen solid for two days. The bloated yellow clouds had cleared and sunlight dazzled the land. Vineyards and apricot orchards terraced the slopes, pruned back and desolate, and the thought of apricots made me wish powerfully for summer. Suddenly my eyes yearned for colour, for respite from these frozen whites, a longing for sweetness so physical it was almost painful.

The valley dropped fjord steep to the icy river. Yellow houses huddled like settlements in the Arctic, and bulky-jacketed men were cutting the ice from their boats with chainsaws. In Rossatz my morale was restored with three cups of coffee and a plate of eggs, and at Krems I crossed to the northern bank and backtracked, as Paddy had done, a couple of miles upriver to Dürnstein.

Above this turreted, belfried town – still the 'little town of vintners and fishermen' that my predecessor had discovered – spreading on its hill like a rotten fungus, was the ruin of yet another castle. This was where Richard the Lionheart had been imprisoned in 1192, on his way home from raising hell in the Holy Land, and the riverscape couldn't have looked much different from when he gazed from his cell. Agriculture stippled the white and grey land, the slush-sliding Danube reflected the sky, and far away the abbey of Göttweig glittered on higher ground. I was intensely reluctant to leave these enveloping slopes, the protective shelter of rock walls, and pass into the featureless floodplain I saw was coming. Earlier I had wished for colour, but now the thought of exchanging the frozen whiteness of that valley for the dull greens and sludgy browns that stretched to the east filled me with depression.

It was Valentine's Day. Back in Krems I thawed off in a bar full of couples swigging cocktails and eating white sausages, an unglamorous combination. A young waitress waiting for her lift forlornly sniffed at a long-stemmed rose, while next to her a cleaning lady morosely battered the pavement with a broom. This was the end of the Wachau, a sad departure.

~~~

Winter was literally behind me as I walked on the next day; a ferocious wind propelled me from the valley, blasting me along the river as if the Wachau was blowing its nose to eject a foreign body. The season was confused, the weather veering from snow, sleet and hail to blinding sunshine and back through the course of the day. After a couple of hours my back was caked in dripping sludge, but suddenly it was warm enough to take off my gloves for the first time in weeks, and my breath was once again invisible in the air. Heaved along by that powerful wind, I covered an immense distance.

Dejectedly, I found the land turning ugly again. Pylons sang in the wind, and the roads were lined with scrap metal and wrecked cars. Swastikas were scrawled on underpass walls, along with what had become a returning motif of suburban walking: the glyph of the ejaculating penis. Future archaeologists, perhaps, would examine these signs and conclude the existence of an early twenty-first-century fertility cult, secret messages exchanged by hormonal young men across the continent.

In Tulln, half a day's walk before Vienna, I stayed with a couple called Maike and Heinz, friends of my cousin in Rotterdam. Maike was Dutch, and blue and white china plates depicting windmills and dykes decorated the walls of their flat, evoking Netherlandish landscapes I only half remembered. She and Heinz had been brought together by a curious quirk of war: her father had been taken to Austria by the Nazis as a slave labourer, welding ships on the Danube, and his father was an American soldier stationed here after the end of the war and later shipped out to Korea. When he grew up, Heinz discovered his family was part Shawnee Indian. 'Years before he found that out, he got a tattoo of a wolf,' said Maike. 'The wolf is the Shawnee totem animal. Babies know how to drink milk, and people know memories like this. It's in the blood. He has always loved wolves – when he sees wolves on TV the hair stands up on his arms.'

It seemed as confused as the weather outside. The same cataclysm that had created Mauthausen, obliterating so much of Europe, had brought together the daughter of a Dutch slave labourer and the son of a Shawnee Indian. It felt as if I was crossing the continent on a tapestry of stories.

Another mighty wind heaved me to Vienna. I crossed the bridge to the Donauinsel, a narrow island penetrating the city like a splinter; towers, bridges, radio masts, steeples, smokestacks and skyscrapers threw themselves up on either side as if I was watching fast-forwarded footage of urban growth. Flyovers and railway lines whooshed past, speeding towards some calamitous convergence. Graffiti in a mix of languages read 'Vote Communist', '*Juden Schwein*', 'All Coppers Are Bastards', and then the city's core unfolded into façaded squares, boulevards, tramlines, pitted fin-de-siècle buildings resembling stone hives. A one-legged beggar accosted me waving a takeaway Starbucks cup, while a well-dressed fat man in a restaurant window picked through the smashed remains of crab shells, like a Bolshevik propaganda poster of capitalist injustice. Below Saint Stephan's Cathedral, old-fashioned cabbies with bowler hats queued in a line of carriages while horses with pointed ear guards scuffed their hooves on the cobbles.

This was where I waited, too. Something extraordinary was about to happen. Around the time I'd left that morning to follow the river in the wind, my girlfriend Anna had been passing through the X-ray at London Luton Airport. As I was traversing the town of Korneuburg, of which I remembered nothing, she was already thirty thousand feet above Germany. And as I was inching down the Donauinsel a train was catapulting her into the heart of Vienna, perhaps on one of the very lines I had walked beneath. Since putting my boots on the road that day I'd travelled fifteen miles, while she had covered a distance of seven hundred. Yet here we both were, in exactly the same place, at two o'clock in the afternoon.

'It's amazing you walked here,' she said.

'It's amazing you flew.'

The journey hadn't, in these three months, taken us far apart. There was perhaps a moment of partial unrecognition, an astonishment of familiarity, and the next few hours were a process of gently relearning one another. But happiness at being together overrode everything else. Vienna was close to a halfway point between Rotterdam and Istanbul, a pivot on which so much turned, and a place of such natural convergence it felt inevitable we should meet here. Almost at once, the aloneness of walking vanished from my mind.

We had a week. For four of those days we rented a shabby, delightful apartment on the eastern bank of the Donaukanal, on a street called Große Schiffgasse. Anna had discovered it, and it was only later I spotted the Salvation Army hostel down the road and realised that Paddy had stayed there when he found himself penniless in 1934. There was another one of those psychic reverberations that cropped up now and again, fleeting points of synchronicity with my predecessor's journey. Paddy had also stayed some nights in an apartment on Schreyvogelgasse – I only remembered this because it meant 'Shriekbird Alley' – and walking in the old town one morning I was struck by certainty a particular street would bear that name: 'When we see the sign at the end, it will say Schreyvogelgasse.' And that's what it said.

Other than these points of correlation, there was little connective tissue between our different eras. When Paddy had arrived, a full-scale uprising was taking place – armed Social Democrats were fighting a pitched battle with the army in the Nineteenth District, and the air rumbled with distant explosions – and Nazi influence was creeping through the country. 'It was a desperate time for Austria,' he wrote with the benefit of hindsight. 'All through 1933, the country had been shaken by disturbances organised by the Nazis and their Austrian sympathizers ... They culminated five months later in a Nazi *coup d'état*. It failed, but not without bloodshed and heavy fighting and the murder of Dr Dollfuss. Afterwards there was ostensible quiet until the final disaster of the Anschluss in 1938, when Austria disappeared as an independent nation until the destruction of the Third Reich.' By contrast, mine and Anna's Vienna was a city with its struggles behind it, drifting gently along in retirement. There was a sense of nostalgic contentment, a feeling that some vital force had long ago moved on, which provided our time together there with a suitable dreaminess.

Most of our hours were spent in a state of pleasant disorientation, giving ourselves over to the joys of wandering and watching. The streets were darker at night than in other capital cities, inky pools intermittently lit by suspended electric lamps, rattling in the Siberian winds. The leaping shadows gave a film noir aspect to solitary strollers in flapping coats; as in Salzburg, I got the sense the inhabitants were playing up to the architecture.

There was much more dereliction than either of us had expected at the heart of a country as rich as Austria. Grand nineteenth-century mansions were boarded up and abandoned, left behind like enormous cakes that nobody wanted any more. It wasn't until several weeks afterwards when I reached Budapest, Vienna's sister-capital from the days of the Dual Monarchy, that I was able to recognise this as a symptom of post-imperial decline. But Budapest had moved on since then, had been transformed and transformed again, while Vienna hadn't quite kept up with the century's changing moods. With all the trilbies and kidskin gloves, the fur coats and trotting leather shoes, the city seemed stuck, at least visually, at some point before the 1960s.

Everywhere we kept coming across tableaux of amazing slaughter. I'd always imagined the Hapsburgs as stuffy and rather dull – a caste of bureaucrats and opera-goers – but their taste in statuary suggested something quite psychotic. Outside the Spanish Riding School hapless victims were being slain by bearded maniacs with clubs, and on a monument elsewhere a furious baby stood poised to ram a flaming torch into a screaming hag with wrinkled breasts. These fetishes of violent death – like baroque palaces and hydroelectric dams – said a lot about the mentality of their age. As I continued east into the lands the Austro-Hungarians once ruled, I would be walking in the shadow of extraordinary violence.

The days ran away from us. We crisscrossed the city on foot, on bike, by tram and train, filling in the blanks on the street map, leaving invisible lines. How many times did these trails cross Paddy's, who stayed in Vienna for weeks? We smoked cigarettes in local bars with ice hockey blaring on television, the tables set with bowls of dusty bonbons. We sampled Sacher Torte in the Hawelka Coffeehouse, where monkey-suited waiters yelled in voices cracked from decades of abuse, and left without paying after our gestures were studiously ignored. Back in the flat on Große Schiffgasse we drank wine and lay around naked. I satisfied my Wachau Valley craving for summer with apricot jam. We queued for hours to get into the opera, compelled by a sense of reluctant duty, and as the ticket booth opened ran away to go ice skating instead, in a labyrinth of frozen water like something designed by a visionary child with no concept of health and safety. It was an immeasurably better choice of entertainment.

In the Kunsthistorische Museum, one of our last acts before leaving, we paid our respects to a beautiful painting: Breughel's 'Hunters in the Snow'. The bone-weary trudge through a winter landscape was something I could relate to now, and there, unchanged, was the eisstock game I'd played on my fourth day in Austria. It was a painting I knew well, but my walk had given me different eyes. I understood the tension, the way the image tugs two ways: the relief of reaching your destination – that homely *Gemütlichkeit* of china stoves and winter warmth – tempered by the yearning to go on, to plunge into a green-watered landscape, into the white, smoky world, towards a vanishing horizon. It was a painting about the conflict between leaving and coming home, between the adventure and the safe return, between the need for companionship and the delight of being alone. There could be no more appropriate painting for this point on my walk.

It was only thirty miles from Vienna to the Slovakian border, where Eastern Europe, and the unknown, loomed ominously ahead. Leaving the West and leaving Anna became conflated in my mind, and the thought of imminent parting was suddenly appalling. It felt like we'd spent four weeks together rather than four days, and self-sustaining loneliness – the silence, the space, the accumulation of eccentric and unsavoury habits – was something I would have to learn all over again.

Before this severance, however, came one more adventure. Anna accompanied me for two days to the ends of Austria, through the forested Donau-Auen, one of the Danube's last remaining natural floodplains. This national park was a glimpse of what much of the river must have looked like before the advent of hydro-power: a boggy and mysterious realm of shuffling yellow reeds, frozen ponds and knotted entanglements of vines. It was warm enough for rolled-up sleeves. The sky was blue, the sun was gold, and a desperate sweetness lay on the land. The only other soul we met was a man with a handlebar moustache riding a gleaming penny-farthing, clearly some mad apparition from a previous century.

We were lucky our journey was possible; the polymath's vision had almost come to pass here also. In the early 1980s the Austrian government had planned a dam here, which would have destroyed the last stretch of untouched river outside the Wachau, placing these riparian forests deep under water. Protests had rocked the country, activists had taken to the trees and, unprecedentedly, the government had backed down. The clearance of the forest was halted, and a decade later sixty square miles of wetland were declared a national park. Now the only dams in this region were built by beavers.

I thought of the seeming inevitability of the other hydro-projects I'd seen. Why had those been constructed and this opposed? It was partly due to economics, and partly to the growth of the environmental movement – Austria's Green Party was born from these protests, and further downriver the Danube Circle, opposing another dam on the Czechoslovakian border, became a political force in Hungary – but perhaps the rejection also stemmed from a more primal urge. The destruction of the Donau-Auen might have been too great a loss, as if people sensed it represented the snuffing out of some last echo of the wild that was everywhere disappearing. Perhaps a little of the polymath's anguish – his cry of 'never, never, never!' – had resounded in those demonstrations, carrying across the years.

We spent a final night together in Hainburg, the last Austrian town. Its defensive walls were studded with cannon-balls from Ottoman invasions – the pass between the mountains ahead was the gateway to, and from, the east – and the knowledge of being on an old frontier added to the sense of impending departure. We slept in the incongruous setting of a guesthouse above a pirate-themed pizzeria, and in the morning the bus arrived to carry Anna to the airport.

The driver's punctuality gave us time for one kiss, the doors snapped shut, and she was gone. By the time I stopped for lunch, she'd be seven hundred miles away.

I had no idea what to do. Anna was about to be flung through the sky, and Eastern Europe glowered ahead like a malignant spectre. I went a few paces and stopped, unprepared to be with myself. I'd forgotten how to walk. It was the same reluctance I'd felt on the first steps of my journey, blinking in the North Sea light, a sense of having to gather myself and tell my feet to move.

The sun was climbing in the east. The river bent sharply around a rocky protuberance blocking my view, hiding whatever it was that might come next. The only reason I started walking was to see what lay behind that rock; I felt no particular sense of purpose, just curiosity to know what was around the next corner.

Around the next corner, of course, was the next corner. This was the simplest trick of the road, and it fooled me as it always did; straightaway I was back in that Breughel painting, chasing the vanishing horizon. A narrow path drew uphill to a ruined watchtower strategically placed on the elbow of the river, an old frontier position; under the trees the first snowdrops were out, imparting the sense of crossing into another season. Woodlands blocked my view again, and when I reemerged at the river a distant radio mast heralded the environs of Bratislava.

The last Austrian buildings I saw were shabby fishing huts with nets dangling over the water. Trophies of the heads of conquered fish were mounted on wooden shields; knowing how much she would have loved that, I missed Anna with a sharpness that stopped my feet again. The Danube tightened and my path along its bank became a muddy tractor track winding through sycamore trees. A dog barked from across the river, and I had to check my map to confirm that it was barking from Slovakia. This, I was soon to find out, was indicative of the reception most Slovakian dogs would give me.

Austria quietly petered out while its neighbour took shape on the opposite bank. A city was beginning to form there, expensive-looking modern apartments ranged along the brow of hill, and then a white fortress appeared that could only be Bratislava's castle.

'I was wandering across a field when a man in uniform began shouting from the dyke-road overhead. Where the devil did I think I was going? It was the Austrian frontier post. "You were walking straight into Czechoslovakia!" the official said reproachfully as he stamped my passport.' That encounter of Paddy's must have occurred exactly here, but, in the post-Schengen EU, there were no officials and no frontiers. In a rustling yellow wood I came upon a tin sign that read 'Medzinárodná Mariánska Trasa, International Virgin Mary Pilgrimage Route', the only confirmation I'd crossed from the Germanic to the Slavic world.

Soon came a sharper clue. Deeper into the trees was a Communist-era border post, derelict and graffitied, half-absorbed back into the forest in which it had been concealed. Weeds had found root in the cracked concrete roof and the dark eyes of its gun emplacements were lidded with old man's beard. Only a couple of decades ago, the invisible line I had just strolled over would have been one of the hardest barriers to cross on the planet.

Even at walking pace, things changed so abruptly it was startling. When I emerged from the wood I was in a country that was utterly altered. Suddenly the roads were potholed, the signposts hung at irregular angles and even the concrete of the tower blocks was stained in a different way. The colour spectrum had shifted into browner, murkier tones; the grass appeared yellowish-green rather than greenish-yellow. I climbed a bridge topped by an observation deck shaped like a UFO and crossed the Danube into the city, following a general shuffling of anoraks down a dripping walkway. A mauve-faced tramp lay slumped against the wall, under graffiti that read, in English, 'capitalism = fascism'.

The old part of the city was full of sunlight and shadows, the pavements scrubbed scrupulously clean. Feeling pleasantly displaced I rambled through the streets, under buildings with green tiled roofs, up steps and through archways. A congregation of old women was spilling from a church, outside which beggars waited for coins. The begging style had altered too, as if there was a requirement to demonstrate greater anguish here: these petitioners were on their knees, hands outstretched in supplication, or else crouched motionless with foreheads pressed to the ground.

Already I could see a difference in the people. Hair was darker, cheekbones higher, faces bonier yet somehow rounder. The new impressions rushed in so fast it was hard to keep up with them. On a bench by the Magistrat, a municipality building decorated with a double cross over three round hills, I tried to absorb something of this new culture by osmosis.

An angry demonstration was taking place in front of the Carlton Hotel, policed by paramilitary gendarmes in high boots and berets. Speeches roared over a crackling megaphone, accompanied by furious chanting, was an excellent way to take in my first words of Slovak. An amiable punk explained that tapes had been leaked from a secret wire tap that implicated the government in a corruption scandal. 'Of course everyone else is corrupt too,' he said in effortless English. 'But we still protest.'

Minutes later I was speeding away in a 4×4 the size of a small tank. Arrangements had been made for me to stay with the friend of a student I used to teach in London; I had an idea she was slightly embarrassed I'd witnessed the demonstration. Petra was strikingly beautiful and ruthlessly efficient, and my student had told me she moved in the highest echelons of Bratislava's media life, but I didn't quite know what this meant until I saw her apartment. Nothing could have prepared me. The apartment was vast and everything was colour-schemed either white or purple: white walls, white designer furniture, white orchids in white vases, purple carpets, purple sofas, purple easy chairs and, most arrestingly, a balcony beyond the French windows laid with purple AstroTurf. Petra showed me around, then announced that she was leaving immediately for a weekend in a spa resort with her husband. In ten minutes she was through the door, leaving me alone in the mulberry mansion.

The flat was up the hill from the old town, with a clear view over the city. I stood on the AstroTurf balcony watching the sun go down. It seemed a very long time since the morning.

EAST

Between the Woods and the Water

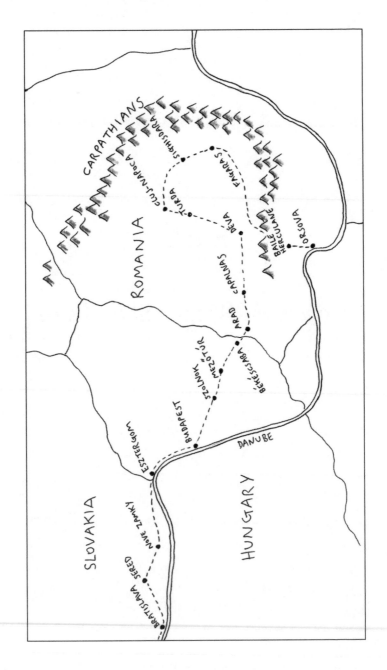

From Bratislava to the Iron Gates

5

The Yellow Lands

Bratislava to Budapest

The juxtaposition of tongues made me feel I had crossed more than a political frontier. A different cast had streamed on stage and the whole plot had changed.

A Time of Gifts

PASSING FROM AUSTRIA TO SLOVAKIA WAS A WATERSHED MOMENT in my journey. All the way from the North Sea to the border I'd just crossed, change had mounted gradually, one culture merging into another at such an incremental pace it wasn't a process I was ever consciously aware of. But the single step I'd just taken, back in that yellow wood, had carried me across several fault-lines.

It was a step from the Germanic to the Slavic, across language groups marking ancient tribal boundaries. It was a step from the West to the East, cultural and political concepts that hadn't existed in the same way on my predecessor's journey, when this region identified itself neither as West nor East but *Mitteleuropa*, Middle Europe. In the seasons of my journey, the broad colour palette of my walk, it was a step from winter to spring, from white to yellow. And as that overgrown border post showed, it was a step across the old Iron Curtain, from NATO to the former Warsaw Pact. Despite EU integration, globalisation and other supposed tendencies towards homogenisation, the differences were probably starker than when Paddy took that step. Since 1945, these neighbouring countries had spent half a century on different sides of the planet.

Another significant change: Paddy's Bratislava was a provincial backwater on the fringe of Czechoslovakia – many still called it Pressburg, its imperial Hapsburg name – but since 1993 Bratislava had been the capital of an independent country. Away from the genteel centre, decrepit townhouses spoke of decades of neglect, but under the surface was a sense of bubbling energy. Ducking in and out of bars in visibly subsiding buildings I found no Hungarian farmers with Hunnish whips looped around their wrists, no Slovak peasants in canoe-shaped moccasins, but arty, well-dressed crowds knocking back shots of pálenky. The castle, in Paddy's day a gutted shell that 'sulked on its hilltop as a memento of fled splendour', had been rebuilt and was now illuminated dazzlingly white, as if an attempt was being made to wash away its former reputation as a harlot's nest. There were no harlots now, no Gypsies or Carpathian dancing bears, only gangs of underage drinkers and couples quietly necking in the shadows.

Gone, too, was the thriving Jewish population; through emigration or deportation by the pro-Nazi regime in the war, the Yiddish-speaking community had been almost entirely wiped out. The Heydukova Street synagogue still stood – its seven pillars gave it the look of being behind a protective cage – but of beaver-hatted rabbis or Talmudic students there was no sign. 'Bratislava was full of secrets,' wrote Paddy – both the harlots and the Jews were initiations into worlds previously unknown – and from above, lit up at night, Bratislava still resembled a termite mound of twisting alleyways and sloping streets. But much of its pre-war diversity had been destroyed, its polyglot character effectively Slovakianised.

Beyond the Danube spread vast plains, a welling expanse of nothingness alarming in its scale. Squinting, I could make out the haze of towns and the tracery of roads, wind turbines twizzling in the distance, although the horizon absorbed them, swallowing everything. A statue of the Moravian king Svatopluk I brandished a sword towards the south, out of which so many enemies had marched, as if defying the emptiness itself.

The sight unsettled me deeply. It was through such lands that I would soon be travelling, unconcealed by woods and valleys, exposed beneath that enormous sky. The old familiarities were gone. The colours were different, the smells were different, people's facial expressions were different, and it was too early to know how Slovakia treated its walkers. The cure for this trepidation, as always, was abrupt immersion into local life; on my second night in the city I took myself to a music bar in the old town.

I picked the place because the band's name amused me: the Hugo Cáves Orchestra, a Slovak wordplay on Hugo Chavez. In a smoky room I bought a glass of Budvar that tasted like old dishcloths, and watched a nine-piece brass and strings ensemble pound out a mixture of Balkan beats and Gypsy electro that wouldn't, oddly enough, have been out of place in East London. An hour later, not quite knowing how, I was at an after-party upstairs in an attic chaotically heaped with hardback books: antique German gynaecology journals from 1879, Russian biochemistry manuals from 1963, and selected works by Joseph Stalin, which various members of the band were using to roll joints on. The room filled with more and more people, bottles of vodka and plum pálenky circulated frantically, and whenever a glass smashed on the floor everyone broke into clapping and chanting; broken glass, I was told, brought Slovak luck. A dog with a handkerchief round its neck leapt and barked about the room, and someone was going around painting people's faces with charcoal stripes. A few shaven-headed kids stuck their heads round the door, scanned the room and left. One of my new friends spat as they departed.

'Skinheads. Fascists,' he said. 'You know about our history? We fought with the Nazis in the war. It was a good thing we lost.'

Another man loomed over me, a tall fellow with a solemn, secretive look. He ushered me into a corner and launched into a complex account of his latest business venture; he seemed to have a vague idea I might be able to help him. He was acting as an agent for an ex-soldier, trained by Russian Special Forces in every conceivable art of killing, 'like a cross between Bruce Lee, Arnold Schwarzenegger and Steven Seagal, but with a very powerful mind'. This formidable man, he said, could pull down a tree with a length of chain and propel assailants across the room with a flick of his wrist. The plan was to sell his services to whoever needed them.

'He will come in useful when the government falls,' he said rather ominously. 'But now I'm deciding whether to hire him to Brussels or the Arabs.' He pondered for a moment, frowning. 'I think probably Arabs.'

'Everything changes in the East,' a woman told me in the early hours, after I'd extricated myself from potential involvement in the mercenary business. 'Even the colours change. It is much greyer here. The Communists did that to us. But perhaps the greyness is not really there, perhaps it's only in our minds. Slowly, I hope, the greyness is being washed away...'

Washed away, certainly, was my previous trepidation. The night had been an initiatory rite, disinhibiting me from this new culture; after one more day in the apartment, nursing a pálenky hangover, I went rattling in a tram to Bratislava's eastern fringe, past shabby kiosks and market stalls flogging off old Soviet junk, Red Army hats and

Lenin pin badges, to cross the threshold into the new land. Leaving the tram on the outskirts, and skirting an iced-over lake, past overturned pedalos and leaf-covered barbecue stands, I set out through yellow scrubland ringed by motorways.

The logistics of walking were different already: no cycle paths or footpaths threaded along these roads, so I picked a route over apparently unowned and abandoned fields, unsure whether or not I was trespassing. In parts my path was a mirror of Paddy's – 'through a hazel-wood where young roedeer bounced nimbly away, their white rumps twinkling in the undergrowth' – but the reflection was distorted by concrete bungalows, branching highways, electricity substations. Politicians grimaced from billboards; those from the ruling party, at the centre of the corruption scandal, had been defaced with red paint. Some had bullet holes.

Near a deserted construction site I encountered my first Slovakian dogs, two raggedy strays that came foaming through the long grass, veering away when I brandished my walking pole. Through every village I was accompanied by a chorus of canine aggression, and I would remember places as much for their dogs as their architecture: in Bernolákovo I was confronted by a pack of yapping lapdogs, more irritating than frightening, and in Veľký Biel a Doberman hurled itself against a chain-link fence, maddened at my presence. I began to travel more warily, scanning the land for hostile signs, taking diversions to avoid possible points of ambush.

In Senec I found cheap accommodation in a pension called Skórpiona. It was a town of tower blocks and deserted boulevards; something about it was recognisable, and when I came to the lakeshore, dotted with boarded-up holiday chalets, I identified the rather comforting gloom of an out-of-season resort. In a nearby bar, whose walls were hung with faded Communist memorabilia – busts of Lenin, Stalin and the Czechoslovakian premier Husák peeking from between the brandy bottles – I listened to the unfamiliar hubbub of Slavic, the treacly sounds full of sloops and chushes, inkys and ankas, the letter *c* pronounced *ts* like the clash of cymbals.

When I awoke, ice was hurtling from a slate-grey sky. Winter wasn't finished with me yet; wearily I dug hat and gloves from the depths of my bag. By the time I reached the lake the surrounding fields were ankle deep, and I followed rapidly whitening farmland to a village called Reca – pronounced 'Retsa', with that cymbal clash – where an old woman with a single tooth gestured towards a bus stop. Using my few words of Slovak, scissoring my fingers in mime, I tried to explain my intentions; eventually she abandoned her entreaties, throwing up her arms in exasperation. Five minutes later I looked back to see her standing in the middle of the road, glowering after me.

The snow was piling down thick and heavy, turning the world opaque. The road dawdled towards the south, so I set my compass and struck east over the fields, taking my marks from trees glimpsed vaguely in the blankness. Two animals I took for deer turned out to be hares, legging away at amazing speed over the white ground.

The road forked at the village of Pavlice. Two old men were loudly conversing – one in a grubby baseball cap, one in a huge fur hat, and both with wads of tissue stuffed in their ears against the cold – and I asked them directions to Majcichov. Should I take the left-hand road? The man in the baseball cap nodded energetically, while the one in the fur hat bellowed 'No!' Confused, I pointed to the right-hand road. Was that the one I should take? 'No!' the fur-hatted man yelled again. Both of them were grinning. Whenever one nodded yes, the other would shout out 'No!'; the more I questioned them, the louder they shouted. I assumed that one disagreed with the other and, like the old riddle, couldn't work out who was telling the truth and who was lying. Finally it dawned on me: they weren't shouting 'no' at all, but '*áno*', Slovak for 'yes'. But even with this revelation I couldn't tell which road to take, so I set off down the left-hand one hoping for the best.

After ten minutes came a honk, and a battered Lada rattled up with the two men inside. They were concerned I would get lost and had set out to find me in the middle of another blizzard. They drove several miles down a pitted farm track I would never have found on my own, cheerfully yelling at astounding volume, and deposited me at the edge of Majcichov just as the snow stopped falling.

It was a miserable last stretch to that day's destination, Sered', along the side of a motorway past tenement blocks and 1960s prefabs coming apart at the seams. But Slovakia, I had discovered, was also scattered with providential internet hosts, and I'd arranged to meet one here: a mysterious woman called Margita, with a broad, expressive face and amber eyes. She met me beside a pretty Catholic church and took me back to the house her parents had built thirty years before.

The conversation we had over dinner, as my sodden boots dried above the stove, was my introduction to what would become a familiar theme. Having seen the dual-language signs, in Slovak and Magyar, outside every village, I enquired about the status of the Hungarian minority.

Similar attitudes were to be voiced by every Slovakian I met; and, leaping ahead a bit, by practically every Romanian. Hungarians, they all complained, refused to learn or communicate in the language of the country they lived in. They resisted integration, educating their children in separate Magyar-language schools, and generally regarded themselves as superior and different. It was irritating, arrogant behaviour, but what could be expected? They were still obsessed with the empire they'd lost in the Treaty of Trianon in 1920, when Hungary was stripped of two-thirds of its territory and population; after almost a hundred years, they still hadn't got over it.

What was extraordinary about these opinions, which resurfaced in countless conversations over the next few months, was their similarity to the ones Paddy had encountered. 'They had been under the Magyars for a thousand years and always treated as an inferior race,' went the complaint of a Slovak schoolmaster in 1934. 'Even when they were fighting the Austrians in defence of their nationality and language, the Hungarians were busy oppressing and Magyarizing their own Slovak subjects.' And, from a Hungarian peasant, the counter-argument: 'All the local inhabitants, though Hungarians, are compulsory Czech citizens now. The children have to learn Czechoslovakian; the authorities hope to turn them into fervent Czechoslovaks in a couple of generations.' If that was the intention, it clearly hadn't worked. The attitudes of Slovakians towards Hungarians, Romanians towards Hungarians, and Hungarians towards absolutely everybody hadn't shifted even slightly since Paddy's time. The tenacity of dislike was almost admirable: the Second World War and fifty years of totalitarian government, nominal Cold War comradeship and supposed EU integration, hadn't made so much as a dent in the old antipathies. The only thing everyone agreed on was a mutual hatred of Gypsies.

Apart from this implacable and depressing anti-Roma prejudice, my normal experience was to find that I cravenly tended to agree with whoever was talking to me.

My sympathies generally crept towards Slovakians in Slovakia, Hungarians in Hungary and Romanians in Romania, and whether this showed empathy or extreme gullibility I wouldn't have liked to think about too much. So at Margita's house, I found myself thinking that those Hungarians did sound pretty awful.

I woke up on the sofa bed in the kitchen. Sunlight was moving through the rooms, making the curtains glow with a green, velvety light, touching on the glass necklaces of a chandelier. Outside was a bright spring morning, as if yesterday's blizzard had never occurred.

Margita directed me to the Váh, a tributary of the Danube. 'It's the longest river in Slovakia. That's why we put the accent there, to make a long sound. It's not the Váh, it's the Vaaaaah...' And so I set off, following the vowel, along a dyke strewn with heaps of rusted metal and old mattresses, discarded shoes frozen into the ice that still lipped the banks. It felt like a more rubbish-strewn version of the Netherlands.

Around Šoporňa, the river bloated into an enormous lake. The water shone like mercury. Waterfowl crashed in the rushes, and occasionally the onion bulb of a church bobbed up in the distance. '*Rovno! Rovno!*' cried a man attacking a very small tree with a chainsaw when I asked for Štrkovec: 'Straight on! Straight on!' Such exchanges were always delivered at the highest volume.

After another half hour's walk, I thought I could see it. Something lay ahead, at least; but from this distance, across the fields, it was hard to tell if I was looking at a once-grand country house, the *kastély* I was searching for, or a collection of derelict barns huddled beneath the trees. Up close it wasn't much clearer – a shamble of outhouses, broken machinery, pigs and goats in muddy paddocks scattered around collapsing walls – but at the gate I encountered a young man in plastic slippers, pacing back and forth outside a twin-steepled chapel. His shaved head and soft, misshapen face were a sign I had reached the right place. The kastély of Štrkovec, which Paddy knew by its Hungarian name of Kövecses, had been nationalised by the Communists and now functioned as a hospital for the developmentally disabled.

A kastély was a Hungarian version of a schloss, though Kövecses was dismissed by its incumbent as a mere 'shooting-box'. Paddy had stayed here for weeks as the guest of Baron Pips von Schey – a Proust-devouring aristocrat 'of a half-patrician, half-scholarly kind which even then felt threatened with extinction' – his days spent reading, walking, hare-shooting and immersing himself in the glittering scandals of a Middle European noble strata that was soon to disappear. Industrialisation and modernisation were rumbling on the horizon, Nazism loomed across the border, and five years after Paddy's stay this blissful idyll was shattered by war. After 1945, the Communists would obliterate what the war had left; like the kulaks, the aristocracy would be liquidated as a class.

For Paddy, Kövecses-Štrkovec was the beginning of a string of aristocratic connections threading his journey from here to Transylvania. For me, seventy-eight years on, it was a trail of ruins. Gutted and derelict country houses, the visible symbols of vast social upheaval, were to become as recurrent a theme as hydroelectric dams.

The young man guided me into the building with elaborate courtesy. I was surrounded by a curious crowd of patients in vests and tracksuits, slipper shod, with troubled smiles and sweet, bashful faces, anxious to shake my hand. They escorted me down the corridor in expectant parade, and in an overheated office I tried to explain to a member of staff why I was there.

The staff were perfectly happy to let me look around, though they'd never heard of Baron Pips von Schey and knew little about the building's past. My questions were received with the same bright smiles and polite lack of interest I'd encounter in Hungary and Romania; a kind of protective blankness that arose at any mention of life before 1945. I had the sense they were humouring me; perhaps a professional reflex. First I was taken to the dining hall, where a tray of potato soup, boiled cabbage and bread was brought before me, and an assistant fetched a book about the hospital's history. Under the inquisitive smile of the only patient to escape her shooing, a tiny man with ears like satellite dishes, I leafed through the pages. The lost world of Baron Pips flashed past in a few grainy photographs - people in hats having picnics under trees on shaded lawns - and I wondered how many of those faces Paddy might have known. What had become of them all and how had they been scattered? As if in answer, a man began howling in the corridor, his voice ascending and descending, like an air-raid siren.

The assistant returned and led me from the ground floor, where the patients wandered freely, to upper levels where the more severely disabled were housed. In one room, two men in wheelchairs sat as motionless as statues, solemnly watching the glow of a silent television. In the next, a man with haphazardly jointed limbs clambered spiderlike over a foam floor; the assistant held his hand and giggled, making him giggle too, and for a few seconds the two of them clung to each other, laughing. In the next room disabled children, their bodies distorted and distended, lay in cots among teddy bears, toys and plastic flowers. The assistant bent to kiss their foreheads with great care.

As for the building itself, its libraries, portraits, roe-buck horns, shaded lamps and leather armchairs had

been stripped out long ago. Its walls were painted institu-
tional green or covered in wipeable surfaces, its corridors
flickering under fluorescent tubes. Not the faintest trace
remained of the life that had been lived there.

By mid-afternoon I was walking again, tracing the banks
of the Váh. My sojourn had lasted just a few hours, but
the place had afflicted me with something of its sadness.
The river bottlenecked at a hydroelectric dam, and I lay
on a pebbled beach among washed-up plastic scraps and
watched the slow clouds heave. The kastély was a monument to a culture that had been erased. The story it told
was one of pain, and yet there had been much kindness
in what I'd seen. Only then did it occur to me that there
may have been meaning to what I was shown. My questions
about the fate of its former inhabitants had been answered
starkly with images of present need: the hand holding the
hand of the man who could only crawl, the gentle kiss on
the foreheads of deformed children. There had been a message there, and I carried that house and its inhabitants in
my mind for a long time. They were very beautiful people,
and I was glad they were there.

'We had four different phases of property seizure. In
1918 the Czechoslovakian state took land from many aristocrats. Then the fascists confiscated Jewish property during Aryanisation in 1941. The German minority had their
property taken in 1945, and in 1948 collectivisation started
under the Communists. Those were our four big land-grabs.'

Miloslav, with whom I stayed at the end of that day in
Šal'a, was a bespectacled, tie-dyed man who had studied
history. He also ran a New Age teashop incongruously sit-
uated on the ground floor of a Soviet tower block – his
attempt to bring 'world culture' to the town – and we were
sitting on embroidered cushions sipping tea while nag
champa incense billowed in the air.

Šaľa had the look of a village forced to become a town against its will. Now it was less a town than a village of high-rises. Miloslav took me to see the last farmhouse, a cottage of dark thatch and whitewashed walls, a preserved oddity, the last of its kind. In the contrast between this peasant dwelling and the brutalist blocks looming over it, I had an understanding of how absolute the transition must have been. Communism had flung a peasant society into the industrial age within a single generation; people who had grown up living in cob-walled houses with their cattle found themselves crowded into concrete hives full of other human beings. The shock was almost palpable. Like Štrkovec, this house was the relic of a lost civilisation.

I slept on cushions in the teashop, and in the morning followed the river again. The land glared many shades of yellow, saturated like an overexposed photograph. The trees were full of chattering birds and the rattle of woodpeckers, but apart from a dark-browed man on a bicycle, who gave me a formal nod, and a fox slinking through a field, nothing moved in the vast countryside. My boots kicked up waves of dust. For the first time the horizon wobbled with heat haze. After an hour of silence and sweat, notions of an industrialised society felt vanishingly distant.

There were no tower blocks in Zemné, the village into which I diverted desperate to find water. Its tiles had slipped, its roofs had sagged and the holes were patched with plastic sheets; its yards were full of squabbling chickens and dogs standing guard over dead refrigerators, tyres and machine parts. A hunchbacked grandmother went by, covered in gold jewellery, and when she opened her mouth to smile her teeth were gold too. Girls stalked down the street with plumes of black hair, heavy mascara and gold hoop earrings, trashy and elegant at the same time, and young men watched with disinterested interest as I passed.

It was a Roma village, or the Roma part of a Slovakian village, or the Roma part of a Slovakian and a Hungarian village, for these communities were segregated by borders I didn't know how to spot. Suddenly I felt myself to be in a more foreign country.

My host that night confirmed the divisions. We were eating *bryndzové halušky*, dumplings with sheep's cheese and ham, in the provincial town of Nové Zámky – New Castle – named for a six-bastioned fortress built to defend against Ottoman attack. Julia was German, a language teacher in the local Hungarian school, and echoed what Margita had said: Hungarians studied separately, and lived in separate villages. Despite carrying Slovakian passports, they defined themselves as Hungarian people, resolutely unassimilated. 'What about Roma?' I asked, though I already guessed the answer. 'There are no Gypsy children in my school. Maybe they don't go to school at all. The people here hate them. *Hate* them. Even educated, intelligent people. I used to try arguing with them, but there is no point. Then the mother of one of my colleagues was killed by a Gypsy man two months ago. He was trying to rob her house, and he killed her with a pillow. Things like that don't help, I suppose.'

Leaving Nové Zámky in the morning I saw the local municipal symbol: a sandy-bearded knight slaughtering a Tartar with an axe. The cartoon image alluded to centuries of territorial brutality, and I was reminded of something Miloslav had said: 'In the flatlands each wave of colonisation displaces the one before. Only in the mountains do cultures hold.'

But the flatlands were coming to an end. South of Pribeta, the horizon lifted at last towards faraway hills. The sight of high ground quickened my pace, although I was walking through fields of black earth that turned my boots into pendulums of mud, giving me a comical leg-swinging gait. Drivers slowed to offer lifts, and each time I would have to go through the charade of explanation: '*Pešo, pešo! – on foot, on foot!*' They drove away discontented, as if they had failed to make me understand what was being offered.

The village of Gbelce – Köbölkút to Paddy – was a tranquil settlement of tiled cottages with vineyards stippling the hills. In a bar modelled on a saloon I greeted the barmaid in my best Slovak with a cheerful '*Dobrý deň!*' and received a scowl in return. After taking my seat I understood why: the words *szia* and *igen*, 'hello' and 'yes' in Magyar, were a clue that this was still very much a Hungarian village. Presumably there were all kinds of signs I hadn't yet learnt to pick up on, a certain look to the houses perhaps, a subtle modulation in the atmosphere, by which these communities set themselves apart. Watching the folk around the bar I thought I could see a difference in the faces – their cheekbones seemed less defined, their noses longer and more chiselled – but the more I looked around, the less consistency I saw. A ferret-faced man was talking rapidly to a companion with heavy brows and sadly sloping eyes. The other drinkers at that table were squat and meaty-looking toads, cigarette smoke pouring from thick lips.

This would be my last night in Slovakia: the hills I had seen earlier announced my third meeting with the Danube, which formed the border with Hungary. The little country had slipped by in a golden blur, a rug being pulled from under my feet. It was bewildering. Somewhere in these parts Paddy had slept his first night rough and been apprehended by the police on suspicion of smuggling saccharine. Tonight would be my fifth or sixth – did abandoned castles count as rough? – and at dusk I climbed the hill behind the village, past a farm of baying dogs, and crashed into inviting woodland I hoped would conceal me. Leaving Gbelce I'd seen the ominous sign of a carload of men in camouflage gear unloading hunting rifles, but under my shelter of sticks and leaves – a ceiling was needed, however symbolic – I laid out a salvaged plastic sheet and settled myself to the creak of trunk against trunk in the wind.

Sleep came surprisingly quickly. The half-moon rose so bright I woke a couple of times in a panic, imagining someone was shining a powerful torch through the trees. But no hunters, or suspicious excise men, ever came. Birdsong woke me at dawn, the sky blue and peach above the branches. I demolished my shelter, and went down to last night's bar for coffee.

It looked even more like a saloon by day, wreaths of smoke brightened by the sunbeams slanting in. A different selection of men were there, drinking beer and pálenky at seven in the morning: men with squinting eyes, thick brows, tangles of curly hair poking from sun-bleached baseball caps, greasy fringes, matted beards. 'Things had become much wilder in the past hundred miles. The faces had a knobbly, untamed look: they were peasants and countrymen to the backbone,' wrote Paddy of Köbölkút's villagers; apart from the lack of sheepskin cloaks, fleece hats and homespun frieze, things hadn't really changed. They came and went, shaking the same hands they probably shook every morning, with the effortless familiarity of men who had known each other their whole lives, who had been to school together, worked together, been to each other's weddings, had fights and made up again, and drunk together every morning and night, and probably in between as well. These bonds were tribal, knitted so tight they couldn't easily be picked apart; suddenly I had an idea of how the Hungarian minority had survived almost a century of attempts to assimilate them.

The land was saffron coloured, the sky clear as water. There was a great communication of larks, wood pigeons and other small chatterers. It wasn't far to Štúrovo – Párkány to Hungarians – to which I followed the railway line I'd heard from the woods the night before. Far across the fields to the southeast appeared a distant green bubble, a blister on the horizon swelling larger with every step; it looked as if it might detach from the skyline and float away. This carbuncle was the dome of the Catholic basilica of Esztergom, my first glimpse of Hungary.

Štúrovo-Párkány reminded me oddly of border towns in Mexico: chain-link fences, discount bars, vacant plots of land for sale, the sense of being the last stop before a larger neighbour. But it ended in a leafy boulevard terminating at the Danube, the natural frontier between these and so many other countries. The five-humped green steel bridge I would shortly cross was a facsimile: the original was destroyed in the war, and it's a sign of the two nations' mutual antipathy that they didn't get around to rebuilding it for another sixty years.

Across the river, elegant Esztergom rose in ramparts of stone. Steeples and towers were scattered above the upthrust of defensive walls, and above it all the basilica loomed like improbable cover artwork for a sci-fi novel. Under that gleaming dome, verdigris against the sky, human figures were circling clockwise like tiny mechanical guardsmen. Even though it was only midday a half-moon hung above the scene, teetering on the crossbar of the topmost golden cross, and something about those things combined, in dazzling sunlight and cold air, gave the vision the intensity of a hallucination.

The longer I looked, the more the feeling of sheer unlikeliness grew. I had walked through winter to get here; now it was spring, and the snowdrops were out, and ahead was another country. A ship came quickly downriver, a cargo barge called *Linz*; it was only a month ago I was there. The barge must have passed through the lock at the Persenbeug power dam.

Another ship slid past, flying a German flag this time, and turned a clumsy right angle at the river bend. The waters flexed around the pilings of the bridge, as if trying to drag them wherever it was going. A solitary canoeist shot downstream in pursuit of the ships, almost comically vulnerable against the muscle of the river, and its motion allowed me to tear myself from this watching trance and cross the bridge halfway.

Paddy had lingered here a long time, 'meditatively poised in no-man's air', in the unfilled space between two countries and two books. This was the exact point where *A Time of Gifts* ends and *Between the Woods and the Water* begins. 'The air was full of hints and signs,' he wrote of that moment. Storks were soaring overhead, birds of good omen, and on the Hungarian side of the river an assembly of frogged and braided noblemen, hussars, bishops and candle-bearers was gathering for a Holy Saturday service in the great cathedral. In telescopic detail Paddy's memory picks them out: 'strolling, gossiping, glancing at their watches, leaning on their scimitars ... as he talked and nodded, the monocle of a tall dandy flashed back the sunset in dots and dashes like Morse code.' There were no storks in my no-man's air – I wouldn't see them until Romania – and rather than monocles, the wing mirrors of turning cars flashed on the Magyar bank. Nevertheless, there were hints and signs around me: a strange coincidence had come about, one of those inexplicable moments of contact between our journeys. The notebook I'd been writing in since stepping off the ferry at the Hook of Holland, the first book of my own walk, had serendipitously reached its final page. Crossing the bridge meant the start of another book, for both of us. The occasion needed to be marked.

I laid my copy of *A Time of Gifts* underneath the railing. The book was swollen with rain, muddied, torn and scribbled on, exactly how all books should end, if they are done justice. My boot slid it towards the edge until it was hanging in the balance, meditatively poised, and a final nudge tipped it over. It landed with a splash, spreading ripples that elongated in the Danube's brown flow, pages detaching and floating around it like petals. At surprising speed it raced downstream, chasing the canoeist and the barges towards the river bend. When the book was just a white speck in the current, I continued over the bridge to Hungary.

It was a high-ceilinged house that smelt of roses and polished wood, with a spiral staircase winding around the type of glazed tile stove that in Austria they called a *Kachelofen* and here was a *cserépkályha*, the pronunciation of which alone told me everything I needed to know about the impenetrability of Magyar. The staircase led to a gallery, off which slanted attic rooms supported by nests of beams looked down on an oval table where parents and siblings were laying out a loaf of bread as big as a torso, two hunks of glistening meat, mashed potatoes, paprika and horseradish sauce. Soon we were gathered around it, and my glass was being filled with *pálinka* made from pears, one of countless welcoming toasts in the weeks ahead.

My first Hungarian contact, a medical student called Sámuel, had met me by the basilica at the toll of the three o'clock bells. Arriving at his family's house was like coming home in a life I might have once imagined. I immediately felt relaxed with the way the eating proceeded, anyone picking from any dish when they desired. The youngest boy – who, they said proudly, had an extraordinary sense of smell – strategically moved around the table to get the best pickings. Wine was poured, and the youngest boy was given his own small glass, a custom that invariably marks a civilised society.

They took me to mass the next day: not in the basilica, sadly, but in a smaller, modern church that practised a trendier kind of Catholicism, with acoustic guitars and schmaltzy hymns. After communion the three priests drifted down the aisle to flute music, like credits rolling at the end of a film. Sámuel led me through the riverside part of town he called the 'water city', where the ruin of a seventeenth-century mosque hinted at Esztergom's Ottoman past. Now it couldn't have felt less Turkish: the city had grown dozy and sedate, the kind of place that always has woodpigeons cooing under the eaves and the rumble of cars on cobblestones, caught in a perpetual Sunday. Back at the house, the table was being laid with food again, and from behind a door came the sound of Sámuel's sister playing piano. 'I kept wondering if all Hungary would be like this,' wrote Paddy, and I thought the same.

The family, I learnt over lunch, were originally German blacksmiths who had emigrated to Hungary after the Ottomans were expelled, part of Maria Theresa's policy of Germanising the empire. It hadn't worked in the long term: they were Hungarians now. As if to emphasise the fact, they playfully chided me when I went to clink beer glasses. Beer glasses were not to be clinked – wine and pálinka glasses yes, but beer glasses never – in memory of thirteen patriots executed for taking part in an anti-Austrian conspiracy in 1848. Actually the prohibition was only meant to have lasted a century and a half, so the deadline had technically passed, but it was still observed, even if jokingly. It seemed an innocuous quirk, like saluting magpies for luck or not walking under ladders, but the next few weeks would demonstrate how deeply national pride – and resistance against perceived foreign domination – was lodged in Hungary's psyche.

I set out from Esztergom with half a loaf of bread in my bag and a hip flask of pálinka. The track elevated me past ramshackle houses and mouldering car wrecks to the brow of a hill from where I could look back over my route, perhaps one of the greatest pleasures a walker can know. The Slavic land beyond the river shimmered in a golden haze; I could even see the woods where I'd slept above Gbelce. This was the start of the Pilis Hills that rolled south towards Budapest, and daubs of paint would, theoretically, mark my trail through the forest. In reality the markings had often flaked away, so I navigated mostly by the knowledge that the Danube looped east, then south, and if I kept it vaguely on my left I couldn't go far wrong. This, too, was a notion that didn't quite match reality, but it was a beautiful place to get lost in.

The track rambled through hilltop meadows, the grass still lank from winter, then into leafless oak woods carpeted with acorns. Mulch crunched underfoot with frost, and my body was filled with a sense of buoyancy and power. The air was clean, the sky was clear, my ankle had finally stopped aching even at the end of long days, and I felt as if I could walk for ever into the blue loom of hills. In the silence of those woods every quiver of leaves was amplified, every startled flutter of wings; small rocks cascaded down the slopes, dislodged by unknown creatures; and when I surprised herds of deer they crashed away making more noise than I did. Infrequently through the trees a glimpse would come of the lower world: tiny villages I identified as Pilismarót and Dömös, Szob on the opposite bank, and always, reassuringly, the bright sheen of water. Ahead was the famous Danube Bend, where the river kinked south and north. Abandoning the track, I tried to maintain a straight line through the trees.

For hours I rose and fell, descending slopes so steep it was more like coordinated falling. Frequently the land plunged into narrow gullies sliced by streams, at the bottom of which oak leaves had formed leaf drifts as high as my knees. It was exhausting work, but the beauty of the hills made weariness impossible. Exhaustion and weariness are entirely different sensations.

I met only two other humans in those hills. The first was an old man in a clearing, gazing around as if uncertain how he had ended up there, who gave me a friendly wallop with a fist the size of a grapefruit. The second was a younger man with sandy hair and a lumpen face, who replied to me in German when I asked for Magyar directions. At first I assumed he thought I was German, and then realised he was German himself, but speaking in an accent that sounded altogether different, something gnarled and guttural I hadn't heard before.

When I emerged at the town of Visegrád, I realised he must have been a Schwob: a descendant of the Swabian settlers who once voyaged down the Danube. 'As much German as Magyar was to be heard on the half-awake quay of Visegrád,' Paddy wrote. 'Their language and their costumes on feast days were said to have remained unaltered since the time of Maria Theresa in whose reign they had taken root.' The costumes had probably changed, but there, on the wall of an inn, was a mural of the famous box boats that had come all the way from Ulm, and the German name for the town, Plintenburg, in Gothic script. It made me think of Dierk and Dora, and Michi and Waldi, far upriver. I wondered if any of their distant relations had ended up around these parts.

Visegrád was also connected to another point on my journey. In 1984, as Austrian police were trying to evict protestors from the wetland forests of the Donau-Auen, the Czechoslovak Socialist Republic and the People's Republic of Hungary were constructing a series of barrages to regulate the Danube's flow. It was the kind of grandiose public work scheme Communist governments excelled at: this stretch of the river would be dammed and flooded, thousands of people displaced, the ecosystem trashed, and the Danube Bend transformed into an industrial reservoir.

Like the loss of the Donau-Auen, it was too much. Environmentalists and intellectuals founded a group called the Danube Circle to oppose the construction of the dam, which increasingly came to be regarded as a symbol of the regime itself. History was on their side: in a few years, this small environmental group ballooned into a movement ten thousand strong, part of the anti-Communist wave sweeping the Eastern Bloc. The dam was abandoned only months before the Berlin Wall fell.

The Czechoslovakians were furious at the betrayal of their plans, and after 1993 the new Slovak state went ahead with the sinister-sounding 'Variant C', which involved diverting the Danube into their territory upriver and damming it there. This was still a subject of dispute and gave Slovakians and Hungarians another excuse not to like each other, but the Danube Bend remained intact, dazzling in the sun as it must have done when Paddy stopped here.

At dusk I climbed the slope towards Visegrád castle.

The ascent was marked with the Stations of the Cross; I couldn't imagine anything worse, when toiling up a long hill at the end of a tiring day, than a succession of images of a man being gradually tortured to death. It made the going tangibly harder, just as the beauty of the hills had made it easier. When I reached the castle, I found it defended by a one-eyed nightwatchman with an Alsatian, both of whom seemed to guess my intentions. The place had been built to repel the Mongols, so sleeping here didn't look likely. In gathering twilight I headed back towards the dimming forest.

It was that uncertain time of day. The rising moon gave almost as much light as the sinking sun; for a moment both hung in balance, poised between day and night. Then the sun plunged and the moon soared free, and suddenly the land was black and the sky ridiculous with stars. Beside an iced-over pond I found a wooden picnic shelter, pyramid shaped, with an earthen floor. It wasn't big enough to stretch out in, but curling up in my sleeping bag, on a carpet of dry leaves, proved to be quite cosy. I slept soundly and opened my eyes to see the leaves starched white with frost, the hills outside touched with sunlight under an orange sky.

All morning I tramped south through the woods, never meeting a soul. I followed a friendly-looking road for a while, but it started taking turns I didn't agree with, so I set my compass and went back to rustling, crashing, snapping, crackling and thrashing my way through the brush until I hit marked trails again. The paint was fresher on these trees, guiding me down, with much deviation, into Szentendre.

This was a diffuse town, its suburbs nibbling into the forests and doing their best to scale the hills, the old centre lying on the far side of the highway zooming south to Budapest. Cobbled lanes led between coloured houses, bell-shaped cupolas topped the churches, and there was a rather self-consciously arty atmosphere; a sign in several languages informed that it had been colonised variously by Scythians, Celts, Romans, Avars, Magyars, Turks, Serbs and artists. After coffee and an overpriced slice of cake, I was back to the Danube.

The riverscape alternated between woods and wetlands, urban edgelands and industrial belts, the river rolling smoothly on, unaffected by these changes. A pack of dogs in a rubbish dump sang broken-heartedly at the passing of a fire engine's siren. Roma were burning off the dry grass, managing to turn the job into a community event: half visible through the rising smoke were gatherings of men and women, ancient grandmothers and children, swapping cigarettes and laughing; some had even fashioned armchairs out of blocks of polystyrene. We exchanged *szias* and hellos. They watched me pass with a mixture of curiosity and entertainment, as if they knew something I didn't.

On the long approach to the great double city came riverfront houses, moored houseboats, waterside cafés with owners scrubbing up for the coming season. I crossed a railway bridge over the river and in the distance the emerging entities of Buda and Pest gathered solidity beyond a furze of trees. The conjoined halves took shape like the cardboard scenery of a puppet theatre: domes, spires, towers and bridges silhouetted in two-dimensional tones. With my slow progression down the river I had the impression I wasn't moving, but the city was reeling me in.

Under the first of its bridges, through a sudden rattle of trams, past the wooded spit of Margit Island, without awareness of the transition I found myself in the city's dirty heart, surrounded by the clatter and hum of millions of strangers self-absorbedly going about their daily routines, living out unknown lives behind countless windows. With mounting exhilaration I passed beneath the warlike spires of the parliament building, under the peeling façades of faded Austro-Hungarian grandeur, the damp expanses of biscuity walls, balconies and fire escapes that looked like ancient mining machinery. Already, I could feel myself falling in love.

An old friend called Lucy had lived in Budapest for years, playing the fiddle and mastering the agglutinative intricacies of Magyar. She didn't live here any more but had told friends about my journey, and it was to one of these friends I was heading now. On a street of tall apartments near the terminus of Oktogon, past a row of Szex Shops and a striptease joint advertising the spectacle of 'Girl with a Snake', 'Soldier Girls' and – it sounded sweet – 'Girl with Candles', I buzzed a buzzer and was admitted to a clammy hallway. Several floors up, a woman called Agape welcomed me into her flat, a happy chaos of dirty dishes and clean clothes. 'Something to drink?' she said at once. 'I have only tap water, pálinka, vodka and beer.'

Agape was the second person I'd met in my brief time in Hungary – Sámuel's sister had been the first – who had a certain clear-eyed, windswept appearance, a sort of camp-fire look that was very appealing. I felt instantly comfortable with her; as in Esztergom, there came a sense of indefinable familiarity. She served toast slathered in paprika paste, then led me out of the flat, across the road and onto a tram that whooshed us south and over the bridge to the Buda side, where her father was doing some kind of performance on a boat.

The boat turned out to be a floating club, aboard which artists were gathered to commemorate a dead friend called Sándor Bernath, painter and techno producer, who had played a leading role in Budapest's underground art scene. There were many goatee beards and berets, piercings and ponytails; a painting depicted a group of devils masturbating over the Hungarian flag. It was only when I'd been in the city longer that I realised how much this gathering represented everything the government despised.

A white-bearded man with a ponytail leapt onto the stage. This was Agape's father, a sound artist, accompanied by a chubby guy operating a box of knobs and dials, and a frumpy-looking woman in a velvet dress. Together, these three unlikely characters launched into the most extreme avant-garde noise-chaos imaginable: Agape's father stomped and roared in guttural fury while the velvet-dressed woman made inhuman shrieks and yelps, hideously distorted by the chubby fiend on his techno-box; it sounded like Tom Waits being tortured in hell. After my solitary rural days, it came as a total shock.

The audience clapped politely. The next act was tamer – the dead man's daughter sang Allen Ginsberg's 'Father Death' translated into Magyar – but then a bald man took the stage and announced: 'Those of you with delicate nerves should leave the concert hall now.' After several minutes of excruciating industrial grinding, most of us did.

<hr />

So began my time in Budapest. I was to stay three weeks, not that I knew it then. I was content to let the city draw me in, to lead me down whichever alleys it desired, to lose me in its crumbling core.

When Paddy was here he stuck mainly to Buda, in a house near the Vár, the fortress palace that projected the spirit of Hapsburg militarism over the sprawl of Pest across the river. It was the civil, moneyed quarter, abutting the Coronation Church with its whimsical white follies, conical towers that looked like wizards' hats. The view was fantastic, but I preferred Pest. Gentrified Buda was a fossil; below it, Pest teemed with maggoty life.

'It spread insatiably across the plain and I could see great Oxford Streets, like the Andrássy út and the Rákóczi út, slicing their canyons through the boom city.' My predecessor's description still held: Pest's streets resembled hollowed-out ravines, the buildings deposits of sediment left after the drying-up of some dirty river, and I wandered its geology for days on end. Balconies stuck crookedly from walls like the sides of deep pits, the netted stone heads of lions and bulls embedded in the brickwork. There were covered markets lit by bare bulbs glowing through mists of grease, where old regulars in cloth caps drank beer and ate *lángos*, fried dough smothered in sour cream. The more I walked, the more I felt I had found the perfect place, with all the seediness and enchantment a city should contain.

Seediness, enchantment and pain: successive waves of suffering had left visible tidemarks. The walls of apartment blocks displayed the bullet holes made by Russian soldiers in the doomed 1956 uprising, when the city rose against Soviet rule. Sudden gaps opened up between buildings, denoting places where bombs had fallen and nothing had ever been rebuilt; traces of doorways and landings were visible six storeys up. In the gardens of the Dohány Street Synagogue were buried unknown numbers of Jews, murdered by the Nazis and their local allies, the fascist Arrow Cross; the headquarters of the latter had subsequently, with grim inevitability, become the headquarters of the Communist secret police. Budapest had absorbed all of the twentieth century's bloodiest moods, and trauma lingered in its courtyards like a bad smell.

I moved to another part of Pest to stay with more of Lucy's friends, Gergő and his girlfriend Eszter, who lived in an artist colony behind Kerepesi Street. Dynasties of sculptors had lived there, the studios handed down from one generation to the next. 'If you see a sculpture in Budapest from the last hundred years, there's a good chance it was made here,' Gergő said. His parents' careers had bookended Communism: his mother's first big commission was for the Socialist Party headquarters, while his father's last major work was to celebrate its fall. The statues of the Soviet era had now been exiled from the city to a place called Memento Park, half an hour's bus ride out of

Buda, where social-realist heroes of labour stood in perpetual defiance of capitalism, shaking granite fists at the sky.

Bicycles hung from the ceiling in the studios, attached to a clever system of pulleys, and Gergő winched three down to carry us into town. Soon we were drinking in a gutted mansion transformed into a warren of graffitied chambers. Again I was reminded of Heidelberg's Roten Ochsen inn, but this was like a version constructed from a rubbish dump, cluttered with broken furniture, figureheads, coloured lanterns, rubber trees, abysmal paintings, haphazardly stacked television sets, tables and chairs salvaged from skips, its ceiling held up by girders. I would spend many nights in 'ruin bars' like this, hedonistic dives hidden behind the walls of dilapidated nineteenth-century townhouses. Some were legal and some were not – most lay in an indeterminate zone between toleration and disapproval – and they fostered a bohemianism that seemed more urgent, more genuinely felt, than the affected artiness of Western European cities. The longer I stayed in Budapest, the more I came to understand why. People here actually felt they had something to react against.

Politics surfaced inevitably in every conversation. 'You are a stranger here?' a woman asked me once in a café, pulling up a chair to my table. 'Do you know what's happening in this country?' Agape had talked about it, Gergő and Eszter talked about it, and so did practically everyone else I exchanged more than pleasantries with: the right-wing government of Viktor Orbán – once a hero of the anti-Communist revolution, who had swept to power two years before – was now systematically destroying the democracy he had helped establish. Everyone had their own outrage to add, a litany I soon knew by heart. Freedom of speech was being curtailed: new media laws threatened journalists with fines if they published anything deemed 'unbalanced'.

The constitution had been rewritten, giving government appointees the power to nominate judges, and the symbolic 'Republic of' dropped from Hungary's official title. Anti-Slovakian and anti-Romanian sentiment was being stoked up, and the government was flirting with irredentist fantasies of restoring the lands Hungary had lost after 1920. Violence against Roma and other minorities was on the rise. The director of one of Budapest's biggest theatres had been replaced with a fascist – a supporter of the openly anti-Semitic Jobbik party – and arts venues and cultural centres were being shut down across the city.

'Places like this are being destroyed, any cultural place they don't approve of, anywhere doesn't promote a nationalist agenda. They're doing this just to prove they can,' Gergő said gloomily. 'They're sending a message, to show they can do anything they feel like doing. No one knows how far this purge will go.'

Around us drinks were being drunk and music being played. The conversation later shifted onto lighter paths, but this sense of political attack was never far away. Anger simmered under the surface of every discussion, waiting to bubble up. It became increasingly oppressive.

The next day, forgetting such matters as foreigners can so easily do, I did something I'd dreamt about while shivering in hunting hides in the snow of Austria, watching my breath freeze into crystals on the windows. I took myself to Rudas, a sixteenth-century Turkish bath, to steam three months of aches and pains out of my battered body. It was a relic of Ottoman culture, with squat pillars supporting a mineral-encrusted dome through which daylight filtered through dirty panes of coloured glass. Old men wallowed in steaming pools, sprawled naked on stone benches like gross parodies of Renaissance nudes, or sat stoically, glazed with sweat, enduring their private trials; in the event of overheating a rope emptied a bucket of freezing water over the puller's head. I plunged from one temperature to the next, alternating between extremes, until achieving a state of mindless delirium. One of my toenails fell off; I could do without it.

At dusk, strolling back over Erszabet Bridge, the bridges either side of me simultaneously flooded with light, mirrored perfectly in the Danube. Someone had given me a cigar, and I lit it now. Nothing, it seemed, could be better than this. Back at the art colony the house was filled with guitars and violins, and everyone was singing.

I moved again, this time to Buda. My host on the posh side of the river was a middle-aged journalist called Judit, razor-witted, passionate and fiercely intellectual, seething with indignation about the state of her country. She had a spare room in her flat on the seventh floor of an apartment block, and said I could stay as long as I liked. On one wall she pointed out photographs of previous guests: 'Three Finnish theologians. Two Argentinian dancers. An Iranian dissident. Two Chinese Australians. A gay swimmer. A very nice English girl. Two French financial analysts...' It sounded like a bizarre version of 'The Twelve Days of Christmas'.

One night, she invited me to an opera she was reviewing. Politics seeped in here, as it did everywhere else: all I got from the performance was a feeling of mild claustrophobia – opera had the same effect on me as baroque architecture – but Judit came out fuming. 'The director is another one of Orbán's lackeys,' she said furiously, 'another government man put there to restore traditional, conservative theatre. They won't be happy until our cultural life is back to how it was in the 1930s.'

Drinking wine in the kitchen later, she showed me the diary her mother had kept in the Second World War. Her family had been lawyers in a small Transylvanian town, well-to-do, middle class, part of the intelligentsia. Sepia photographs showed a world of tennis and piano lessons, pretty women in spotted blouses, men in shirtsleeves and high-waisted trousers larking around on sun-dappled lawns; transposed three hundred miles east, it was part of that same enchanted culture as Štrkovec. All this vanished after 1920, when Magyar-majority Transylvania was severed from Hungary and absorbed into the Romanian state. Judit's family left for Budapest. In 1945, having already seen one world destroyed, her mother spent six weeks hiding in a cellar while the Red Army fought the Germans street by street through the city above.

'We expect the Russians any day now,' Judit translated from yellowing pages scrawled with delicate green ink. 'How will they start? At one house they threw a hand grenade into the cellar. I try always to think of beautiful things, the landscapes and places of my childhood. I see how much beauty and how much richness was in my life, and how good it is that I can live off these things now...' As the diary progressed the Russians drew closer, taking house after house, until they were in the building next door. The women covered their faces in grime to deter potential rapists; numbly, everyone waited for the end. Eventually, a single soldier stumbled drunkenly down the stairs. They bribed him with a wristwatch and he went away. 'We were occupied by one Russian soldier,' Judit's mother wrote.

It was right there on that page, the source of so much of Hungary's grief. The phantom limb of Transylvania, the beauty and richness she had clung to when she thought she was going to die, was still something that caused Hungarians much pain. That feeling of injury, unconsolable after almost a century, hadn't changed since Paddy's time. Outside the liberal enclaves I frequented in

Budapest, other Hungarians I met remembered the injustice of Trianon as if it had happened last week, and spoke bitterly of how Magyar-speaking minorities in Slovakia and Romania were still persecuted. This sense of victimisation – of Hungary against the world – underlay many xenophobic trends, as well as the paranoid nationalism on which Orbán based much of his power.

Before leaving Budapest, I witnessed Orbán give a speech for the commemoration of the 1848 revolution, when Hungarian patriots rose against Austrian oppression. March 15 was supposed to be a day of national celebration, but society was so divided that the crowds had split, like the city, into pro-government and anti-government factions. The government march was spectacular, led by a column of mounted hussars in uniforms that would have sent Paddy into raptures of sartorial bliss – frogged, beribboned, gold-braided, with scimitars, tight dolman jackets and plumed shako hats – accompanied by falconers with hunting birds hunched on gauntlets. The marchers were joined by a jolly contingent of skin-headed Polish nationalists, invited as part of a right-wing front against the EU. Flags fluttered in their thousands, turning the boulevards into rivers of red, white and green, and the pavements were lined with war veterans cheering themselves hoarse. At the anti-government march, there was hardly a flag to be seen. As ever, the right wing put on the better show.

'Eastern Europe has always needed strong leaders, strong beliefs,' said a young man I met in the crowd. He was smooth with slicked-back hair, flawlessly well spoken. 'Hungarians have never liked being told what to do. First the Austrians, then the Russians, now the EU – we've been dominated by foreign powers for ever. We want liberation. Mr Orbán is making us strong again, standing up to the EU socialists, throwing out all the old Communists who never left their jobs. For a long time we have been living in darkness – now he is bringing us light.'

The bringer of light took the stage after a display of traditional dance. He had a pugnacious, hectoring voice and played his audience like a pantomime performer, producing a chorus of hisses and boos when he named the baddies of the drama: EU technocrats, socialists, liberals, whinging journalists, foreigners in general. Occasionally my companion translated: 'Mr Orbán is saying that we are free people.' 'Mr Orbán is saying we will not be a colony of the EU.'

Elsewhere in the city came a more unsettling sight. The youth wing of the far-right Jobbik party were parading in black uniforms, mini-fascists waving flags adorned with runic script. This was *rovásírás*, an archaic alphabet promoted as a symbol of Magyar exceptionalism; across the Great Hungarian Plain I would see it emblazoned on village signs, part of the government's nationalist revival. The effect was rather spoiled by the fact that no one could actually read it; in a similar way, the menacing effect of these adolescent Nazis was marred by the way they were swigging from beer cans – less parading, now I looked, than tipsily swaggering – but it was still another nasty echo of the 1930s. They looked more silly than threatening, but perhaps this has always been the danger with fascists.

After March 15 I began to think about moving on. The weeks had gone barrelling by and my journey had dissolved. Over the past few days blossom had appeared on the trees, prompting thoughts of change and fresh starts. I set a date, then rolled it back. Then I rolled that back too. Friendships had made me comfortable and they seemed too much to lose; I had grown close to people quickly and couldn't easily pull away. At the same time, part of me longed to escape the poisoned politics that saturated every conversation, the ever-present sense of grievance and attack, and to head, once again, into open landscapes.

In SRLY, the ramshackle café on Király Street where I'd spent many nights, I gathered the friends I had made for farewell drinks. On the tram back to Judit's apartment, I was amazed at how quickly the city had drawn me inside itself. It felt as if I was turning my back on another life; a life that could be mine, if I only stayed.

Judit saw me off the next morning, waving in a red dressing gown, a cup of coffee steaming in her hands. On the photograph wall in her flat she had pointed out two new pictures: one of me writing on a laptop, one of me lacing up my boots. I was glad that something of me would remain.

6

No Horizons

The Great Hungarian Plain

Carts drawn by horses and oxen easily outnumbered the motor-cars. Gypsies were on the move in long, jolting waggons that made all their gear clatter ... By the approach of evening, all trace of the capital and the western hills had vanished. We were in the middle of a limitless space.

Between the Woods and the Water

THE HILL OF BUDA WAS THE LAST HIGH GROUND I WOULD SEE for days. Beyond the terminal suburbs of Pest, the concrete net enwrapping the city – bursting in places, the further I went, to spill out scrappy woods and fields, suburbs bleeding into satellite towns, satellite towns into villages, past tower blocks and warehouse zones, into fields consumed by weeds and seemingly devoid of life – nothing stretched but flatness.

This was the start of the Alföld, the Great Hungarian Plain. Most Hungarians called it Puszta, deriving from 'empty' or 'bereft', and it comprised the westernmost of the thrilling-sounding Eurasian steppes across which the colonising Magyar tribes had swept. In previous centuries, this vast swathe of grassland and freshwater marsh was known as the haunt of *betyárs*, Robin Hood–style outlaws escaping the yoke of feudalism; Paddy had glimpsed a shadow of that outlaw sensibility when he camped with a tribe of wandering Gypsies, complete with dancing bear. Since then, much of the grassland had been turned over to agriculture; Communist collectivisation programmes had forced the Roma to abandon their nomadic way of life. Towns had nibbled at the emptiness, and here and there could be seen the orange twist of a gas flare's flame, desultory smatterings of light industry.

My predecessor had crossed these miles on a chestnut horse called Malek, on loan from a benefactor in Budapest. A horse would have suited me nicely as well, but the artists and ruin bar–frequenters I'd befriended had none to offer. Someone had warned me the Puszta would be mind-numbingly dull: a monotony of yellow horizons, stubbled by villages and crisscrossed by highways, sort of a Hungarian version of the American Midwest. The thought of so much emptiness produced a similar trepidation to what I'd felt overlooking the featureless spread of Slovakia from Bratislava's castle: an itinerant's fear of being exposed, without the comfort of valleys or woods in which to sneak unnoticed. Amid the parched, unmoving fields, under the cloudless wasteland of the sky, I had the impression at first of walking into a desert.

In Szolnok, one of my first small oases, I stayed with an incongruous family of Buddhist soap-makers. They lived in cheerfully slovenly style with a kitchen piled with dirty plates, and served me a curious meal of fried bread and tiramisu. The town initially looked little more than a nexus of railways and superstores – Tesco seemed to have won whatever war it was fighting here – but at its centre lay pleasant streets of Austro-Hungarian municipal buildings, pastel-shaded architecture in comfortable disrepair. I could imagine well-to-do farmers coming to settle their paperwork. There was a sleepy, indolent air. The political hive of Budapest, with its conflicts and divisions, already felt several decades distant.

After Szolnok, scrubby fields stretched to the south. The land grew wider, emptier: there was a feeling of multiplying space, as if the volume of the sky had increased, an adjustment of scale that was slightly alarming. It was like a telescope suddenly zooming out and I saw myself as a moving speck in a milky yellow vastness. But as my mind acclimatised, the trepidation I had felt was replaced by intrigue. The Puszta was monotonous, certainly, a purgatorial threshold, but under the surface domestication of roads and infrastructure the ghost of the steppe remained, its emptiness a physical presence, bubbling up between settlements.

Summer was truly upon me now and the texture of the air had changed: not scalded hot by sudden sun but warm in the way a lake stays warm after days of sunshine. The paths were dry enough for my boots to kick up thick grey dust, and dust devils corkscrewed ahead, always collapsing into nothing by the time I reached them. The sky was baked pale blue, the colour of distressed plastic. I wouldn't see a cloud for ten days; after a while this flawlessness started to feel unnatural, as if the workings of nature had stopped, the weather as featureless and unchanging as the landscape.

Following a dyke along the Tirsza river I met a group of farmers lounging by propped-up bicycles, machetes and scythes scattered about, seemingly the only living things in the landscape. Cracked faces peered from under tattered baseball caps, eyes squeezed into permanent squints, like extras in a cowboy film. They motioned me to Mesterszállás with forceful jabbings of the thumb – '*húsz kilométerre*', 'twenty kilometres' – gave courteous nods goodbye, and when I looked back five minutes later they were still staring after me. Nothing disturbed the silence of the land but the crunch of my boots in the dust and the tweedle of skylarks. In late afternoon the horizon's flatness was broken by the steeple that announced my destination, where I'd been offered a place to rest; the faster I walked towards it the more it kept its distance, hovering always on the skyline as if unsure of my intentions, finally creeping up to me with extreme shyness.

No one had offered me a horse, but the emptiness of
the Puszta was scattered with benefactors nonetheless;
friends of friends I had met in Budapest, or strangers who
had somehow heard of my journey through the mysterious channels of the internet. In Mesterszállás, I'd received
instructions from a woman I was never to meet to call at
the Városháza, where someone called Edit was expecting
me. The Városháza was the village hall, a low stone building snared in ivy, and Edit was a cat-faced woman who led
me unquestioningly to a house nearby. She showed me
into a dormitory furnished in dark wood and a bed with
crisp white sheets; we were mutually tongue-tied, but she
made it known I was a guest of the village.

Spindly trees bordered the garden, black against the
pinkening sky. Dogs trotted along the pavements on important private assignments. The evening was hazy with wood
smoke, and from cigarette smoke drifting along behind
cyclists returning, with impressive slowness, from the fields.
It felt like the village was heaving a great sigh after no great
exertion.

Farmers in padded coats were drinking pálinka in
the only bar. Magyar pop blared from the speakers, and
a fat man with a white moustache was manhandling the
barmaid in a dance; when she'd managed to get away he
plonked himself down at my table, his face flushed with
bonhomie, and talked without pause for the next half-
hour. The Magyar pop inexplicably changed to earsplitting
thrash metal. Three younger drunks in camouflage gear
were pretending to have a fistfight at the bar, handing out
boisterous stage slaps and testicular bootings. My companion downed his beer, and then the beer he'd bought me,
and went back to shuffling like a happy bear. When I left,
his drunkenness had passed its exuberant peak and plunged
him into despondency; I tried wishing him goodnight but

he only moaned in despair, burying his face in his thick hands.

I had a recollection of something someone had told me in Budapest: '*Sírva vígad a Magyar* – Hungarians rejoice in crying. It means a kind of sweet pain. One eye might be smiling, but the other is weeping. You get together with friends, you drink pálinka so you don't feel the weight. Nationalities have souls, just like people do. This is one way to explain our country's soul.'

The next day's halt wasn't far and I meandered slowly. Every so often on this journey I would find myself displaced, filled with incomprehension as to how I came to be there. The narrative of my walk fractured into component parts that had no chronology, that didn't connect at all. The white winter was so far away it might have happened years before, the rain of the Rhine was further still, and Holland was just a brown smudge beyond my memory. None of it bore any relation to the cracked fields around me now, the sweat dripping off the end of my nose or smearing up my glasses.

That sense of disembodiment followed me all day. I stopped frequently to sit and smoke, hiding from the sky in the meagre shadows of hazel trees bordering the fields. Insects had woken in the heat: scuffling red beetles that were either mating, or fighting, or both; bronze-coloured millipedes clambering in the dust. Cars were infrequent interruptions to the silence I had grown used to, gathering like physical manifestations of sound, entities formed from pure momentum. Tossed untidily along the verge were the skeletons of deer, the tattered remains of foxes and hares, and once the long, lithe body of a polecat: one hooked fang in a mouth of blood, red beetles working in its fur.

The town of Mezőtúr assembled itself on the horizon. A haywain clattered down the road, pulled by two dappled horses with crimson pompoms bouncing round their necks to ward off the evil eye; it was the first horse-drawn transport I'd seen, and it made the sight of the town infinitely more exciting. A large, potato-headed man was waiting by the petrol station, flanked by four beaming teenage girls. 'I am Péter Hollosvolgyi,' he announced in carefully enunciated English. 'Don't worry, even Hungarians find it hard to pronounce. These girls are Heti, Beti, Nora and Petra. We are delighted to welcome you to Mezőtúr.'

The connection had come via Esztergom: Sámuel's cousin was a teacher at the local Teleki Blanka Gimnázium, and had arranged for me to stay the night at the school. In return I was to give a presentation to the students in the morning; Heti, Beti, Nora and Petra had volunteered as my guides and helpers in the meantime. They strolled with me around the sights in the dying hours of daylight, dutifully pointing out the usual statues of patriotic heroes: the revolutionary Kossuth, the national poet Petőfi. They seemed to know every face in town and greeted the adults with 'csókolom', 'I kiss', which Paddy had heard in Transylvania. It derived from the antiquated 'I kiss your hand', a throwback to feudal courtesy – the Magyar equivalent of forelock-tugging – that had stubbornly outlasted Communism's levelling attempts.

Another intimation of the old order came when they took me to a small museum in the school grounds. Alongside the famous Mezőtúr pottery, dog-headed drinking jars and intricately embroidered cotton were a pair of tall leather boots and a lidded, long-stemmed bamboo pipe. Paddy had described the drovers here as 'tough, tousled and weather-beaten fellows in knee-boots' who 'smoked queer-looking pipes with lidded metal bowls and six-inch stems of reed or bamboo'. Could the artefacts displayed – stripped of human meaning now, the boots unworn, the pipe unsmoked – be the same ones he had seen on the feet, and clenched between the teeth, of riotous drunks in the local inn? The *mulatság* – 'the high spirits, that is, the rapture and the melancholy' – into which those peasants had descended was certainly the same 'sweet pain' I'd seen in the bar the night before. The costumes may have changed, but the Puszta's highs and lows – in spirit and topography – had remained the same.

I was given my own small room in the school dormitory. The students seemed unfazed by the presence of a pungent, bearded foreigner, and I whiled away the hour before bed playing chess with Heti. The girls had been given the task of organising my breakfast; I requested bread and cheese, coffee, maybe a piece of fruit. In the morning the table was heaped with a loaf of bread, two cheeses, a large salami, a packet of ham, a jar of instant coffee, two chocolate bars, a packet of biscuits, assorted yoghurts, four oranges, a bunch of bananas, an onion and a leek. The girls spectated proudly as I tried to make a dent in this pile, refusing to eat any themselves, and when I could manage no more they crammed the leftovers into every available space in my rucksack. Stuffed and dazed, still half asleep, I was led to the assembly hall to explain, to two hundred puzzled students, what I was doing there.

When I left Mezőtúr, I was turning my back on the last hospitable oasis for a week. There were no more benefactors until the Romanian borderlands; days of solitude and silence lay ahead. This was the point on Paddy's journey that he began to get passed along from aristocrat to aristocrat, rounding off his days' wanderings with hot baths, dinners and bicycle polo, 'strolling from castle to castle, sipping Tokay out of cut-glass goblets and smoking pipes a yard long with archdukes instead of halving gaspers with tramps'. On my post-aristocratic walk, this was the point at which I started to look, and feel, like a tramp myself. The constant sweat, and drying of sweat, created Rorschach patterns on my clothes, discoloured from the effects of dust and sun. My forearms and neck tanned purplish-brown, and my beard, untrimmed for weeks, took on an alarming aspect. Sometimes I became aware of a cloying, homeless stench I didn't recognise as my own. There was something transcendental about it; my body was starting to smell like another person's.

From Mezőtúr I followed rivers dribbling south and east: first the Hortobágy-Berettyó, more a dried-up drainage canal, and then the reluctant, green-brown sluggishness of the Körös. The earth was baked so hard it wasn't much different from tarmac. Occasionally I passed a farm, to be met by the predictable fury of dogs, and just as often an abandoned cottage with furniture smashed to kindling, wallpaper sloughing from the walls, dusty clothes piled on the floor. In one, as I wandered through the rooms, I picked up a framed photograph of a woman and a little girl standing neck deep in water, beaming happily. It was as if the family had left one afternoon, thirty or forty years ago, and never returned. Was their story connected to the land upheavals of collectivisation, urbanisation, the economic hollowing-out of the countryside? There was no one around to tell. It only added to the Puszta's sense of peculiar desolation.

I reached Gyoma, where Paddy had delivered his borrowed horse. Since then the village had merged, Budapest-like, with neighbouring Endrőd to form Gyomaendrőd; but that was where comparisons with the capital city ended. Chickens drifted in the lanes like inflated plastic bags, competing for pecking space with guinea fowl, little speckled zeppelins with giblet heads. Two workmen stood gazing at a puddle, the effluvium of some infrastructural flood, with expressions of fathomless depression. Having no horse to return, I crossed the bridge to the river's northern bank where an entanglement of forest seemed to offer the perfect place for my first night of camping.

Gergő had helped me choose the tent back in Budapest. It weighed just a couple of kilograms and packed down to the size of a sleeping bag, but even this modest extra weight had added to my daily aches over the past few days. The increased pain was worth it, though, for the freedom of crashing where I pleased; the tent was a happy medium between a stranger's hospitality and sleeping in a ditch. On that first evening I picked my way through knotted vines and old man's beard, under an overspilling nest of wasps dropping like slow hail, until I came to a crescent beach framed by fallen trees. The tent went up authoritatively, magically transforming my status from potential rough sleeper to temporary resident. Having established this claim to the land, I sat on a trunk jutting over the river and murdered mosquitoes. The Körös turned molten at dusk, a murky golden soup lit with magnesium-bright flecks from the dying sun. Clumps of twigs floated past like knots of hair.

It was the first of many such times in the months ahead. That undecided hour between evening and night was always a process of adjustment, a gradual settling of nerves in potentially ominous surroundings. Pigeons whooped in the trees, pheasants clattered melodramatically, and deer crashed through dry leaves with unexpected violence. From inside the tent the rustling of small beasts in the under-growth, magnified by the silence of night, could sound as big as horses. Noises carried from nearby villages were louder than seemed possible: the evening outrages of dogs, the bells of churches, the yells of children, each marking the end of the day with their own form of music. I hadn't quite got the hang of it yet – sudden noises could still make the blood jump in my veins – but I slept well that night, with no disturbed dreams. It seemed as good a sign as any that I was accepted in the landscape.

The next day's walk was virtually indistinguishable from the day before. Once again the land was yellow, the sky blue, the dust grey, and heat haze made the horizon roll like jelly. Infrequent columns of farmers passed, mounted on tool-laden bicycles, each nodding '*szervusz*', '*szia*', '*halló*', trailing his own plume of dust. Sometimes I came upon a pink-fleshed, shirtless fisherman by an amputated snip of river, disconnected serpentines created by waterway regulation, and once a walnut-faced man with missing teeth emerged from woodland to seize my hand; when I told him where I was from he bellowed '*Angol!*' into the trees, where presumably concealed spectators were watching. 'My answer "Angol,"' Paddy wrote of a similar encounter, 'induced a look of polite vagueness; an Angle meant as little to her as a Magyar might in the middle of Dartmoor.'

Körösladany was the next stop, and trudging through the beginnings of the village I was suddenly exhausted with the role I had to play: the eccentric stranger, announcing his friendly intentions with a smile, a clumsy sentence or two, a round of handshakes. A couple of glances from the locals, half-challenging and half-shy, were enough to drive me straight towards the dark bolt-hole of the church, a medieval impulse for sanctuary from the surveilling world. It was as cold as a fridge inside, and the varnished wood and silent stone were wonderfully familiar. Best of all, it was totally empty; I didn't have to explain myself to anyone. I stayed there a long time, clawing back my mood. The sweat dried on my skin and the aches subsided. When I left, I felt as though something had been rebalanced.

Later I worked it out: that church had once been the private chapel of the family of Count Johann Meran, another of Paddy's noble connections. The schoolhouse lying off the park – 'a long ochre-coloured late eighteenth-century building' – was the family kastély, while the park was part of their estate. Now children were playing there and Roma were laying out picnics on the lawn. Körösladany no longer felt so unfamiliar.

At dusk I crashed through tinder-dry woods to camp south of the Körös. Bells tolled from the Meran church, bats flickered after mosquitoes. I woke at dawn to see a polecat leaning in through the mesh of my inner tent, its little clawed hands outstretched, like someone gazing through a shop window. I clapped, and it didn't move. I poked its belly, and it still didn't move. On its snub, two-tone face was a similar expression to the one I'd seen on those of yesterday's locals.

The Körös branched into the Sebes-Körös, and the Sebes-Körös into the Holt-Sebes-Körös – the Swift-Körös and the Dead-Swift-Körös – and I followed these confusingly titled rivers all day through the dull-coloured world. Beyond the occasional hello I had spoken to no one in two days and silence was becoming addictive: when I reached Vésztő that evening, solitude was wrapped around me like a protective blanket. Vésztő gave the impression of having been dropped from a great height; for such a small town it was too spread out, its houses haphazardly scattered, like the debris of a messy landing. Plaster was peeling from walls held up by scaffolding, and even the newly constructed houses looked derelict. There was nothing in the shop apart from sweet, loaf-sized sponge cakes; I bought one knowing it would be horrible and hurried out of town, setting my sights on the distant trees of the Körös-Maros National Park.

Already I was becoming adept at scoping out camping places. Trees were good, and rivers were good, and hills were good – but the Puszta had no hills – and the woodland ahead offered both trees and water. Unfortunately the trees turned out to lie behind a swathe of bog, and my first attempt to find a path ended in sodden feet. My second attempt took me halfway before my boots sank in slime, and when I tried backing out they sank that way as well. I made a panicked sideways leap, which landed me, to my surprise, on a concrete beam. Another beam lay a short jump away. I'd discovered a line of stepping stones, a secret pathway.

Beyond that protective moat lay an aspen forest. I sprawled contentedly under the trees, relieved to be invisible again. But as I was putting up my tent I heard crashing feet: instinctively I hid my face, shrinking low against the ground, and three men with hunting rifles passed within thirty feet, looking neither left nor right, before vanishing into the trees. I stayed dead still. I couldn't retreat deeper into the woods without crackling through dry leaves; all I could do was wait, and hope they didn't come back. Ten minutes later they did come back, crossing the wood from another direction; they passed even closer that time, but still they didn't see me. It was inexplicable; perhaps I really was invisible. I stayed motionless until dark, when I was sure I wouldn't be found, and once inside the tent was struck by the ludicrousness of the situation. What on earth was I doing sneaking around a wood in Hungary, hiding from the local population? The Puszta was sending me weird. I felt as if I was slipping between the gaps.

In the morning, slightly shamed by my instinct to hide from the locals rather than meet them, I returned to Vésztő and sought out coffee in the roughest-looking bar I could find. Inside was a strangely beautiful scene: glasses sparkled in the sunlight, and blue cigarette smoke hung in aurora borealis-like veils. It was barely eight o'clock in the morning, and seven old men in a variety of headgear - fishing hats, baseball caps, a beret and a service cap that looked like something a Second World War tank commander might have worn – were already on their second or third glasses. My arrival silenced the room. I requested coffee, a mistake soon remedied by a man called Sándor, who cancelled my coffee and ordered me pálinka instead. The clear spirit was solemnly poured from a battered plastic bottle, and beer arrived as back-up. Sándor clearly believed in starting the day as he meant to go on.

We swapped cigarettes, that time-honoured ritual for familiarisation with strangers, and attempted conversation in a mix of Magyar, English, German and Russian. What was I doing here? '*Gyalog*,' I said, 'on foot', a word I remembered because it sounded a bit like 'dialogue'. '*Gyalog? Gyalog?*' he cried in delight. Where did I stay last night? I gestured vaguely out of the window. '*Lány?*' he enquired, 'girl?' I nodded to keep him happy and he bellowed his approval. Encouraged, I made my way through the rest of my Magyar vocabulary, which consisted mostly of geographical features: *falu*, 'village', *erdő*, 'forest', *hegy*, 'hill'. Apart from the latter they went down well, and I wasn't sure if it was because I'd pronounced the word for 'hill' wrong, or if, this being the Puszta, it wasn't part of his verbal landscape.

The other denizens of the room were enjoying our interaction immensely. They took it in turns to order drinks and slide them down the bar. After a while we were joined by a character who could only have been the town fool – in communities like this, a role as important as the mayor or the local policeman – who cackled and chortled, hopped and jigged, while his friends alternately laughed along and shook their heads sadly. With his long oily hair, knee-high boots and greasy jerkin he could have come from any time in the last few hundred years, and his hat caused hilarity because it looked like an even filthier version of mine; much amusement was derived from swapping them back and forth. Outside the window the early-morning sun-beams were replaced by the white light of midday. I was on my fourth pálinka and another round of beers was coming. I didn't know how to get away. Sándor clung to my arm and implored me not to leave. When I finally departed, huge disappointment overcame him; he shook my hand resignedly, as if I was making a terrible mistake, and when I turned to wave he was staring dully at his glass, all humour drained. I felt quite guilty.

I followed the road, morning-drunk, the sun high in the sky. Once the alcohol wore off the track was interminable, stretching ahead without deviation to a horizon with as little imagination as itself. My hangover started early. But it wasn't far to Doboz, a village shaded by rustling trees, where the air itself seemed to be cooled by the cooing of doves. In one of these now-dilapidated houses Paddy had been given a pistol with a mother-of-pearl handle for ward-ing off Romanians, but I had no clues which house it was. The only candidate I saw was an enormous crumbling struc-ture something between a mansion and a barn, although I couldn't tell if it had once stored grain or aristocrats.

On the other side of Doboz I found the Körös river again – the original Körös, stripped of its modifiers – which had become wider, slower, fringed by driftwood-strewn mudflats. Reeds concealed a pungent beach whining with leggy mosquitoes, and here I erected my tent on a bed of mouldable river mud and waited for the day to die. I was in limbo again. The hangover didn't help. I hadn't washed for almost a week and had eaten practically nothing but bread, cheese and salami. It took a long time to relax to the sudden pop-clunk of plastic bottles as the tempera-ture dropped, releasing mysterious pressures, and during the night a wind blew up; my dreams were of flash floods sweeping my tent away.

I was coming to my last Hungarian town: the Romanian border lay two days distant. The closer I got, the more I experienced jolts of apprehension. I'd been in Hungary for over a month, long enough to absorb certain of its attitudes, and many Hungarians still considered Romania enemy territory.

'My days on the Slovakian bank of the Danube, where many of the inhabitants were Hungarians, had given me the first hint of Hungarian irredentist convictions,' wrote Paddy. 'The bias against the Slovaks was strong; but, since the loss of Transylvania at the Treaty of Trianon, the very mention of Romania made them boil over.' Once again, nothing had changed. 'They are all robbers and crooks! You can't trust them. They'll take everything you've got,' he was warned in 1934, and those words might have been spoken by people I met in 2012; even the Buddhist soap-makers of Szolnok had told me to beware, and Sándor had practically spat in disgust when I said that's where I was heading. Hungarians had confidently told me I'd be savaged by dogs, robbed by bandits, tricked by Gypsies, menaced by bears, that the people were shifty and dishonest, the land polluted, the villages drab; and even though I knew these were partial, tribal views, the cultural osmosis had done its work. The prejudices of the cultures I walked through affected me like the seasons or the cooking, and I found it impossible to inure myself against them.

Perhaps subconsciously trying to delay the horrors of what lay ahead, I stayed two nights in Békéscsaba, the capital of Békés County. It was a rather shocking return to urbanity, with neoclassical buildings framing tree-lined boulevards, dotted with espresso bars and cafés that didn't serve pálinka first thing in the morning. The city was large enough to support a caste of alternative kids with facial piercings and styled hair, a specialisation of appearances that only becomes possible above a certain population size. On one street was a monument of a guillotine severing a block of stone. The blade was inscribed with 'Trianon'; Hungary lay on one side, and Transylvania the other. Soon I would be crossing into the severed block.

I had benefactors here. The first was Adrienne, a pretty young woman who worked in a dog shelter. In the apartment she shared with her parents I washed the filth from my body, turning the water in the plughole grey, and had my first proper meal in days: cherry soup and stuffed cabbage leaves smothered in sour cream. Her mother worked in a tanning salon – catering mainly for prostitutes, she said – and her father was employed at the dog shelter, having lost his construction job in the economic freeze. They entreated me to cycle out and visit them at work the next morning.

I borrowed a bicycle and did just that. The shelter was an hour's ride east – a road sign for Bucharest caused another brief wobble of fear – and in many ways it resembled hell: four hundred baying dogs, with the stench of four hundred dogs and the piss-stained bedding of four hundred dogs, the shit of four hundred dogs and, by far the worst, the dinner of four hundred dogs, bad meat boiling in a blackened tub the size of a jacuzzi. The fug was overwhelmingly awful, but Adrienne bounced through the canine squalor as if she was at a picnic.

Luckily I had an excuse not to linger: the night before, her father had helped me identify Póstelek, the most likely match for the kastély where Paddy had stayed. It was a short cycle away and arriving by bike was appropriate: this was where my predecessor had played bicycle-polo on the lawn, before leisurely evenings of smoking a chibook – a relative of the Turkish narghile pipe – in the immaculate company of Count Józsi and Archduke Joseph. Conjuring up such rose-tinted scenes was quite an effort now.

I had gone from dogs to ruins. The house was so comprehensively gutted it might have been destroyed eight centuries ago rather than eight decades. Its 'pinnacles, pediments, baroque gables, ogees, lancets, mullions, steep slate roofs, towers with flags flying and flights of covered stairs' had been reduced to rubbly heaps, like digestive biscuit crumbs. It was as broken as a building can be, smashed to smithereens. There was something extraordinary about the thoroughness with which this world – in all its comfortable wealth and self-assurance – had been annihilated.

The same peculiar cultural amnesia I had observed at Štrkovec made it hard to find out exactly what had happened. Adrienne's father vaguely supposed the house had been destroyed in the war, while other people thought it had been an accidental fire. No one mentioned Communism, which was certainly the cause, if not of the destruction itself, then of the decades of subsequent neglect that had atomised the building. When I crossed into Romania I would see this again and again: the dereliction of these country houses was deliberate and systematic, part of the ritualised disgracing of the dispossessed ruling class.

In Póstelek's once-famous arboretum – its magnolias and tulip trees growing wild above the weeds – I thought back to the first ruins I'd seen on this walk, squatting in the crumbling castles of the Rhine. Those citadels of knightly power were destroyed centuries earlier, as kings extended their dominance over lesser rulers. The twentieth-century despoilment of the kastélys of Hungarian nobles was a fundamentally similar process: an autocratic national government exerting control over the local power bases of landed gentry. Communism was only an extension of the centralising process begun by monarchs in medieval times; as with much else in the East, it had simply taken place a few centuries later here.

It was tempting to return with my tent to camp in the grounds that night, but an unusual offer had come my way. In Budapest I'd received an email from a place called the Panorama Wellness Hotel, offering a night's accommodation; its owner had somehow heard I was passing through Békéscsaba. So after leaving Póstelek I found myself in an otherwise empty hotel behind a petrol station, in a room with an en suite shower and cable television. My arrival was expected, but the staff spoke no English and I was unable to discover the whereabouts of my host. I imagined he or she would knock on the door at any moment – or join me in the restaurant downstairs, where I was served goulash and chocolate pie – but I finished my meal alone. The next morning the waiter brought me something called a 'peasant's omelette' and photographed me eating it from a dozen different angles. My mysterious benefactor never appeared. Full of grease and paprika, I set out for my last day's walk on the Great Hungarian Plain.

It was one straight path to the border beside the railway line. The land was green suddenly, with rustling yellow reeds. On the horizon, distant hills were visible for the first time in days; with a rush of excitement, and a jangling of small fears, I knew I was looking at Romania.

Several hours down the track, I was stopped by a car containing two stubble-headed country cops in sagging boiler suits. They were the Rendőrség – it was a last reminder of the perverse uniqueness of Magyar that the word for 'police' sounds nothing like 'police' – and they wanted to see my passport. When I explained I was walking to Romania, they waggled chubby fingers. 'Nem. Tren,' they said, pointing to the tracks. Paddy had been told the same in 1934; despite all that had happened since, the border still wasn't crossable on foot.

In Lőkösháza I boarded a train to carry me to Curtici, the first town over the border. It rattled through frontier nowhereland, the landscape identically derelict on both sides of the divide, fields and farms and abandoned houses, with clouds advancing across the sky like columns of infantry. The Rendőrség checked my passport again; the Romanian Poliție did the same half an hour later. I was still in EU territory, but was the end of the passport-free Schengen zone.

~~~~~

Bracing myself for instant attack from bandits, Gypsies, dogs and bears, I stepped onto the platform. A sleepy mongrel lying in the sunshine lifted its head and dropped it again, making no attempt to attack me at all. A group of rather courteous policemen pointed out the road to Pâncota, showing no surprise that I wanted to walk, as if it wasn't much business of theirs. These were encouraging signs.

On foot, small differences were immediately apparent. The first change was in the rooftops, which were steeper, narrower, witchier looking, with a preponderance of slightly creepy turrets and dragon-scale tiles. The architecture had assumed a folkier, more whimsical aspect, and the guttering was embellished with peculiar armoured decorations. More spectacularly, there appeared palatial concrete edifices crowned in outrageous adornments of tin, glittering arabesques like fantasy pagodas; the opulence of the roofs contrasted starkly with the mansions below, which were all rebar and bare cement, their windows plastic wrapped. These were the famous 'Gypsy palaces', more status symbol than home, kept permanently under construction to avoid paying taxes.

No less striking was the shift in language. From the assembled men in berets and women in shawls and heavy boots, I caught snatches of a Latinate tongue, and its lilting, southern-sounding cadence brought a rush of familiarity that was quite unexpected. Magyar had been impenetrably alien. Here, I could actually guess at the meaning of things.

One night in Budapest I'd gone drinking with a man called Sean, an American translator who spoke Magyar and Romanian fluently. He'd talked of Hungarian psychology and why it was that Magyar-speaking people felt exceptional, isolated in the middle of Europe, under threat on all sides. It was partly explained, he thought, by the uniqueness of the language. 'If you look at Romanians, they're actually very open to new ideas and influences. They feel themselves part of Europe because they have a linguistic link with Italian, Spanish and French, and they can understand a lot of the Slavic languages too. Magyar is utterly unlike any neighbouring language, so Hungary has no sense of connection or shared culture. I think that might explain why the country is so inward looking. Why Hungarians have this fear of the outside world.'

As I left for the blue hills, curiously watched by old men and women with faces so wrinkled they looked as if they'd been creased and smoothed, creased and smoothed for a hundred years, I thought of something else Sean had said about Romania: 'People have faces there.' I knew now what he meant.

I followed a newly surfaced road with infrequent traffic. The late-afternoon light was intense and rain swept the horizon, streaking the sky like brushstrokes on canvas, but none fell near me. Naïvely painted Christs were nailed to crucifixes of hammered tin, and grubby sheep waddled the fields, another difference from Hungary; this was a transition from a farming to a shepherding culture. A Dacia, Romania's national car, slowed to offer me a lift. A horse and cart jangled past. A disproportionate number of dead dogs lay along the roadside.

I kept walking until I was too footsore to continue. In a village called Sântana I was directed to a pension that looked boarded up, with only a couple of dogs yapping from the balcony to alert me to inhabitation. After ten minutes of knocking and waiting, the door swung open to reveal a smiling man who introduced himself as Kitos; he led me upstairs to a cheap yet surprisingly pleasant room with a view over tiled roofs, blossoming fruit trees, dogs and chickens squabbling in a yard. Rubbing his arms in a mime of cold, he went out and returned with an electric heater that filled the room with the smell of burning hair.

By the time I came downstairs, the lower floor had become a bar and Kitos had morphed from manager to barman. He poured me two shots of homemade *ţuică* – the Romanian version of pálinka – powerful moonshine from the inevitable battered plastic bottle. On the television a handball game was in progress between Romania and Hungary, and when the Hungarians scored Kitos delivered a matey attack on another man at the bar, a guy with most of his teeth knocked out so he literally sported fangs. 'Magyar man,' Kitos explained, pummelling this ethnic enemy in a mock-aggressive way, then linking fingers together to symbolise their friendship.

I ended up at the only table on a salvaged car back seat, while Kitos delivered more beer and liberally handed out ţuică. My new drinking buddies were one very brown man, one very white man and one very red man; the hands of the very red man so huge, his fingers so thick and strong, that I felt embarrassed to display my own puny specimens on the table. A deck of Romanian cards was produced, suits I'd never seen before, and a complicated game ensued.

The red-faced man talked and talked, desperate to communicate something. He scrawled on a sheet of paper and I dimly understood that he was giving me a lesson in Romanian history. The name 'Decebal' I recognised, the last king of the Dacians, the civilisation that had ruled these lands before the Romans came. Then he leapt forward to 1848 and a picture of a tree, then 1947, 'Mihai', who I guessed was King Michael I, the word *'abdicat'* with a scrawl of a train, an aeroplane, then *'comuniști'* and a symbol that – with elaborate mimes – represented the act of fucking. I was more or less following him – King Michael abdicated in 1947, left the country by various means of transport, then the Communists came along and proceeded to fuck everybody – but after that the plot became confused. He had scrawled over the words so much that written communication was hopeless, so he launched into a series of charades that grew less and less comprehensible: a very realistic impression of a bear (Russia?), water being drawn from a well (irrigation? resource exploitation?), then a cow, a Chinese person, a fat man getting drunk, and finally, I deciphered, Napoleon's penis. This went down a storm at the table: a pun on the word *pulă*, 'dick', to make Na-pula-eon. I was glad I'd kind of understood the joke, but integrating it into the wider historical narrative was tricky. This wasn't greatly improving my understanding of Romanian history, although I couldn't have asked for a better introduction to the culture.

I woke with an aching head on a cold, bright morning. Cockerels were crowing in the yard and my breath steamed in the air. Downstairs Kitos served me coffee, brushing aside the coins I offered with gentle firmness. Another card game was in progress with the deck from the night before, and cigarette smoke was already billowing over the table.

7

People Have Faces There

Romania

*Every part of Europe I had crossed so far was to be torn
and shattered by the war; indeed, except for the last stage
before the Turkish frontier, all the countries traversed by
this journey were fought over a few years later by two merci-
lessly destructive powers; and when war broke out, all these
friends vanished into sudden darkness.*

Between the Woods and the Water

My fear of Romania was gone. I'd crossed the threshold
and been accepted, and as I journeyed east in the cool of
the morning my delight increased by the mile.

Paddy had walked this road alongside peasants in homespun tunics, sheepskin jackets and foot-tall hats. The trap-
pings may have changed since then, but for the first time
on my journey the change didn't feel so absolute. Suddenly
the word 'peasant' wasn't a throwback to a lost era, but an
accurate and literal term to describe the people I met, those
who inhabit the land; when Romania joined the EU, the
number of small and subsistence farms in the community
increased by a third. In Curtici I'd noticed that most of the
men wore berets, but after only one day's walk the style of
headgear had changed: the men in Pâncota preferred felt
porkpies pushed back high on their heads. Fleece waistcoats were worn alongside baseball caps and secondhand
sportswear. Roma girls swished down the street in random
colourfulness: a clash of lurid stockings, patterned skirts,
jumpers of neon spots and swirls, garish shawls pulled over

very black, very shiny hair, and lots of gold. Their gaze was open and direct, with the faintest hint of a smile and much humour behind the eyes, something between a challenge and an invitation to intimacy. It was immensely self-possessed, and immensely separate; it struck me as the look of a foreigner to another foreigner.

Not far out of town I was overtaken by a moth-eaten horse pulling a wooden barrow on rubber tyres. The driver slowed and jerked his thumb, an offer not to be refused, and cleared a space among rusty scythes and bundles of wire. He was a young man called Moise, and his face wouldn't have been out of place in Rajasthan. With him was his wife, a beatific woman in a Stars and Stripes bandana, and their little son, who regularly leapt down to salvage useful scrap from the roadside: a smashed computer, a circuit board, dumped electronic waste, to be cannibalised for profitable parts. Moise attempted communication in Romanian, Magyar and German, and then, as an afterthought, '¿Hablas español?' It was the one language we shared; he had worked, like many Romanian Gypsies, as a farm labourer in Spain. That job had been swallowed by the crisis; now he was scrap collecting again. Along the road we encountered other scavengers on carts and bicycles, whistling greetings to one another, exchanging tips on promising sites, a tribe of modern-day hunter-gatherers living on the verges.

A couple of miles up the road our paths diverged. Moise scribbled his number on a cigarette paper. 'Perhaps you can help me one day. If you hear of any work when you get back to England, remember me and my family.' Gold flashed in his mouth as he smiled. His wife and son were already picking through a pile of rubbish in a nearby field.

Throughout the afternoon I had the sense of incrementally climbing. These were arid steppes no more; the hot sun and cold air spoke of a mountain climate. Hills folded into hills, with snow dashed on the peaks. With my water supplies depleted, I was delighted to discover a conical stone structure that turned out to be a natural spring, at which two men were filling up dozens of plastic bottles. They let me jump the queue, and burst out laughing as I drank and then practically threw it back up; the mineral water tasted overpoweringly of rotten eggs.

Near the country town of Ineu I diverted down a sun-dappled driveway towards the Spital de Psihiatrie Mocrea, the Mocrea Psychiatric Hospital. The link between old country houses and mental health institutions was strong; this was where Paddy had stayed as the guest of another Hungarian count, luxuriating in a life of picnics and after-breakfast cigars, the start of a 'blessed and happy spell' of leisurely sojourns with cultured hosts that carried him to the vales of Transylvania. The former kastély of Count Tibor was a hulking custard-yellow building at the end of an avenue of trees. A bemused gatekeeper escorted me to the hospital's director, a broad, bald man named Augustin, who led me inside. The interior was a facsimile of Slovakia's Štrkovec – the same over-lit, disinfected corridors, the same compulsively smoking characters shuffling between the rooms – and once again, not a trace was left of its previous incarnation.

'Here is where the old Tibor used to drive up on his horse,' said Augustin as we reached the annexe, but when I asked more about the building's former owners, his expression went blank. 'I think perhaps they moved to Hungary. They donated their land to the Romanian state. No one really knows...' Again came that sense of historical vagueness, softening the sharper edges of the past.

A violent and glorious sunset was bursting over the land. The hospital was an island in a warbling sea of birdsong, and the conical hill of Mocrea – Mokra in Paddy's time, the name, like the estate itself, having since been

Romanianised – glowed in golden light. 'Do you have a place to sleep?' asked Augustin. I suggested camping in the grounds, but he didn't think it was a good idea. 'Not because of the patients, because of the dogs. This place belongs to them at night.' Instead he offered me a bed in Ineu, ten minutes down the hill, in a dormitory attached to the special-needs school run by his wife. It sounded suitably strange, as appropriate for my journey as staying with aristocrats was for Paddy's.

The school adjoined a crumbling fortress with trees growing through its windows, patches of sky visible through its roof. It used to be an orphanage, Augustin mentioned briefly. The school itself was empty apart from a young man who worked as a caretaker, and when Augustin was gone he served me macaroni cheese and sat watching as I ate with unusual concentration. At first our interaction was smooth – he found my attempts at Romanian amusing – but halfway through the meal something in him altered. His expression grew dark, his facial muscles twitched, as if he was suppressing great fury; he began swinging back and forth, compulsively rubbing his knees. His questions, which I couldn't understand, became increasingly threatening in tone, and his anger built and built until I managed to deflect it with a question of my own, a clumsy Romanian sentence or two, which made him giggle. But once the laughter died away his anger built again, the rocking restarted, his fingers clenched and clawed tormentedly. It was a nerve-wracking half hour, and he seemed as relieved as I was when at last I escaped to my room.

Only later did I guess a connection between his anger and this place. The orphanage, I learnt the next morning, was one of those horror stories I grew up hearing about in the 1990s: six hundred infants penned in cribs in the corridors of that ruined castle, by-products of Ceaușescu's disastrous fertility drive to strengthen the Romanian state. Communism had criminalised both abortion and contraception, pregnancy tests were mandatory for women of childbearing age, and tens of thousands of unwanted children were traumatised and neglected in the years leading up to the regime's collapse in 1989. Romania's accession to the EU had prompted the closure of these institutions; the special-needs school at Ineu was set up, largely, to deal with the mental health fallout from those times.

'My wife and I work hand in hand,' Augustin had said. 'Often it happens that the kids she teaches end up in my hospital. They go from one institution to another.'

The road the next day threaded southwest, back towards the Hungarian border, through villages of dilapidated bungalows with tiled roofs undulating as if in a frozen wave. The colours splashed on the walls – lime green, neon pink, bilious lilac and lavender – had been unleashed after 1989, an attempt to wash away half a century of uniformity. In the fields along the road I glimpsed my first Romanian sheepdogs, the ferocity of which I'd been warned about: enormous woolly beasts, dreadlocked with matted hair, that looked less like dogs than sheep-demons protecting their flocks, their status marked by horizontal sticks hanging under their throats. They eyed me warily as I passed, but the road was neutral ground and I was allowed to make my way unmolested.

Despite the lack of cars on the road, the corpses of car-struck strays appeared frequently. The ancient Dacians, I'd been told, rode to war under the standard of a snarling wolf's head, trailing a tube-shaped length of fabric that produced an unearthly howling as they charged. I'd also heard that contemporary myths said their warriors underwent the ritual of lycanthropy – transformation into wolves – which may have explained the popularity of werewolf legends.

Could the enormous number of strays, part of everyday life in this country, exist as some collective consciousness of Dacian wolf culture? It was more fun to think so.

It rained, stopped raining, rained again, and I broke my no-lifts rule to accept a ride to reach the city of Arad before dark. The sprawling industrial outskirts, smokestacks and electricity substations gave way to an ebony-domed Orthodox cathedral. Black-garbed priests, with angular headwear and trapezoid beards, congregated on the steps like soldiers in some dwarf army. In the park along the river, catkins bobbled the branches. Old gentlemen strolled by in long tan coats, hands clasped behind their backs, followed by respectful envoys of peaceable stray dogs.

My first Romanian Couch Surfing hosts arrived in their own time. Paul was a blond-bearded, loose-limbed man slouching along in baggy green trousers, while his girlfriend Alexandra was dark, petite and precise of movement. They were representative, they said, of two sides of Romania: he was from the west, where people were known for being lazy and relaxed, while she was from the Black Sea coast, where people were busy and efficient. 'You want some wine? You want to smoke a joint?' were Paul's first questions to me, as if emphasising his regional stereotype. So we sat beside the river, drinking homemade red wine and smoking local grass, and then repaired to their regular bar for more of the same.

The river was the Mureş, which flowed into Hungary to become the Maros, which I had walked and camped beside for much of the previous week. 'We like that it goes in that direction. It takes all the rubbish into Hungary,' said Alexandra, only half-jokingly. Even though they were liberal and young, anti-Hungarian sentiment surfaced frequently. 'They refuse to learn Romanian. Fucking bastards!' she laughed, a perfect echo of what I'd heard in Slovakia. 'We don't hate them all, of course. We have Hungarian friends.

But as a culture, they still see themselves as an imperial power. They still think Transylvania is theirs, even though it's in the middle of our country. They can't let it go.'

Up until then, I hadn't really thought of Hungary in terms of a former empire; Hungarians saw themselves, if anything, as victims of other empires, first Austria in the west and then the USSR in the east. But for Romanians, Hungary itself was the historical tyrant. Once again, my preconceptions spun around in the air and fluttered down to land in different places.

Romania was the only country in Europe where the anti-Communist revolutions of 1989 turned bloody – over a thousand people died in the uprising and its aftermath – and Arad was the second city to rise against the regime. Paul had been four years old, and remembered the rattle of guns in the streets, people heaping portraits of Ceauşescu onto bonfires. 'Every book printed back then had his picture on the first page, so there was plenty to burn. It was a big, angry party.'

Like every other Romanian I met, they were cynical about the democracy the revolution had delivered. The current president had dubious links with the Securitate, Ceauşescu's infamous secret police, and the political class was largely comprised of ex-Communists. Paul talked nostalgically about the 1990s, the cowboy years, when everything was up for grabs: 'The '90s were better than today. Life was more free. Gangs beat you up in the street, but things were easier.'

'Gangs beat you up in the street, but things were easier?'

'There was an openness, a sense that we could do anything. Now it's all been closed again. Under Communism we had money, but there was nothing to buy. Now we have everything to buy, but we have no money.'

I'd planned on leaving the next day, but was easily discouraged. We went back to the river, drank more wine, smoked more grass and returned to the bar. An ever-shifting kaleidoscope of hedonistic friends came and went, bearing jugs of homemade booze. The same thing happened the following day, and after that I began to lose track. I sank into an indolent life of mild intoxication and heavy conversation; my time in Arad was as leisurely as Paddy's country-house sojourns, only with more marijuana and fewer domestic servants. There was a subtle but significant shift in the language of hospitality: the question had changed from 'When do you have to leave?' to 'How long can you stay?' 'Two more days? A week? Why hurry? We're having a picnic by the river tomorrow, we're meeting friends on Friday night, someone's having a party. Maybe we can borrow a car and drive to the mountains...'

On one of these long, loose afternoons we built a fire by the Mureş, upriver from a Roma family camped with dogs and horses. A feast was prepared of pork and *slănină*, cured fat melted on willow switches over the flames and dripped on bread, a Romanian version of marshmallows. The ţuică-fuelled conversation turned to the EU, which Paul, Alexandra and their friends regarded with deep misgiving. This was a notable difference from Hungary, where left-leaning people I'd met generally saw the EU as a counterbalance to nationalism, but it was rooted in pride in Romania's peasant culture. These young, modern, urban people were intensely proud of the fact that country dwellers still raised their own crops, ploughed with horses, made their own wine, butchered their own pigs, produced their own cheese, and retained some knowledge of how to harvest traditional medicines from the forest; this culture was threatened by EU regulation and the free-market ideology espoused by their government.

'Every year on St Ignatius Day, each family sacrifices their own pig,' said Paul, his face lit up by the flames. 'It brings everyone together, and every bit of the animal is used: the meat, the blood, the bone. We make slănină out of the fat. It feeds the family all winter. Now people in Brussels are saying these pigs should be sent to an abattoir, where they can be killed by electricity. What's the point of that? Is it better for the pig? And the peasants must pasteurise their milk, buy a licence to sell it to their neighbours, they won't be allowed to sell țuică from the cherry tree in their own garden. They want to turn us into Western Europe.'

'Our government is embarrassed by the fact we still have peasants here,' said Alexandra. 'They think it's backward, primitive. They're trying to force peasants off the land so foreign multinationals like Monsanto can grow modified crops here. No capitalist government wants its people to be self-sufficient – self-sufficient people don't go shopping. They are trying to make us dependent, to take away our freedom, so we can be controlled.'

This appreciation for wildness and tradition cropped up again and again over the next few weeks. It was a kind of hippy nationalism that dovetailed with something else that emerged as the fire burnt low: a mystical admiration for the ancient Dacians. 'The Dacians were free people, a highly advanced civilisation. Look at the beauty of our country – we have mountains, rivers, forests, we are rich in salt and gold. It was paradise here. The Romans invaded, destroyed the culture, destroyed the language, stole our resources. Now the EU wants to do the same. It's a new Roman Empire.' These words resonated with something I'd heard before. It took me a moment to work out what, and then I remembered Harry, the broken-toothed drunk I'd met beside the Rhine, babbling about the freedom of Germanic tribes against imperial oppression. The sentiment was identical. Both versions of history were wildly over-romanticised, but accuracy wasn't the point. This mythologised affinity with suppressed ancient cultures spoke of a similar yearning for a long-lost age of greater freedoms, unbounded by rules, that bubbled under Europe's surface like a buried river.

On my last day in Arad, Paul got hold of a car for a long-planned trip to the mountains. His objective was an Orthodox church, to stock up on the mineral water that flowed from a nearby spring; he spoke of this water as being so pure it was almost miraculous. As I was helping them fill the bottles, I became aware of a rattling rhythm sounding from somewhere above – at first I thought it was a wood-pecker – a complicated paradiddle punctuated at intervals by the clang of a bell. A black-robed priest was drumming on a suspended plank with a pair of wooden sticks; this was the *toacă*, played every day from now until Easter. We sat and listened, sipping the sweet, achingly cold spring water, as the rhythm grew in speed and complexity, culminating in a frenzy of tapping before rather bathetically fading away.

That was my call to move. The next day was damp and grey, but I was set on departure. Hymns drifted down the streets as I headed back towards the Mureș. It was Easter Sunday, for Catholics at least – referred to rather dismiss-ively as 'the Hungarian Easter' – the Orthodox version wouldn't take place for another week. I passed the charred remains of our fire, and when I looked back Arad was only a jumble of steeples and power lines on the horizon. The river wound scrappily east and south, its banks occasionally mounded with trash, overhung with blossoming trees that looked like frozen explosions. I met no one that day. It felt good to have escaped the city.

The E68 hummed to the north, and beyond it surged a procession of hills that marked the beginning of the Mureș Valley; I considered climbing up to camp, but a week of indulgences had left me lethargic. Instead I pitched my tent by the river, and woke at dawn to see the grumpy face of a beaver scowling from the shallows. After kicking off downstream it gave a final intolerant glare and disappeared underwater, slapping its paddle tail to warn other beavers that an Englishman was camping there.

As the valley rose around me, I had the sense of being enfolded in a wave of green. Pale blossom spattered the slopes, the trees throbbed with new leaves, and vineyards lightened the darker green of the hillsides. I was in an excellent mood: the piles of garbage and discarded plastic bottles only enhanced the prettiness of everything around them. By noon I had reached the Franciscan monastery of Maria Radna, where Paddy had played skittles and conversed in Latin with a monk called Brother Peter.

Today there were no brothers in sight. The basilica had seen better days. Wooden ribs protruded from one of its twin steeples, and torn plastic sheeting fluttered in the wind. The statues of two battered saints, Francis and John Nepomuk, flanked the steps exhaustedly as if recovering from a bruising wrestling bout. I was here to meet someone called Ileana, who had contacted me several weeks before in a rather mysterious fashion: the email had simply said she was researching abandoned country houses and wanted to help me locate the places where Paddy had stayed. Once again, I was aware of the rhizomatic network of fans spreading across the continent, popping up when least expected. Nevertheless, there was something slightly different about Ileana's message. She was driving from Bucharest, a journey of six or seven hours, and our meeting was clearly of unusual importance to her.

I had several hours to wait, and spent much of this time studying the votive paintings inside: hand-painted offerings of thanks for deliverance from various disasters. They were naïve, beautiful paintings, charting a folk history of everyday catastrophes: housewives being consumed by flames from gas stoves, a builder plunging Icarus-like from a crane on a construction site, and one, unintentionally humorous, of someone getting stuck head-first in a cement mixer. In every scene, the Virgin Mary regarded these events with concern, but never appeared to be in a hurry to physically step in. The faces of the crushed, the mauled, the bleeding and the burning showed the same gloomy acceptance, impassive in their suffering.

Ileana was younger than I'd expected, a slight girl in her mid-twenties. We sat on the steps outside the church in the afternoon sunshine.

'There is something I didn't tell you,' she said. 'I am the great-granddaughter of Count Jenö Teleki.'

~~~~~

'A tall, spreading, easy-going middle-aged man, with gold-rimmed spectacles and a remarkably intelligent, slightly ugly and very amusing face ... he had all the instincts of a polymath: everything aroused his curiosity and sent him unwieldily clambering up the library steps. He delighted in gossip and comic stories, and he had a passion for limericks, the racier the better.' That was Paddy's description of the count, with whom he had stayed blissful weeks as a guest in Kápolnás - now Câpâlnaş - thirty miles east along the valley. A scholarly, cultured and generous man, historian and butterfly collector, his speech inflected with Scottish from his upbringing by a Highland nanny, the kindly figure of Teleki represented the best of the privileged culture that the war, and Communism, had torn apart.

The story of Ileana's family was a permutation on a narrative that was familiar by now. Their estate was nationalised in 1948, and they were preparing to flee when they were betrayed by a former servant, arrested and imprisoned. Their property was confiscated. 'Recently we obtained an inventory of the things taken from the house. It was obvious no one had any idea what they were dealing with. Very valuable items were marked as "ring", "piano", "painting", "chair". We asked the National Bank what happened to it all. They said it was sold to help pay off the external debt in the 1980s.'

Throughout the Communist era, the remaining members of the family were disgraced and humiliated. After being tortured in jail, Jenö's son Eugen was given a menial job in a railway station and became an alcoholic. When people used to jeer at him, asleep in the waiting room, he would say: 'Let me be. This is how the last Count Teleki wishes to die.'

Ileana had grown up knowing nothing of this. Her grandmother had kept it secret, knowing the Teleki name was a black mark against the family. But after Ceauşescu's televised execution in 1989 and the fall of Communism, they pieced the story together. Ileana's father had won back the house – used for decades as a psychiatric hospital – in a legal case, but as they had no idea what to do with such a property, they continued renting it to the state.

'Have you ever slept in an asylum before?' she asked. 'There's a room we can use. You can stay as long as you like.'

But first, she wanted to show me other broken houses in the valley: the continuation of the trail of ruins I had followed since Štrkovec. In nearby Odvoş – formerly Otvos – we broke in through a shattered door to explore the shell of the house where Paddy had stayed with Mr v. Konopy, a learned wheat-breeding enthusiast. Dust motes swooshed as we passed through the rooms. Traces of silver-patterned wallpaper still gleamed on the walls. In the family chapel the ceiling had collapsed in a downward sneeze of straw, and a crack running down the wall bisected the painted face of Christ. Since Ileana had last been there, the pews had been stolen.

'This vandalism was deliberate,' she said. 'The library at Căpâlnaș contained communications with the Vatican, illuminated manuscripts written on calfskin. When the house was nationalised the peasants didn't know what to do with them, so they turned these manuscripts into socks to line their moccasins.'

We went next to the kastély at Bulci, where Paddy had attended a party, rubbing shoulders with monocled Francophiles and ladies in gorgeous gowns. Now the house was Sleeping Beauty's castle: weeds prised through the broken tiles of what might once have been a break-fast terrace, shutters hung at crazy angles from boarded-up windows, and paint flaked from the doors like tiger bread. Since Ileana's last visit, the portico had collapsed. I tried to imagine the windows lit up, the hallways humming with life. Now there were dogs sleeping in the ruins and the only sound was birdsong.

My ruin guide left me there, to camp beside the river while she drove on; we arranged to meet at her asylum the next afternoon. I pitched my tent beneath a white willow on the bank of the Mureș, and woke to a field of frost. The sky was the colour of a smashed blood orange. On Bulci's overgrown lawn, a man was quietly cutting grass for his animals with a sickle.

For most of the day I followed the river, struggling through jungled woods and tripping over vines. The river had widened since Radna, here and there narrowing into bottle-necks or forking to enclose wooded islands. 'Everything in these reedy windings was inert and hushed under a sleepy spell of growth and untroubled plenty,' wrote Paddy, but now much of the land had grown wild. As I neared my destination I fought through a stubble of charred stalks from the burning of the winter grass, pushing my way through scorched willow that whipped across my face and arms,

giving me charcoal stripes. Coated in ash and sweat, I came
to Căpâlnaş looking like I'd escaped from a fire.

'I loped exhausted through long shadows to the kastély
at Kápolnás. Double flights of steps mounted to a balus-
traded terrace, where people were sitting out in the cool
moment before sun set; there were glimpses through
french windows of lighted rooms beyond.' If I squinted
it was almost the same, though the people on the terrace
wore dressing gowns rather than evening wear. Dogs slum-
bered in the sun, and a stocky, powerful-looking man was
strolling in the garden. He was wearing what looked like
a walkie-talkie, and from his authoritative bearing I took
him for an attendant. It was only after he'd seized my hand,
linked arms and marched me to the house that I realised
he was one of the patients; the walkie-talkie was actually a
blaring radio. Weirdly, he looked a lot like Jack Nicholson.

'Ion,' he introduced himself. 'Like the singer, Elton
Ion.'

'Nicholas,' I said.

'Sarkozy?' he cried, then slapped himself on the forehead and erupted with laughter. '*Vive la France!*' Then he
seized me by the head, a slightly alarming turn of events,
and landed two bristly kisses on my cheeks.

A curious circle of patients gathered round, shaking
hands and smiling: men and women, old and young, in
plastic slippers and woolly hats, smoking furiously. One
young man with a shaved head and white socks pulled up
to his knees approached me with an expression of rapture.
Ion impatiently shooed him away, circling his finger in the
air and giving me a meaningful look.

'Crazy,' he explained.

Double doors of polished wood led to a dim, tiled hallway. A marble staircase laid with dirty rugs climbed to the
upper floor, where an ornate gallery looked down on the

glass-panelled ceiling of the room below: once the famous library, from which the moccasin-socks were made, now a recreation room scattered with stained sofas. The dining room was a dormitory, where daylight from the French windows spilled onto hospital beds piled with slumbering forms, disordered heaps of pyjamas and legs, men in various stages of exhaustion or depression. The rest of the house was a mildewed warren of corridors and mysterious half-closed doors, lit by flickering chandeliers, where patients shuffled in semi-darkness in a fug of tobacco. Women in shawls scowled around door frames. The upstairs bathroom was occupied by aggressive stray dogs. Unlike Štrkovec or Mocrea there was nothing sanitised here: this hospital looked more like the set of a low-budget horror film.

Ileana showed me to the room set aside for her family's visits: three hospital beds and a ceramic stove the colour of a glazed pie dish. She showed me family photographs – Count Teleki staring owlishly through round spectacles, with a spotted bow tie and a toothbrush moustache, Eugen glaring at the camera in traditional costume – and took me on a tour of the estate: the overgrown gardens reverted to nature, the half-collapsed stables and outhouses, the attic, the roof, the labyrinthine cellars.

As evening wore on, I started to feel curiously at home. Under the surface creepiness was a gentle, even tender sense, as if the house and the gardens around it were, like the patients themselves, deep in convalescence. We visited Teleki's grave in the woods; he had died during the war, before the estate was nationalised, and his resting place was surrounded by lichened columns and vaulted with trees like a chlorophyll cathedral. In Communist days the family was forbidden from setting foot here, so they couldn't lay flowers on his grave. They used to throw them over the wall; it was the closest they could get.

As her great-grandfather had done with Paddy, Ileana drove me down the valley to Hunedoara the next morning, on the now traffic-snarled E68, to visit the famous castle. This was the stronghold of Ioan Hunyadi, a medieval ruler with the rare distinction of being a hero to both Romanians and Hungarians, who had defended these lands against Ottoman attack. She told me the legend of the well in the courtyard, dug for fifteen years by three Turkish prisoners on the promise of freedom when it was done. Hunyadi's widow later broke the promise and ordered them put to death. The story said they'd left a message carved at the bottom of the well: '*apă ai, inimă n-ai*', 'you have water, but you have no soul'.

From Hunedoara we ventured on, winding through the hills to the Hațeg Valley to see the church at Densuș, constructed on a Dacian place of worship with pillars made of Roman tombstones; thousands of years of history layered into an edifice that resembled a collapsing cake. The eyes of the saints on the icons had been cut away; powerful charms in witchcraft, Ileana said. She told me local vampire stories – 'not like Dracula, you know, more like energy-sucking beings' – tales of female forest spirits that people went blind if they saw, went deaf if they heard, went dumb if they talked to. Perhaps there was something of Teleki in her passion for these tales. To the south lay snowcapped mountains, forming a seemingly impassable barrier to whatever lay beyond. This was the massif of Retezat, one of the highest and wildest parts of the 'wolf-harbouring Carpathian watersheds' Paddy had set out to find, and my desire to walk through those peaks was overwhelming. It was a bit like falling in love: a breathlessness and a sense of dizzy possibility, accompanied by an immediate fear of somehow losing my chance. It affected me like a chemical shift. But for now I had to turn my back: following Paddy's trail, my route lay north and east in a loop through Transylvania. In a month, I would return this way.

Back at Căpâlnaş we shared a bottle of wine on our hospital beds. The night was cold, so we summoned someone to light the stove in our room. 'Excuse me, one fire!' the assistant yelled, charging through the bedroom with a flaming log balanced on a shovel; as soon as he thrust it into the stove the room filled with smoke, flowing through cracks in the tiles and pouring into the corridor, where patients gathered anxiously, prepared to evacuate. Luckily, there were no smoke detectors in the hospital.

Dogs sang in the garden and patients griped in the corridors. The lights intermittently brightened and dimmed as if controlled by an unseen pulse from the overworked heart of the building. The house itself, I had come to see, was the victim of a trauma; it seemed an appropriate sanctuary for people who, in ways I'd never know, had been through traumas of their own. It was like the special-needs school in Ineu, built to deal with the damage caused by the failed orphanage system: traumatised children housed in the ruins of a traumatised culture. Căpâlnaş, like its current inhabitants, was in recovery from history, refugees from the modern world. Ileana repeated something Ion had said, when she'd told him of her family's plans to renovate the house.

'Why renovate?' he'd replied. 'Objects, like people, get morally damaged.'

I left on a grey, overcast morning, the birds singing as if before rain. Ion shook my hand and planted two last tobacco-smelling kisses on my face. He was standing at the gate to say goodbye, hand raised in salute.

'Long live the Kingdom of Great Britain!' he roared as I went by. Then greenery closed over the house, and Căpâlnaş was gone.

The inward migration of storks had begun. Storks were a recurring motif in Paddy's journey, and I was delighted to see their return; cumbersome and awkward birds, all joints and pivots, hinges and elbows, settling in giant nests on telephone poles and rooftops. The sound they made was extraordinary, less a song than a knocking together of pebbles in the throat. I followed an unmetalled road on the south side of the Mureş, and was gobbled at by turkeys in the villages and rushed by gangs of geese that lowered their heads to attack, hissing like evil lizards.

There was one final stop on my tour of ruination. In the hills above Gurasada I climbed through a broken window into the kastély where Paddy had spent his longest, and happiest, country-house sojourn, befriending an ex-hussar called István and falling in love with a married woman, with whom he embarked on a love affair in a grand loop through Transylvania. This house was smaller than the others, and I wasn't sure I'd found the right place until I recognised the octagonal pillars, the ochre walls of the arcade, the fanlight of green and purple glass, amazingly still intact.

Nothing stirred inside but dust. The rooms were empty apart from piles of musty agricultural pamphlets. In lieu of the 'fine portrait of an ambassadorial ancestor', the centrefold of a porn magazine was pasted to the wall.

I'd considered sleeping the night inside, but there was nothing to stay for. I'd had my fill of ruins. So I spilled my last drop of ţuică on the steps and headed to the woods. Acorns crunched under my boots. As I was putting up my tent, I heard the first spring cuckoo.

~~~~~

I'd got myself on the wrong side of the river. The next day's walk was dominated by the E68, the so-called 'international road' on which half the trucks of Europe seemed to be racing for the border. There wasn't much option but to follow, squeezed precariously into the kerb, sometimes having to leap aside when traffic careened too close. Shepherds in conical felt hats tended flocks of longhaired sheep either side of this zooming stream, as if refusing to notice. The valley narrowed into steep hills and widened out again, and I followed the river past a cluster of cooling towers huffing water vapour. This was the industrial overture to the city of Deva.

I wasn't much in the mood for cities and my time here was fleeting. I stayed with a young mixed couple: he was Romanian and she was Hungarian, or more properly a Csango, who, she explained, were descendants of Szeklers, a separate Magyar-speaking tribe that had guarded the eastern frontier. These bewildering subcategories were a sign that Transylvania was close, with its patchwork of ethnic groups. The idea was slightly unreal. Thanks to the Dracula industry, probably nowhere else in Europe occupies the same hinterland between fact and imagination, and the proximity of that magic-sounding region – the loss of which drove Hungarians into such masochistic grief – urged me swiftly on. I left Deva early the next morning, taking a shortcut through a riverside slum towards open fields.

The price I paid for my impatience was nearly rabies. A series of huts, roofed with plastic, abutted fields scattered with waste like a parody of healthy crops. The reason for the frequency of rubbish soon became clear: these hovels lay in the shadow of the dump, a broken mountain of trash that soared from the earth, spilling its innards, layer upon layer of compacted garbage like an archaeological dig of twenty-first-century culture. The wind changed direction and the smell of it hit me, a stench so thick it filled my skin. As I passed its perimeter, there were movements within. Scrawny dogs emerged ghoulishly from nests of rotting mattresses, seeping out from behind broken fridges, watching me with mustard-yellow eyes. They were the same colour as the rubbish, perfectly camouflaged.

These hyena-like hounds were the worst I'd yet encountered. Sensing that something bad was coming, I stopped to fumble for my walking poles, telescoped up and strapped to my rucksack since I'd stopped using them weeks before. Seeing me clumsily arm myself, the dogs launched into attack. I'd just managed to extend one pole before the pack came foaming in, rushing me from the left and right; I was forced constantly to dodge and wheel, striking out first in one direction then lashing the other way, while more and more dogs rushed from the dump, outraged by my defiance.

A rangy Roma man was leaning on an axe nearby. He had paused from chopping wood to watch as I hopped and swung towards him, his expression as impassive as the Virgin Mary's in the votive paintings at Radna. I had the impression it was some kind of trial: that only once I'd fought my way through the gauntlet of dogs, proving my worth in some way, would he deign to help me. And so it seemed: when, at last, I managed to reach his little hut, he shouted something that made the dogs swiftly draw away. Then he fanned cigarettes in offering.

My nerves were rattled. I didn't stop walking until the town of Simeria, by which time it was pouring with rain; the downpour was a deliverance, driving the dogs under shelter. I crossed the bridge and turned east under a mesa-like rock to where the land was greener, cleaner. Gradually the rain eased off. The cloying stench of garbage was replaced by the sweetness of blossom.

'*Drum bun*,' called an old woman in the village of Bobâlna. She wore a red and gold shawl, and her back was so hunched her upper body was parallel to the ground. The words meant 'good road', and it started to become one. To the north the land rose into rocky outcrops snarled with hawthorns, while to the south, beyond the river, across a sweep of agricultural land, the furrowed wall of the Carpathians glowered beneath a belt of clouds. The houses grew squatter, their stone walls thicker, giving an impression of greater permanence.

The next village was precisely divided between Roma and non-Roma neighbourhoods. First came a commotion of hooves and a cartload of children clattered past, pursued by a pack of hounds; wild boys zoomed around on motorbikes, naked infants hunted in the river for useful scraps along the banks, washing flapped between cob-walled houses, and stout old ladies bellowed conversationally through windows. Then I crossed an invisible border and the streets were deserted, the houses neatly fenced and gated. After that lay empty fields again.

With a loaf of bread and a lump of sheep's cheese, I branched at last off the road and hiked a steep track into the hills, through terraces and pastures, until the tree line. I hadn't stopped walking for eleven hours and the effort almost did me in. I sprawled shirtless on the grass as a stain of clouds spread from the south, between me and the mountains. Thunder thudded distantly, like a car door being slammed. Lightning flooded the valley and dark rain streaked the land, but the sky above me was clear enough to see the first stars. I worried briefly about bears, and then forgot about them. The storm rolled on, and a cuckoo sang like a bird without any other ideas.

I woke to the patter of rain and the tolling of church bells. The valley was obscured behind gauzy cloud, sunk in a yellowish twilight. The bells got louder as I descended. It was Orthodox Easter Sunday.

'Hristos a înviat.'

'Adevărat a înviat.'

My hosts in Deva had taught me the exchange: 'Christ is risen.' 'Truly he is risen.' I tried it out on the people I met, but there were few abroad. The birds were silent under the rain, the stray dogs peering sadly from under dripping bushes. I wandered in a muted landscape with the strange sensation that I was no more than a dream the land was having.

In the afternoon the dirt road ended and became tarmac. The tarmac summoned, as if by dull magic, the inevitable sprawl of cement that heralded a city: Alba Iulia, the seat of Transylvania's Roman Catholic church. Past the cathedral lay a redbrick fortress, a brute of a structure that expanded, the more angles I viewed it from, to a size that appeared completely impossible. Shaped like a seven-pointed star, it was a vaster relation of the one I'd seen in Arad, an outpost of Hapsburg military might to defend against the Ottomans. Its double layer of defensive walls meant that assailants could be cannonballed from two separate angles in a deadly bowling alley. It was like a psychopathic growth, a military super-organism, and given the effort that had gone into making it, it must have been almost a disappointment the Ottomans never came.

A triumphal archway rose whitely above this death machine, from which the two-headed Hapsburg eagle glared defiantly southwards. The monument was carved with reliefs of horses and billowing cannon smoke, topped by kneeling Turkish prisoners, hands bound behind their backs.

'With the erosion from the rain, the sculptor who renovated the statues couldn't work out what the Turks were clutching behind their backs. They each seemed to be holding two objects, but he couldn't tell what they were. In the end, he worked it out. It was their testicles.'

This grisly history was told to me by Vali, a colleague of Ileana's, whom she had phoned to inform of my arrival.

His parents lived beside one of the bastions, and after a fortress tour he led me to their house. His mother and father were white haired, red faced and blue eyed, and they fed me pork wrapped in cabbage leaves washed down with thick, greenish wine that fizzed on the tongue like sherbet. They put me up in a spare room cluttered with unusual artefacts – a bronze bust cast by Vali's brother, a replica tall ship built by his father, his mother's collection of wooden folk masks – and wouldn't hear of me leaving so soon: I must stay at least one more day.

The family had duties in the morning visiting friends in another town. They loaded me up with offerings of cold lamb and nettle stew and deposited me at their local church, where an Easter Monday feast was about to begin. Under the wooden witch-hat steeple, a trestle table was heaped with food. A handful of people were decked out in traditional Romanian costume – pleated skirts and wide white trousers, waistcoats embroidered in black and gold – and the rest were wearing clothes that came straight from the 1950s, with fur collars, elegant hats and kidskin gloves. The priest said a prayer, and dramatically flung up his hands to commence; elderly women elbowed past to shovel cakes onto their plates and children converged on a bowl of dyed eggs – reddened with onion juice and painted with delicate silver flowers – to commence a game like conkers, smashing two eggs together until the first shell broke.

'*Hristos a înviat.*'

'*Adevărat a înviat.*'

I broke eggs with the priest, who spoke good English. He told me his church was located here – outside the fortress walls – because in the past Romanians weren't allowed to build within the city; unlike Hungarians, Szeklers or Saxons, they were not a recognised 'estate' of the province of Transylvania. For much of their history, Romanians had been second-class citizens here.

As my predecessor had been, I was passed from one host to the next: Vali's family arranged for me to stay with friends in the next town. 'But you should probably take that off,' Vali advised as I left. He was pointing to a badge someone had given me at the feast, depicting Avram Iancu, a Romanian hero who had rebelled against Austro-Hungarian rule in 1848. 'Our friends in Aiud are a mixed couple, Romanian and Hungarian. To Romanians, Iancu is a freedom fighter. To Hungarians... well, I guess you could say a genocidal terrorist.'

'Dr Livingstone, I presume?' cried a big man with a walrus moustache waiting by the angled bulk of Aiud's Saxon church later that day. The journey had been a sodden slog, rain falling ceaselessly from morning to afternoon, and I was more thankful than ever at the prospect of shelter. Vali's family friend was named Laszlo – 'like Victor Laszlo, from *Casablanca*' – and the Magyar *sz* gave it away: he was the Hungarian half of the couple. I made sure my genocidal terrorist badge was out of sight. Back at his house we smashed eggs together and drank toasts in various languages: '*noroc*', '*egészségedre*', 'cheers', to which he added, a bit incorrectly, 'God help us!'

I woke in grey submarine light, saw water sliding down the window, and groaned. I was getting tired of rain, tired of boots that never quite dried, tired of my waterproof coat that was no longer waterproof. The accumulative exhaustions of walking had mounted over the past few days: my body ached with a general weariness of the flesh and I longed for somewhere to rest. Twenty miles north lay the city of Turda – I had another invitation there – but a combination of the weather and my overall fatigue made that day's journey exceptionally depleting; from the moment I left Victor's house, everything went badly.

An early decision to escape the thundering E81 led me into a line of hills that looked like a pleasant route from below, but became an obstacle course of deep mud, thorns, barbed-wire fences and unexpected drops, more a fight than a walk, ascending and descending through groves of impenetrable blackthorn that snagged my clothes and pulled me back, ripped the hat off my head, scoring all unprotected skin with bloody scratches. On the highway below vehicles guzzled past in seconds, speeding towards my destination, while I had to struggle for half an hour to round a single hill. I cursed every car I wasn't in. It was one of those days when I was struck by the sheer futility of what I was attempting. Only my fury at motorised transport – fury at the fact it even existed – prevented me from giving up and sticking out my thumb.

Bullying my way through one entanglement I came upon a boy of around seventeen, swathed in a dripping leather cloak with plastic roped around his legs, minding a herd of tender-eyed brown cows. He was so astonished to see me that he couldn't speak. As I fumbled for my map, thinking this was the best explanation, his eyes flicked nervously from my face to my hands, as if half expecting me to produce some kind of weapon. I was conscious of the long-handled axe hanging at his side.

The map didn't do much good. The boy continued staring in scarcely concealed horror, so I wished him *bună ziua*, good day, and continued up the hill. At once I became ensnared in a thicket of thorns that held me like an absurd fly in a spiked, dripping web. More furious than ever, I thrashed and tore until I was free, knowing I looked ridiculous, and when I glanced back he was gone; whether home or to fetch reinforcements, I didn't know.

The rain hammered down with renewed urgency as I approached the final hill before the descent to Turda.

Sheep were scattered wetly about and sheepdogs watched from a distant slope, but they seemed safely far away, and I was too weary to make a precautionary detour. Halfway up the hill, I was stopped by the sound of baying; I'd infringed whatever perimeter was considered acceptable, and a cavalcade of dogs was pouring down the far side of the valley, closing the distance between us with unreal speed. The sight had a dreamlike quality and I could almost have stayed to watch, but survival instincts kicked in: these weren't scrawny garbage-dogs like the ones outside Deva, but hounds bred to bring down wolves. I abandoned all thoughts of appeasement and started running. The dreaminess became nightmarish: my feet were clumsy with exhaustion and, dragged back by the weight of my bag, slipping and sliding on wet grass, I hauled myself up a hill that may as well have been a ladder, hand over foot, in open flight, while the dogs gained the bottom of the valley and rushed unchecked up the slope. I reached the top, found myself on tarmac and was almost mown down by a truck; luckily, my pursuers accepted the road as the limit of their range, and contented themselves with frenzied barking until I was out of sight.

A new landscape opened up. The ground fell away towards cloud-capped mountains, below which was the cleft of the white-rocked Turda Gorge. On the valley floor, I could see the clutter of the city.

Even now, Turda gave itself to me begrudgingly. Sticky agricultural mud stretched either side of the highway, so I followed a concrete drainage canal through a waste of industrial parks, crisscrossed by motorway bridges, into a derelict factory zone where looming gantries sloughed their forms in flakes of concrete. When at last I gained the outskirts my welcome was a rock, hurled by a couple of bored teenagers, which narrowly missed my head and hit the metal gate behind me, the final cymbal clash to the mocking drum roll of the day. I stumbled on until, ten minutes later, I halted beneath the statue of a long-coated man called Dr Ioan Raţiu.

It was a welcome sight. Ioan Raţiu – signatory of the 1892 Transylvanian Memorandum, which demanded equality for Romanians in the province – was a forebear of Ion Raţiu, an eminent politician who had opposed Ceauşescu's regime, himself the father of Indrei Raţiu, the man whose hospitality I was shortly to enjoy. The route that had led me here was far more circuitous than that day's dog-plagued battle through rain: in a ruin bar back in Budapest I'd met Luke and Camilla, a young English couple on the verge of moving to Romania. They had put me in touch with Indrei, who said I could stay as long as I liked in a room set aside for visiting writers. It seemed almost too good to believe.

The Raţiu Centre for Democracy lay just across the square. Depleted in body, depleted in brain, I found myself being led through a courtyard into a homely abode: a glimpse of a winding staircase and a reading room filled with grey afternoon light, antlers mounted on the wall, sofas and armchairs arranged around a fire. Indrei was a late-middle-aged man with heavily lidded eyes, who resembled a kind and intelligent turtle. 'Familiar faces,' he said, pointing towards the kitchen. I couldn't imagine what he meant until a pretty, smiling girl emerged bearing a mug of Earl Grey. It was Camilla, from Budapest. Her boyfriend Luke was having a nap upstairs.

My relief at finding myself in this haven was too much to contain. Rain started pouring again outside. Peacocks mewled in the flowerbeds. I lay in an enormous hot bath and started, for some reason, to cry.

Indrei was leaving shortly to catch a train to Bucharest, so I only had the privilege of his company for a few hours. Fortunately he was a man capable of packing a lot into a short space of time; in a beguilingly tranquil voice he moved swiftly and precisely from one subject to the next, weaving a tapestry of important information. He told the story of his father Ion, who had started his career as a civil servant, fleeing to England when Romania – threatened with imminent Soviet invasion – allied itself with the Nazis in 1940. He remained exiled in London after the Communists came to power, opposing the regime so vocally he was placed on a Securitate death list; framed photographs of him posed with Richard Nixon and Pope John Paul II hinted at his diplomatic standing. After Ceaușescu's death he returned to Romania, made an unsuccessful bid for the presidency, served in the Chamber of Deputies and founded a newspaper. When he died a decade later, his funeral in Turda was attended by ten thousand people.

Indrei himself had been brought up in Cambridge – he was as much English as Romanian – and the Rațiu Centre for Democracy was, in a sense, a continuation of his father's work. Besides giving shelter to visiting researchers, scholars and the occasional English tramp, the centre existed to promote a greater understanding of democracy, and was a hub for everything from environmental to anti-human trafficking campaigns. The totalitarian system Ion Rațiu opposed was gone, but corruption was entrenched at every level of public life. 'Until very recently, Turda's reputation was particularly bad. I didn't realise quite how bad until the chief of police was arrested for keeping girls imprisoned in a locked room in his house.' Between recounting these stories and packing for his Bucharest trip, he was conducting a rapid discussion with an assistant about the visa complications of a Bahraini pro-democracy activist they were trying to bring into the country. By the time he left, elegantly attired – his trilby hat and battered suitcase gave him the look of a benevolent spy – I felt as if I'd received several educations.

My fellow strays Luke and Camilla had the room next to mine. They were travelling around Romania looking for a place to settle, to find a crumbling cottage to restore with traditional building techniques. The longer I spent in Transylvania, the more I realised it was full of romantic English types seeking a cheaper, simpler life, though normally the demographic was older and better heeled. This bewildered me at first, but understanding came one day when I saw a landscape that reminded me of rolling hills in Somerset; rather than the crags and brooding pine forests I'd expected, Transylvania resembled nothing so much as an idealised English shire. With its fields and woodlands, meadows and mountains, its local peasant farmers producing organic, sustainable food, it offered a cross between a back-to-the-land, eco-friendly lifestyle and a return to a rustic idyll, a half-mythologised identity that England had lost. This, I suspected, might have been why Paddy had loved it so much.

There was nothing half-mythologised about Turda. Outside the historical centre – which, as Paddy said, was oddly reminiscent of a Devon market town – post-industrial dereliction sprawled into the valley, horses and carts rattling down potholed roads past abandoned factories, a potent image of the failure of Ceauşescu's modernising vision. It was a slightly depressed and often ugly Romanian city – a very normal Romanian city – and I felt happy there: my week in Turda was a time of much-needed restoration. Madly bearded, with a stench that had worked itself into my pores, feet so sore they felt like they'd been pounded with a tenderiser, I revelled in the luxury of a soft bed, daily baths, and the other pleasures of sedentary life. With Luke and Camilla I wandered the streets, visited the famous salt mine and drank ţuică in the rain, and when they left on the third day I found myself in the house alone, a guest without a host.

I washed my clothes for the first time in weeks, and got to work on rents and tears with a sewing kit. Paddy said that Turda was a town of cobblers and I hoped that was still the case: my boots were leaking worse than ever and worrying cracks were starting to appear in the soles. The thought of replacing them was anathema – we'd been through so much together they'd taken on an almost talismanic quality – so I sought the help of Radu, Indrei's garrulous assistant, who located a cobbler's shop halfway up a tower block. When I picked the boots up two days later they were restitched with twine, leather tongues sewn down the seams, fiercely waxed and scrubbed. They looked reborn.

I tested their powers on a walk to the gorge, that cleft in the white rocks I'd glimpsed when I first saw Turda. An hour's scramble over the hills brought me to the entrance-way, where the Hăşdate River crashed between monumental walls, and narrow goat tracks led to caverns skittering with bats. I branched off the path to zigzag up from the shadowed floor, squeezing between granite juts until I had gained an upper level of circling birds, wild flowers and sunlight. It was precarious enough to feel the enjoyable tremor of risk, before the inevitable disappointment of a safe descent. I stayed there a long time, listening to the wind. According to legend, the gorge was created when a Hungarian king, fleeing from pursuing Tartars, entreated God to grant him passage; the rock parted like the Red Sea.

A market came to town, and for several nights there were musicians and dancers in the square. They were dressed in embroidered waistcoats, absurd foot-tall hats of straw or crested with peacock feathers; the men high-kicked and slapped their thighs, the whirling women's pleated skirts inflating like hot air balloons as they span. Tremulous songs were sung, overflowing with passion and pain, voices ascending and descending to the jerky backing of accordions, clarinets and trumpets.

The crowd watched placidly, barely tapping their feet. The only dancers were the town drunk making alarming lurching motions, and the town fool pirouetting in a pink skirt, his face a mask of snarling happiness. Gypsies looked on as if enjoying a good cockfight: the women in ludicrously clashing clothes with ponytails plaited in bright ribbon, ending in enormous bows that reached to the backs of their knees; the men with moustaches, gleaming teeth and hats of impressive circumference, dressed, as if in opposition to the women, uniformly in black. These were the Gábors – a staunchly traditional and relatively affluent group among the Roma – so called, Radu said, 'because all the men are named Gábor.'

Back in Arad, Alexandra had taught me a Romanian word, *dor*, which couldn't be translated. 'It's the feeling that an animal is tearing you into pieces, but it's still very hopeful. Pain and hope together, like you're going to burst.' It described an emotion similar to the Hungarian sweet pain, where one eye might be smiling but the other is weeping. This music had something of that dor. Watching the inscrutable faces of older people in the crowd, it was impossible to know what they'd lived through: years of deprivation and paranoia in which friends informed on friends, family informed on family. Such a system of total control, of institutionalised mistrust, was something the teenagers in the crowd, in their branded clothes and stylishly tousled hair, surely couldn't understand; or had no interest in.

I couldn't understand it either, but Radu helped somewhat. We took a circuitous walk through town, from the Roman ruins on the hill to the glittering Gypsy palaces on

Turda's outskirts. He told me that he, like many others, had been monitored by the Securitate due to his involvement with foreigners – he wrote letters to pen pals all over the world – and when he asked to see his files after 1989 he discovered that his closest friend had informed on him for years. This was not an unusual story, and he didn't particularly blame his friend; who knew what blackmail or extortion had been used against him? At the height of Ceauşescu's power, it was popularly believed that one in four Romanians was a police informer.

'Things were fine until the 1970s, but then that bloody bastard went to visit North Korea. He saw all the banners saying "Long Live Communism", he saw the children dancing in the streets, people throwing flowers at his car. It was all stage-managed. But the bloody bastard believed it! He fell in love with it! He decided that Romania should be like that, a European North Korea. When he got back from that trip, things started to get much worse.'

Inspired by what he'd seen in one of the world's most repressive states, Ceauşescu launched on a visionary remodelling of Romanian society, aiming to transform its peasants into modern industrial citizens. He called it 'systematisation', a programme of urban expansion that involved the destruction of eight thousand villages; the Hungarian and Saxon minorities were especially targeted. It was the same as I'd seen in Slovakia, where mud cottages had been replaced by high-rise flats in a generation, but carried out with even greater megalomaniacal fervour; the grand scheme for Transylvania included bulldozing castles and fortified Saxon churches, obliterating anything that hinted at the past. In Cluj-Napoca a few days later, I would see the line where the advancing tower blocks, laid out either side of boulevards designed for motorcades and military parades, stopped abruptly at the old town, a cement wave breaking. Like a fossil record, it preserved the point at which the regime fell.

'See this building?' Radu asked as we passed a block like a concrete anthill. 'There used to be cottages here, cottages and gardens. But that bloody bastard decided that people couldn't live in cottages, couldn't grow food for themselves, because that made them self-sufficient. So he knocked them down and built flats. The flats didn't even have kitchens. If families had kitchens they would eat privately, and maybe they would say bad things about the government, so instead they all had to eat in canteens, so their neighbours could hear what they were saying. He wanted machines, not people.'

There was something in Radu's face that I'd seen before: something tight about the eyes that reminded me of people I'd met in the hospital at Căpâlnaş, and also the young man in the special-needs school in Ineu. It had nothing to do with craziness, nor with being angry or sad – Radu, in fact, seemed perennially joyful – but rather an impression of shock, like flesh recoiling after a blow, the memory of impact. In certain lights, history could be glimpsed as a shadow under the skin; I saw it now, underneath the brightness of his smile.

We passed Turda's old concrete factory, closed in the 1990s. 'It was so polluted here,' Radu said. 'The air was poisonous. Now the factory's closed and the birds have come back. There's good and bad in everything. Now we have no jobs, but we do have birds.'

8

The Valley of the Shadow

Transylvania and the Carpathians

Each day in the mountains seemed to contain a longer sequence of phases than a week at ground level. Twenty-four hours would spin themselves into a lifetime, and thin mountain air, sharpened faculties, the piling-up of detail and a kaleidoscope of scene-changes seemed to turn the concatenation into a kind of eternity. I felt deeply involved in these dizzy solitudes, more reluctant each minute to come down again and ready to go on forever.

Between the Woods and the Water

INDREI RETURNED FROM BUCHAREST TO SPEED ME TO CLUJ-Napoca, half an hour by road to the north, and inevitably the landscape smeared into green abstractions. Back at pedestrian pace came streets of pretty stone houses topped by bulbous turrets, cupolas like the conning towers of steam-punk submarines, ending at the Ceaușescu era's frozen concrete wave. In Piata Unirii, the main square, seven irregular pillars marked the dead of the 1989 revolution; above an expanse of cobbles thrust the Saxon church, its elegantly brutal geometry making it look as if it was hacked from a solid block.

This was a different phase of my journey. My predecessor had not walked this stretch, but embarked on a weeklong joyride with István, his friend from Gurasada, and a married woman called Angéla, with whom he was romantically entangled, on a clockwise sweep through Transylvania's Magyar-speaking heartland. The pleasure trip was largely a blind so they could enjoy their love affair away from disapproving eyes. In Cluj-Napoca's New York Hotel they had downed famous cocktails before departing in a hooded carriage to a discrete Gypsy restaurant; now renamed the Continental, the grand fin-de-siècle building was languishing behind tinned-up windows, its owner apparently wanted by the police and in hiding abroad. My own lover was a thousand miles distant and no one had offered me a car, as no one had offered me a horse, so I planned to hitchhike a week in Paddy's wake. No horse, no car, no grand hotel: once again, my journey was a trampier version of his.

Cluj-Napoca was Romania's second-largest city and, after Turda's small-town air, startlingly international. It had enough churches to satisfy every conceivable denomination – Orthodox, Roman Catholic, Greek Catholic, Armenian Catholic, Calvinist, Unitarian – with a mosque and a synagogue thrown in for good measure. It was a university city, and suddenly in the streets I saw Asian and African faces, groups of giggling Malaysian girls in headscarves. This was only an acceleration of what had been happening for thousands of years: Transylvania's ethnic and religious interweave further complicated in modern times by globalisation.

Graffiti in a backstreet reminded me it was still disputed territory: 'aici (nu) e România!' 'this is (not) Romania!' The nu had been added by someone else – presumably a Hungarian – although rather magnanimously they'd written it in Romanian. To Târgu Mureş I was driven by a cherubic-looking student who told me proudly that he was a Szekler, not a Hungarian, and went through a long list of differences I didn't quite understand. He pointed at the gnawed slopes of the hillsides and complained about the number of sheep increasing year by year. I'd learnt enough to pick up on the cultural subtext behind his words: Magyar-speaking people were traditionally farmers, and Romanians shepherds. When he complained of the rise in sheep, he was indirectly complaining about the rise in Romanians.

In Târgu Mureş, Gábor Gypsies strutted like gunslingers in their huge hats and drooping moustaches, while the skirts of the women were as bright as the flowers in the municipal beds, as bright as the red, blue and yellow tiles sparkling on rooftops. It gave me a flashback to München's Hofbräuhaus: as with those lederhosen-clad Bavarians, the livery was as individually defined as pantomime costumes. 'Clothes were still emblematic,' wrote Paddy. 'An expert in Rumanian and Hungarian symbols, looking at the passers-by in a market-place ... would have been able to reel off their provenances as swiftly as a herald glancing along the flags and surcoats of a fourteenth-century battle.' Transylvania's polyglot tribes, whether Romanian, Hungarian or Roma, still proudly and resolutely set themselves apart from each other, and clothes like those the Gábors wore were only the most immediate code. As if further confirmation of this tribalism was needed, I stayed with a dentistry student called Zsófia – a Hungarian, but not a Szekler – who immediately took up the anti-Romanian theme.

'I played with Romanian kids when I was little. But when I grew older my parents said I should have a Hungarian boyfriend. They don't want me to marry a Romanian and the culture to be lost.'

But did it really matter today? I was genuinely curious. If she ate Italian food, listened to American music and drank in a supposedly Irish pub – which is what we were doing at the time – why not have a Romanian boyfriend? Did these things still matter?

'Yes. They don't act like us. They don't control their dogs, they throw rubbish everywhere. They listen to that awful *manele* music, they eat meatballs all the time. And I don't want to sound nasty, but Romanian girls dress like bitches. High heels, skirts up to here, make-up like a cat...'

Her words brought a different understanding of the Hungarian–Romanian divide: the prejudice had less to do with ethnicity than with class. As the old ruling elite, the aristocrats and landowners, there was an innate snobbery to the way many Hungarian people viewed their Romanian neighbours, an intimation of the wellspring of hatred from which the Communist backlash had sprung. While every-one suffered under Ceaușescu – Radu's experience was proof of that – the Magyar-speaking minority had been sin-gled out for especially vicious treatment, and not just those with noble blood. The resentment had been generations in the making.

'The Hungarians over the centuries had handled their alien subjects – and all their own compatriots below a cer-tain rank – with great clumsiness,' wrote Paddy. 'Disdain, oppression, blind feudalism, exclusion from any voice in their councils, rigorous Magyarisation – no blemish was missing.' His own words shed a slightly different light on his rose-tinted vision of pre-war culture, those bucolic rural scenes set against the leisurely life of counts and their liveried servants: the image of an Eden before the Fall. Behind all disparities of wealth and power lies implicit vio-lence, no matter how cultured the ruling class might be. Paddy himself acknowledged the rumours that István, his happy-go-lucky companion, was implicated in Hungary's counter-revolutionary White Terror; many of the young bloods he had picnicked and partied with must, unavoida-bly, have been involved in the viciousness of their age. The brutality that swept away István and Angéla's world, and created the trail of ruins I'd followed down the Mureș Valley, was a reaction to hundreds of years of class patronisation.

And yet, as always, it was more complicated than that. Writing of 1934, when many Hungarian landowners had seen their estates diminished – but not yet seized in the nationalisation that would follow the Second World War – Paddy noted: 'A certain warmth of feeling had managed to outlive the changes of frontier and ownership and the conflicts of the past. "I remember old Count –," I heard a Rumanian shepherd say later on, "with all his horses and carriages! It was a fine sight. And look at him now, poor old man!"' Similarly, Ileana had said that while some jeered at Teleki's son Eugen, drunk in the railway station, others continued providing food, support and sympathy for the dispossessed family. I was often made aware of nostalgia for the pre-Communist past. Even my friends in Arad – hardly conservative types – had suggested Romania might be better off with a king again, instead of the corrupt politicians they had today.

From Târgu Mureș I hitched again, looping southwards. I had a scrap of cardboard for a sign, but choosing what to write was tricky: I was making for the town Romanians called Sighișoara, Hungarians called Segesvár, and the Saxons who'd actually built it called Schäßburg. Most of the Saxons were gone, so Schäßburg could be discounted; remembering last night's conversation, I chose Sighișoara.

Like a magic word, it conjured up a Romanian within minutes. Zsófia certainly wouldn't have approved: he was slick haired and tattooed, with manele pumping from his car – booty-shaking Gypsy hip-hop of the trashiest possible kind – and said he was heading to Brașov to confront the husband of his lover, a respected lawyer twice his age, to demand he agree to a divorce.

I asked whether he'd met him before.

'Met him? I almost killed him. But I don't want to go to jail, so today I'll just talk to the bastard.'

We sped through countryside of quite unreal beauty, the oak and chestnut forests so densely packed they appeared to assume one form, a contiguous spreading growth. The new leaves pulsed with luminous force, and between the woods knee-deep meadows blazed with dandelions.

Sighişoara was a tourist town, but I couldn't begrudge it that. Everywhere I walked I stepped into another camera view, ruined another shot. It was smaller than I'd expected, a settlement of terracotta rooftops slumped in somnolent calm, bright and lazy under the sun, its gardens loud with blossom. I dumped my bag in an empty campsite and climbed the medieval clock tower to see the Saxon architecture spreading in a muddle of slants and verticals, like a diagram of impossible geometry. The old town wall was intact, with its bastions, wedge-roofed, cut with shafts for the unleashing of boiling oil and other disincentives to invade. In the Middle Ages each bastion was controlled by a guild – butchers, tailors, furriers, coopers, blacksmiths, locksmiths – charged with the maintenance and defence of their own tower. Only a fool, I thought, would attack the butchers or blacksmiths. The furriers sounded like the softest option.

A covered staircase scaled the hill to the Lutheran church, inside of which the stone-chilled air rushed over me like a wave. A gothic ribcage of ceiling beams arched dimly overhead, and the faded murals depicting victories over various non-humans – St George lancing a depressed-looking dragon, St Michael hacking away at demons with bird faces and beetle horns – were reminiscent of the gargoyles on Ulmer Münster. The warder told me he was half Saxon, a descendant of Germanic settlers who came here in medieval times; the Hungarian kings invited them as a buffer against invasion from the east, but there were few left now. Having survived centuries of attacks from Tartars, Mongols and other terrors, their walled towns and forti- fied churches had proved no match for the greater terror of the twentieth century. The Soviets deported all men of working age to labour camps after the war, emptying the villages of youth, and Ceauşescu had effectively sold tens of thousands to West Germany, which paid a per capita sum for each would-be emigrant. After the fall of the regime, German citizenship was offered to all those who remained; ninety-five per cent of them packed their bags and left. Now Transylvania's Saxon community was more or less moribund, their abandoned villages resettled by Roma.

'Today in Schäßburg we are only five hundred and twelve,' said the warder. 'But tomorrow we will be five hun- dred and thirteen – my nephew will be baptised in this church. It is a great day for us.' As he spoke, the church bells rang: a simple, repetitive toll that built like the resonance of a singing bowl into a clear, trembling drone while the individual clangs grew softer, mounting and diminishing, before eventually fading back into their own reverberation.

I left Sighişoara on foot, unhappy with the haste of the last few days, following empty lanes into a rolling hillscape. This was farmland, not pastureland – another subtle cul- tural clue – and women were grubbing potatoes from the fields dressed in wide straw hats and aprons, legs like sturdy hams. Hayricks were stacked in beehive form, and the horses that dragged the ploughs were gaudily beribboned, every movement of their heads accompanied by bells. In the village of Apold, huddled around a fortified church – more watchtower than place of worship, and saved from systematisation only by Ceauşescu's death – I stopped, roll- ing with perspiration, to hold my head beneath a water pump, glad to be straining and sweating again. Motorised transport was nothing but destination after destination, slicing everything into disconnected episodes; back at this familiar pace, the world was integral again.

Far away, behind hot hills, the Carpathians sprung once more into view. From this distance they seemed little more than a buckled distortion in the air, as if the sky had crumpled in on itself. Only by holding my vision firm on one part of this illusion, squinting against the glare, was I able to make out a ridge, a shadowed slope, then a peak; if I stared too hard they disappeared, ebbing into the blue of the sky. Summoning them in and out of being was a kind of magic trick, as if by merely focusing I could pull myself towards them.

Heat bounced upwards from the road, and even from the grass. The stagnant ponds in the villages were surfaced with dusty skins, and frogs chuckled weirdly, falling silent at my footsteps. I fell into company with a Roma boy going in my direction, trundling a bicycle with two flat tyres. He claimed to speak both English and French, but looked unhappy when I attempted either, so I took the chance to improve my Romanian, pointing at the things we saw and asking for their names. Some of them I already knew, or thought I did. '*Copac*,' I announced, pointing at a tree, but he only scowled.

'*Stejar*,' he corrected, shaking his head.

I assumed I'd got the word wrong. '*Stejar?*' I asked at the next tree we passed.

'*Cireș*,' he replied, gazing at me as if I was a bit stupid.

'*Cireș?*' I asked at the next tree.

'*Măr*.' He pointed to another. '*Prun*.'

For a moment I was bewildered. Why did the word keep changing? And then I realised, of course, that he was naming different types of tree - oak, cherry, apple, plum - and was confused by my attempt to label them all with one term. For him they were not the same, but entirely different categories. With my encouragement he started naming other things – grasses, herbs, wild flowers, birds, insects, types of rock – but writing them down was not enough. I would never know a place in the way he did. Concentrated in one environment – he had never left Sibiu county – his knowledge went deep, not broad. Compared to him I knew a little about a lot, but he knew a lot about a little. I couldn't help being envious at his way of seeing the world.

We parted ways in Retiş, a village with more horse-drawn traffic than cars, where the heat rolled along the street in visible waves. A dark man dragging a scythe gestured me towards a shaded yard, where I took a seat with a collection of weather-beaten men in battered fedoras, clad in wool and corduroy despite the afternoon being hotter than an oven. They took it in turns to question me, incomprehensibly babbling from the right and the left, and with the stultifying heat and the rhythm of their words I fell into a peculiarly disembodied state; successive beers were delivered, and alcohol was enough to tip me, when I emerged an hour later into saturating sunlight, into astonishment. The mildest intoxication stripped away a barrier of ordinariness I hadn't known was there, and suddenly I couldn't believe a single thing I saw. The moon was out in the middle of the day. The blue, green and yellow world had a hallucinogenic intensity, peopled by medieval-garbed peasants hefting spades and axes. Dust rolled like heavy gas. As I walked on, down a road electrified by the buzzing of insects, it was as if I'd woken up on another planet.

That night, I let the road carry me into the woods above Bărcuţ, where I slept on the edge of a gulley churning with wind-blown trees. The same road carried me in the morning to a village called Şoarş, where an old woman noticed me cranking the handle of a broken pump, and led me to a wooden rig that turned out to be a sweep well. It was the first I'd encountered, though Paddy had seen them commonly on the Great Hungarian Plain: as tall as a telephone pole with a cantilevered arm that swung, counterbalanced by breezeblocks, to plunge a rusty bucket into the water far below. It tasted of cold stone and dark earth. I drank so much I almost couldn't walk.

The Transylvanian loop was coming to an end. With distant Făgăraş in sight, I'd reached the most southeasterly point of Paddy's circuit by motorcar, and was about to swing southwest towards the mountains. Paddy only mentioned Făgăraş in passing – distracted, perhaps, by the sadness of Angéla's imminent departure – but it struck me as a menacing vision after the gentle land of meadows I'd just walked through. The city sprawled across a dun-coloured plain, the dome of its Orthodox cathedral bulging like a blood blister about to burst. The air was blue with meat smoke as I descended the hill – there was a national holiday and families were barbecuing on the slopes – and a sense of indefinable threat mounted through the outskirts. A stocky, brutal-looking man in a rakishly angled hat yelled aggressively at me, thrusting out his chest like a prizefighter; he was being escorted by two policemen who shrugged helplessly, as if they could vaguely guide but not be expected to control him.

With darkness approaching I retraced my steps, avoiding the street with the bellowing brute, to camp in the woods north of the Olt river. Curious insects of all descriptions emerged in timed waves throughout the evening, from small black flies to mosquitoes, small beetles to large beetles, until their attentions became too much and I was forced into the stifling warmth of my zipped-up tent. By the following night, I hoped to be within striking distance of the Retezat mountains.

Retezat was the massif I'd glimpsed almost a month before, with Ileana outside the church at Densuş. Strictly speaking it wasn't Paddy's route – he had avoided the higher peaks, sticking to the forests of the foothills further west – but the sight of those mountains had been so compelling I didn't have much choice in the matter. After the cosy domestication of Transylvania's padded vales, I hungered for a wilder edge: the thought of snow-capped ridges and peaks, glacial lakes, mountain forests roamed by wolves and bears, drew me irresistibly. On the map, the national park was crisscrossed with dotted trails and marked with *refugiuls*, mountain cabins to shelter in; crossing the range southwest, it looked like a journey of three or four days to the spa town of Băile Herculanae, which would place me exactly back in Paddy's footsteps.

First I needed to get to Haţeg, the jumping-off point for the mountains. I left barren Făgăraş behind, sticking out my thumb and getting a lift within thirty seconds from a white-bearded man who crossed himself at every church we passed, and he whooshed me west on the E68, unwittingly tracing the concluding stretch of István's motorcar tour. Through the last Saxon town of Sibiu with its jumbled heavy houses, attic windows like sleepy eyes pushing open through tiled rooftops – 'the last outposts of an architectural world I was leaving for good', both for Paddy and for me – we sped along the Mureş valley beside the railway tracks on which Angéla had departed, waving goodbye with a handkerchief seventy-eight years before. My white-bearded István surrogate let me out at Simeria, not far from the place where I'd almost been savaged by trash-hounds. I lost no time in escaping again: south now, part walking, part hitching, down the road Ileana had driven through the hills to Haţeg.

The Retezat mountains loomed beyond the town, squatting ominously in a nest of cloud. The friendly fields and farms were gone; the Haţeg region felt wider, higher, a land of mountains, not meadows. I rented a room in a small hotel and spent the evening in preparation, stuffing provisions into my bag: two cured sausages, a loaf of bread, several tins of sardines, a lump of sheep's cheese, peanuts, apples, chocolate, instant coffee. The extra weight was worrying, but there was nothing to be done. Now all I could do was hope for sympathetic weather.

Blinding slats of sunlight woke me to a sky the colour of happiness. I hefted my overloaded bag and set out, past the turning to Densuş, with its church constructed of Roman tombstones, through the town of Cârneşti, then southwest towards the vast upheaval of the mountains.

Perhaps my appreciation for distance had been distorted by the lifts I'd taken; I'd imagined reaching the mountains would take no more than a couple of hours, but getting there was a twenty-mile walk in itself. Incrementally and painfully climbing, the heavy rucksack already rubbing a sore in my lower back, I trudged all day into forested foothills, the bulk of the mountains proper hidden above the tree line. There were barns of dovetail-jointed beams, and from terraced fields beside the road protruded wasp-bodied hayricks with poles sticking up like stings. The Râuşor river foamed to my right, cascading from the heights above, sometimes channelled into wooden basins I thought might be for panning gold until I saw women scrubbing clothes in the ice-cold snowmelt. It was mid-afternoon by the time I came to the village of Râuşor, the last friendly halt before the wilderness.

After that, there were no more roads. The deciduous trees ended and the coniferous took their place. A daub of paint on a rock told me where my trail began, and suddenly the world was reduced to the shush of a distant river, the sweetness of resin, the coolness of pines. I closed my eyes and waited.

It was like taking a breath before plunging underwater. I was deliriously alone.

~~~~~

'A kind of spell haunts wooded slopes like these,' wrote Paddy of the Carpathian uplands he'd traversed further west. 'It drives the intruder blindly uphill, knocks ten years off his age ... unlooses a host of immature and atavistic hankerings.' A similar spell haunted these wooded slopes, and the immature and atavistic hankerings took the form of two stories I'd discovered in Hațeg. The first was the legend of Iovan Iorgovan – the Hercules of Romania – who travelled from here to Transylvania to obtain a hammer with which to kill the dragon that menaced the lowlands. In the fury of the fight the dragon scorched the mountains bare, incinerating every living thing and leaving only naked rock; before creeping away to die, it vowed to send plagues of flies to take revenge on Iorgovan's herds. Its smouldering heart roused swarms of angry insects, which had been tormenting cattle on the mountain ever since.

The second story was even more fantastic. Before there were mountains here – before there was even Iorgovan – the Hațeg valley was a subtropical island lying in the Tethys Ocean between the long-vanished continents of Gondwana and Laurasia. The island was roamed by horse-sized sauropods, miniature dragons whose dwarfism was caused over millions of years by their environmental isolation, shrinking to fit their landscape. In these steep, suggestive woods, neither the legend nor the science could be entirely believed or discounted. True, the fossilised remains of dwarf dinosaurs had been excavated; but I'd also heard that on Piatra Iorgovanului, Iorgovan's Rock, two days' walk to the south, the mark of his horse's hoof could be seen imprinted on the summit.

The first refugiul lay an hour up the track. The chafing pain in my back, and the screaming muscle pain in my
thighs, lessened with the joy of the woods as I climbed.
It was startling, the transition from the outside world to
this: the moss-covered rocks resembled hunched forms,
the rounded backs of lurking beasts, a suggestion probably
made more potent by knowledge of bears; frequently my
nerves jumped as one lurched in my direction. The roots
of trees, tentacle-like, clenched and embraced the stones
in innumerable immodest ways, and at one point I was
convinced I heard voices – garbled words and fragments of
sentences – until I realised it was water gurgling over pebbles in a stream, changing its tune with every step.

I stumbled on the refugiul almost by accident: a log
cabin with a slanted roof, a plank bed covered in scratchy
blankets, greasy pillows spilling their stuffing over a foam
mattress. There were paraffin lamps and a wood-burning
stove, blackened pots and a bottle of vinegar that had once
been wine. It reeked of ancient sweat and wood smoke.
Everything was covered in filth. It was perfect.

I located an axe, chopped some timber, lit the stove,
boiled coffee. Water roared whitely outside and logs
crackled in the grate. Waking much later than I intended,
the sun already high above the trees, I reheated coffee,
splashed my face in the stream outside, and set off into
the unknown.

The spell-haunted woods came to an end and I emerged
into a muddle of shoulder-high juniper groves. Before long
the path ran out and a rubble of rocks, marked by daubs
of yellow paint, led me along an ice-lidded stream, with the
last of the pines and juniper groves falling away behind.
Suddenly there were patches of snow, stubbornly clinging
to their winter in furrows that never saw the sun. And
above loomed Mount Retezat, stark from this proximity;

with a jolt of shock, I realised my path led directly to its peak.

The wind nipped colder now. It felt like walking into winter again, and I hadn't been prepared for that; from down below the snow had looked like a decorative touch to the landscape and I hadn't considered the reality of actually walking through it. It was soft, sun-weakened snow and not to be trusted with much weight, repeatedly collapsing beneath me to smash my shins against rocks. Before I'd got far that morning my feet were soaked with slush.

The trail tilted sharply upwards into untrodden whiteness. The painted markings were buried under snow, but the route was obvious: up, and up again, until I reached the summit. Here I stopped to study the mountain properly for the first time, a black-and-white kaleidoscope of plunging diagonals seamed with snow, its complexity more startling every second I looked. The shock transmuted to numb disbelief. Was I really capable of this? My boots were leaking, I had no equipment, no crampons, no ice axe, no partner. I decided to go just a bit further and reconsider from there.

With little awareness of any transition, suddenly I wasn't walking any more but climbing. I was on a ladder of snow, ascending in the foot-sized staircase of a previous climber's boots, melted and refrozen now into shapelessness. The slope grew steeper, the bootprints vanished, and I had to use my walking poles to chisel steps deep enough to hold my weight, until at last with a clumsy leap I was able to grab at juniper branches and haul myself onto solid rock.

It was a ragged fight to draw breath; the act of breathing didn't go far in this thin air. Looking back at what I'd climbed, I saw I'd got myself to a point where I couldn't easily retreat. The realisation simplified things, for it meant I could only go on.

The peak was an abstraction above. The trail markings were splashes of red now, and each time I glimpsed the next it was a small salvation. Some of the snow slopes were too steep, even gouging with the poles – my gradients were limited by the weight of my rucksack, which tugged me alarmingly off balance – and skirting them meant sidetracking up moraines of broken rock, hand over foot, tiny rockslides clattering down with each slip. My legs were shaking, from exertion and altitude mixed with sudden fear of the seeming impossibility of the task. I concentrated on each step, each individual grip of stone, trying not to dwell on the beckoning space around me.

At last, not understanding how, I emerged at a rounded shoulder of snow with nothing beyond but the flawless blue of the sky. There was something peculiarly terrifying about approaching that final rise and knowing nothing else was left, that I could go no further up: it felt like walking towards the edge of the world.

Fear has a transcendental effect: even if it lasts only minutes, it transports you to a different state of being, where nothing is the same. In a kind of exhilarated horror I stood on the summit of Mount Retezat, where a battered tin sign, wrapped about with the blue, yellow and red of Romania's flag, informed me I was at 2485 metres. Two days of walking lay below me: first the snow-veined rock I'd just climbed, then the menacing darkness of pine woods dropping steeply to the chlorophyll green of the lower beech forests, and below that the flatlands, the scattered villages, the road I had followed from Hațeg. Beyond that somewhere, lost in summer haze, would be the line of the Mureş valley I'd traced a month before. Once I descended this peak, I'd be turning my back on that whole verdant world. Ahead, for the next few days at least, there were only mountains.

As I turned the other way the impending mountain-scape opened up, and it was too much. My eyes didn't know what to do with it, uncomprehending the scale. A dizzying plummet to a river-tangled valley hundreds of feet below – I could distantly hear the crash of water, snowmelt cascading into valleys – and far beyond the rock soared to another, vaster chain of peaks, scooped and gouged and chiselled and scarred, utterly empty and utterly strange, hidden from the world below.

Psychologically, there was something different about walking *through* mountains, in order to get from one place to the other, to recreationally walking *in* them. My purpose here was unequivocally defined: I had no choice but to cross that range, because it stood between me and where I wanted to go. Looking back at the way I'd come, knowing I would not see it again, that difference felt fundamental. Again, the realisation was simple; but if I twisted an ankle or fell, if the snow gave way at the wrong time or place... well, that was simple too: it simply couldn't happen.

A more prosaic realisation came to me on Retezat: my trousers had fallen apart. I'd worn them every day since the Great Hungarian Plain, and the exertions of the climb had reduced them to flapping sheets of corduroy. In the weirdly windless calm of the summit I was forced to take off my boots and the shredded remains of this legwear and fumble in my rucksack for spare clothes. All I had was a thin cotton pair better suited to picnics than climbing mountains, only just better than nothing. Clad decently, if not sensibly, I left the old ones draped on the peak like a rival flag, and picked up the red daubs marking the downward trail.

There was less snow on this side, and even the semblance of a path teetering along the ridge, dropping into a wasteland of fissures and escarpments. The trail dipped, rose again, skirted a lower peak and scored its way along the flank of a talus-jumbled slope before plunging, with stomach-dropping steepness, into a stepped bowl of marsh-land and glacial lakes.

This view was even harder to process; it was something like looking at the stars, being able to appreciate their beauty but incapable of taking in their meaning. I gave up trying to fathom the scale and concentrated on the lakes, individual in their characters. The nearest was an improbable robin's-egg blue, with cracks running through its ice, the shape of a giant footprint with splayed toes. It was too huge for a dwarf dinosaur but I thought of Iorgovan's dragon, and wished there was someone here who could explain the legends I was sure must be associated. But the vast land ahead was empty and there was no one to share its stories. Below that footprint lay a darker lake in a scalloped crater, and below that on yet another level two more, all straight lines and angles; still below those a fifth, shattered like an exploded crystal. That was Lacul Bucura, Romania's largest glacial lake, my next place of refuge.

The trail plummeted into this lake-land like a glider los-ing height. The ground grew marshy at the bottom, water glugging and gurgling under ice, forging channels through the softening snow. Around the lakes, the snow drew away to expose patches of soggy grass dotted with purple cro-cuses, and for the first time in these mountains I saw wild-life: a marmot peering shyly from a bank of ice.

It wasn't the only sign of life. Skirting a frozen bog across a patch of dirty snow, I found myself following a line of pawprints I took to be a dog's. Then I realised the prints were too large, too widely splayed; and what would a dog be doing up here, miles from any village? I'd been told that wolves lived in these mountains, but that they kept themselves to themselves. Those pawprints were as close as I got, following that solitary trail for a while before it branched downhill, towards the concealing shadow of the forest below.

Around the middle of the afternoon I reached Bucura. The refugiul here was sparser, with no wood-burning stove, and was surrounded on all sides by swooping peaks and saddlebacks. Here I found my third sign of life: a pair of Romanian climbers sitting on the cabin's stoop gazing wordlessly in opposite directions. I joined them, and no one said anything for a long time; when at last they spoke, it was to offer me coffee from their little gas stove. They had come the same way as me twenty-four hours before; it must have been their bootprints I'd followed up that first slope, and I was grateful for the path they'd forged. Soon they set off again, fastening crampons and swinging ice axes – compared to them I felt much underdressed – leaving me alone in this improbable bowl of ice.

I decided against the refugiul, and instead pitched my tent in a horseshoe of rocks by the frozen lake. There were great movements of clouds, vying with the mountains for spectacle. The curlicues of the snow shone like arcane calligraphy. The sun went down behind the western peaks, though the flanks of the mountains opposite glowed orange long after shadow had fallen over the rest of the land, and apart from the innumerable streams hissing down towards the tree line, everything was silent.

Draining my hip flask as the light slowly leached from the lakeside, I found myself speaking these words, out loud without meaning to: 'When I die, my death will not change the fact that I was here.' That was my best attempt at summing up the feeling of those mountains, my overwhelming gratitude that they, and I, existed. In the same way that my eyes couldn't cope with what they saw from the peak, my mind couldn't comprehend the reality of being here. The same road I'd started following five months before, through suburbs, industrial estates, petrol station fore-courts and supermarket car parks, along canals and cycle paths and railway sidings and motorway verges, and in and out of cities inhabited by millions of people, had brought me to this point. It was only one road – a road with many twists and turns, but still only one road – and it led to this place directly, if followed a certain way.

In the morning, everything hurt. My shins had taken a battering and my legs were a field of bruises. Regretfully, painfully, I packed to leave this otherworldly cauldron of ice and crocuses, and followed the tracks of the wolf towards the forest below.

Soon I was back among pines, tracing the snowmelt river fed by Bucura. I was worried about my supplies, almost depleted in spite of what had seemed sensible rationing: the bread was smashed to crumbs, leaving only a tin of sardines, some peanuts and half a sausage. The slope lev-elled out, and then the path climbed steeply uphill once more, an excruciating trudge back to the heights I'd just descended. When, at last, I reached the top, I recognised this as the waterless ridge I'd been warned about in Hațeg; my bottles were almost empty, so I had to dump my bag and descend to the highest stream. By the time I'd found my bag again, it was getting on for midday.

Cresting the ridge, I expected to see foothills and plains ahead. Instead, to my mild dismay, rose another chain of mountains. The vision didn't last long: an ominous stain was seeping from the south, erasing distance as it went, and the air thickened as I watched. The peaks of the further-most mountains disappeared behind swooping whiteness, and within minutes the dirty murk had swooped on me as well, reducing my world to an opaque twilight.

A horrible mixture of sleet and hail splattered down without warning. I fumbled for waterproofs, but was already soaked by the time I'd pulled them free. Everything beyond my immediate vision had been wiped from existence and I didn't much like what was left: a juniper-tangled wasteland patched with the very worst kind of snow, mushy, corrupted and unstable, on which I slipped and tripped haltingly through the murk.

The same had happened to my predecessor a little further west of here: 'I must have been in the heart of one of those clouds that people gaze at from the plain as they come decoratively to anchor along the cordilleras.' For the next several hours I inched along the white desolation of the ridge, barely able to make out the rocks that marked my trail. The gloom swallowed sight and sound, distance and direction. Occasionally the cloud would lift and forested valleys open up below, allowing a few moments of clumsy orientation, and then descend again, deleting everything. My markers grew further and further apart. Sleet piled up on my hat and coat like frozen porridge.

In a snow-choked valley, the trail abruptly ended. I searched one way after the other, tramping knee deep, trying to guess the direction of the path. It wasn't guessable. I clawed the snow off prominent rocks, knowing the markers must be buried somewhere, but found no daubs of paint, no trace of colour. All I could do was keep going straight, which meant another climb. Scaling a steep-sided gulley filled with collapsing snow, my boots squelching with icy water, was so draining I could manage only five or six steps at a time before stopping, heaving for breath. Cloud poured like dry ice down the perpendicular walls, and the vaguely threatening spikes of pines glowered ahead. It was the worst place imaginable. The journey was shapeless, endless; I could cease to exist in that place, swallowed up inside a land indifferent to my presence.

The gulley seemed to end, and then rose again, and then seemed to end again, and by the time it had actually ended I hated it more than I thought it possible to hate a geographical feature. But I was out, and the cloud was lifting; whiteness bulged through the gloom. After I'd gone on some way, with delirious delight, I saw ahead a smudge of red: I'd hit the trail again.

This side of the mountain felt older, stranger, scattered with lichen-spotted rocks and tussocks of spongy grass. The mist was looser, blown by the wind into ragged veils, and I traced my path through a disappearing and eerily reemerging landscape. It had a confusing effect on perspective: things in the distance looked merely small rather than far away, and glimpses of the valleys below appeared no more than a magnification of the ground before my feet. Then something large loomed ahead, a goitre-shaped protrusion of stone that shimmered into clear form as sunlight diffused across the sky. It was the landmark I'd been looking for, the unmistakable hump of limestone that marked the culmination of this trail. This was Iorgovan's Rock.

I dropped my rucksack and my poles and scrambled to the summit. Below, unexpected valleys plunged into misty depths, a rubble of scree, choked with trees, leading down from these high places. And there as promised, at my feet, the hoofprint of Iorgovan's horse was deeply scarred in the rock: a mighty-sized horse, for a mighty man.

~~~~~~

I'd been counting on another refugiul that night, but I was exhausted, my clothes were soaked and my food was finished. On the map, a trail led down to something marked Casă de Vânătoare, Hunting House, and I decided it was my only hope of finding any dinner. The trail was marked by red triangles I never expected to find, but did, zigzagging down a path of loose rocks towards the tree line. There was no snow on these slopes and forget-me-nots and buttercups were sprinkled down the mountainside. At one point I took a wrong turn and stopped just short of a chasm dropping like a lift shaft, its sheer walls channelling the wind, a great sigh rushing from below. A pair of eagles circled in the geometry of the thermals.

The coniferous trees of the upper slopes gradually became interspersed with beeches, and soon I'd left the pines behind and beeches were all I could see. It was impossible to know how fast I was descending; I had the sense of dropping vertically to the lower world. The light, filtered through the leaves, glowed ever brighter green, a joy after the dingy twilight of cloud level. Then the trees gave way to grass, a sudden opening of space, the brutal gash of a road. I had reached the bottom.

Nothing stirred in those lower depths. It felt like arriving on an ocean floor. I put distance between myself and the mountain and craned my neck back up: Iorgovan's Rock, and the world it belonged to, had vanished from existence.

There was the Casă de Vânătoare, a small building with a tin steeple. It looked abandoned, but as I approached a dog came hurtling from a barn, rebounded at the end of its chain, and bellowed furiously. A little bald man appeared, scowling with darkest suspicion. I pointed at myself, and then the mountain. Immediately his scowl disappeared and I was ushered inside, where an old woman as tiny as him was peering from the kitchen.

When I made it understood that I was looking for a place to camp, and perhaps to buy some food, they lit up with smiles. I could stay here, in the *casă*. They had plenty of *alimente*. They led me to a carpeted room with a bunk bed and fresh sheets, antlers bristling on the walls, and fussed around telling me to take off my boots, dry my clothes above the stove, make myself at home. They seemed aghast that I didn't have slippers, and insisted on finding me a pair. The man, Nicu, served me tea brewed from herbs he collected on the mountain, followed by *apă de foc*, mint-infused firewater to take away the chill. He was a forester, and mimed stalking deer in the foothills, aiming along his arm and making bang-bang noises. He didn't hunt wolves, he assured me – hunting wolves was *interzis*, forbidden – and he didn't hunt bears either, except when they went rogue. During the telling of these tales a meal was in preparation: eggs were fried, bread was sliced, sausage and *slănină* deployed, and soon we were sitting down to eat. Nicu watched me cheerfully, while Suzi packed sausage into her mouth like a happy little hedgehog, filling the pouches of her cheeks and slurping coffee.

The murky cloud cloaking the mountains had sunk into the valley and rain flung itself against the windows. By eight o'clock it was too dark to see; there were no electric lights. Nicu and Suzi went to bed early – through an open door I glimpsed him asleep in neatly buttoned white pyjamas – and when I closed my eyes I saw visions of snow-covered mountains.

When I came to the kitchen in the morning, Nicu was on his hands and knees feeding wood into the stove. He gestured fatalistically upwards. The gloom had not lifted. Drizzle drifted miserably over the pines.

After waiting for the rain to stop and realising it wouldn't, I wrapped my feet in plastic bags and put on every waterproof item of clothing I owned. Nicu and Suzi pointed to the road and told me to keep walking west; eventually, I would get to the village of Cerna-Sat. They wished me '*Drum bun*' and waved from the porch, looking more than ever like a pair of forest creatures. As on so many other occasions, I wished I could have given them something. But they didn't want money, and the only other thing I had was language that they couldn't understand.

The rain fell with unimaginative insistency, as if the sky was stuck on a certain setting. After the first fifteen minutes I was so soaked it made no difference. The air was warm, with plumes of cloud uncoiling through the trees, pouring slowly down the slopes, aimlessly parting and merging. The empty road ended and became a rutted track, puddled with rust-coloured water, dawdling through the beech forests of the Cerna Valley. Again I had the sensation of being underwater, fathoms below the surface of Iorgovan's overworld.

The track went a long way vaguely up and a long way vaguely down, dropping into a rock-walled gorge riddled with tiny caves. The Cernişoara river churned below, fed by a thousand streams. A gap in the trees gave a glimpse of pea-green peaks rising over tiers of cloud, and then the trees closed again and all I could hear was the applause of rain on the upturned leaves.

After the struggle of the last two days, I had imagined descending the foothills would be a stroll in comparison, a mere stretching of the legs to bring me off the mountain. But as beech forests unfolded into more beech forests in every direction, bleared with the distortion of the rain, I slowly came to understand that I was still a long way from anywhere. Only once in the course of the morning did I encounter fellow humans: two shepherds in plastic ponchos who hurried to call off their dogs, which let me pass begrudgingly, as if it was a bad idea. The shepherds wouldn't meet my eye, melting back into the forest as soon as I was gone.

The track grew rougher, weaving uphill and plunging into denser woods. Between the trunks to my left came flashes of green that announced the beginning of a lake: Lacul Valea lui Iovan, a poison-coloured body of water that

I assumed would take a couple of hours to traverse. But the shape of the lake was irregular, its tentacle-like inlets probing deep into the forest, the track running first up one side then back down the other, which elongated time as well as distance. After two hours there was no sign of it ending. The rain intensified to a downpour, the kind of torrent that normally marks the imminent letting-up of rain, but it didn't let up. Two more hours passed, and still nothing had changed. The road mesmerically looped through the trees, each bend maddeningly similar to the one before. With the repetition of trunks and the relentlessness of the rain, the occasional glimpse of arsenic-green water glowing between the trees, it began to feel increasingly like a mischievous trick. The devious lake kept changing shape, wriggling into new alignments, its probing arms growing and shrinking, insidiously subdividing, while the treadmill of the road ceaselessly rolled against me.

It was almost night and I had grown quite paranoid that I was stuck in some inexplicable kink of time, when the trees leapt apart and I found myself at a mighty dam. It was a sheer wall of reinforced concrete, shockingly manmade, below which the world fell away into misted valleys. I had been walking through a vast drainage system, the catchment zone of the mountains behind me; the snow I had tramped through the day before would ultimately end up here. Something about that idea made the lake feel even more baleful, a monster greedily sucking in rainwater, and as the road zigzagged down into lower realms at last I had the sense of escaping from a giant circulation system. I was soaked to the skin and sapped with hunger by the time I staggered into the hamlet of Cerna-Sat.

An old woman in a dripping shawl was driving home a herd of cows, each of which wore a nose belt of spikes to ward off wolves. I asked if there was anywhere to sleep and she motioned me down the road. A man in a shaggy cape like a bearskin stood underneath an umbrella, pointing in the same direction. At length I found myself in a guesthouse – the satin sheets and satellite television contrasting starkly with the toilet, which was a shit-smeared hole in the ground – and a woman brought me soup full of grisly meat, raw onions and slănină, and dried my boots above the fire. I left pools on the floor wherever I stepped. The skin on my fingers was whorled, soaked from my all-day bath.

The morning brought no end to the rain. I pulled on my still-wet clothes, collected my slightly less-wet boots, and continued down the puddled road.

Cloud still clogged the valleys and the watercolour mountain peaks diminished in grey gradations. The sky grew imperceptibly lighter, the rain slackening to a drizzle that felt like a deliverance; but just as I'd wrung out my hat it poured down again with even greater vigour. The swollen river funnelled between cracked and fissured cliffs, brightly veined with small cascades, and defiles led to mysterious ravines I felt a sudden sadness to think I would die without ever exploring. The world felt incomprehensibly large, full of unknowable secrets. I passed farmsteads with trailing smoke, angry dogs and sweet sad dogs, vegetable plots with rows of onions and runner beans on frames. But mostly that day it was beech trees and rain, identical to the day before; though the tumbling river was a better companion that that insane-making lake.

I fell into a walking trance that carried me twenty-five miles without a thought in my head. The valley narrowed and intensified, its emerald walls mounting ever higher into clouds, and my mind became lost in the squelching rhythm of my boots on the road. Suddenly I rounded a corner and came upon an unlikely collection of cars and caravans, washing hanging from lines between the trees.

An old woman in a pink dressing gown was wandering with an umbrella, and then a half-naked man appeared, comically trying to towel himself dry in the rain. It looked like a lunatic trailer park until I smelt the rotten-egg stench and saw the steam rising from the river: this, at last, was the spa town of Băile Herculanae.

When Paddy came here, the Baths of Hercules was a vision of civilisation after the wilderness, a place of casinos and opera houses where fashionable society came to take the waters. The years had left the wilderness intact, but hadn't treated the civilisation so lightly. When the resort town appeared at the bottom of its damp gorge it looked like a collection of dolls' houses mouldering in a ditch. Its roofs had slipped their leaden tiles, its once-ornate cupolas and domes were rusted, its walls visibly rotting; decaying Communist-era hotel complexes loomed from the trees, competing with their predecessors in melancholy. A small bridge led past a stained blue pagoda and a row of slime-covered lumps that once had been classical statues, and I randomly picked a guesthouse from a street lined with pensions plaintively offering reductions in their rates. The coat hook crashed off the wall when I hung up my coat. Everything in Băile Herculanae was as sodden and dishevelled as I was.

I had stumbled on a forgotten valley, a resort that would never again be in season, and its bathos rather suited my post-mountaineering exhaustion. I spent the next morning recovering in the oily waters of a thermal bath that left my body much restored but stinking of sulphur, watching the billow of eggy steam over the bubbling river. Mildewed building followed mildewed building in boulevards of neglect. A statue of Hercules – the same 'lion-pelted and muscle-bound bruiser' that had stood guard in Paddy's day – lurked outside the shell of some once-modish fin-de-siècle hotel decorated with frescoes from Greek antiquity. I won-dered if this was the place where Paddy had been treated to an impromptu performance by a Bucharest opera company. Now the only sign of life was a car that trundled down the road, did a pointless loop around the statue, and trundled back the way it had come.

'People used to come here from Russia, Austria, France, all over Europe,' said the pension manager. 'It was a fash-ionable resort. Now it's abandoned, falling apart. The pol-iticians make themselves rich and leave everything else to rot.' As he talked, I caught a glimpse of the headline scroll-ing across the television, '*Europe e in recesion*', 'Europe is in recession', and wondered what difference it could possibly make in a place like this.

Leaving Băile Herculanae to its nostalgic moulder-ing, I followed the river, the road and the railway south towards Orşova. It was sad to leave the protective gorge that screened that place from the world; now the hills flat-tened out, and as the road widened into a highway I was forced against the verge to be battered by the slipstream of heavy trucks. I fell into company with a man walking the same way, slouching along with a scowl and a mop of greasy hair. He had a split lip and ripped-up knuckles, and his forehead was caked with blood. He had lost his job and his money – I didn't ask if losing his job had anything to do with the knuckles – and spent most of the time com-plaining, in a mix of languages, about various injustices that had been done to him. 'Where did they get the *bani* to build that?' he snarled as we passed a mansion with concrete dolphins leaping from its fountain. 'Where did they get the money? *Corupţie*, that's where.' He was a bitter companion, and I wasn't sorry when he stopped to rest in a patch of woodland. I gave him one of my sandwiches and left him behind.

Further on, a man and a woman were herding cows beside the road, and called me over to ask what I was doing. '*Single?*' asked the man in amazement, '*este periculos?*', 'is it dangerous?' When I said I was going to Bulgaria, he seemed astonished I wasn't carrying a gun. The subject of the economy surfaced for the third time in two days. '*Nu sunt bani,*' 'there's no money,' the cowherd said with a lopsided grin. '*Spania, braf! Italia, braf! Europa, braf! Grecia – kaput!*'

'*Terminat,*' agreed his wife, shaking her head sadly. But I found myself thinking, as I walked on, that if everything did go *braf* – if the EU unravelled and economies collapsed – I'd put my money on Romanians to survive better than most. They had weathered collapses of their own and come out smiling.

Towards Orşova the landscape changed. Finally the rain had stopped – I'd left the clouds behind with the foothills – and there was a sense of space ahead, a rapid lightening of the sky, which flooded suddenly with blue as sunlight spilled across the land. Rounding a corner, I found myself at the Danube once again.

Since I'd left it back in Hungary, eternally dividing Buda from Pest, the river had travelled five hundred miles – perhaps three hundred less than me – looping south through Belgrade and east to irrigate the tablelands of the Banat. It had grown wide and grand, augmented at this bend by the Cerna feeding into it, which poured down from the shapeless lake that had so tormented me. A promenade led past waterfront bars and jauntily bobbing boats, and with the blue sky and strong fresh wind, the unexpected brilliance of the water, the circling and shrieking of gulls, it felt confusingly like the seaside. The green hills of Serbia lay on the far bank, and I had to remind myself that everything before me – the mighty swell of the river, the clutter of the town, even the forested nubs of the hills – would have been unrecognisable to Paddy seventy-eight years before. A visitor knowing nothing of its history might stay days without being aware of it, but the topography of this place had changed beyond comprehension over the last half-century.

For the moment the only thing on my mind was finding a place to sleep. I made enquiries of some drunks arguing over backgammon, who ceased hostilities for long enough to give me slurred directions to a campsite. A long hill out of town, past paddocks and orchards, brought me to a wooden church with cloisters running along two sides, where women in flat-topped wimples were planting flowers in parallel beds. Those winos had directed me not to a campsite, but to the Orthodox nunnery of Sfânta Ana.

I approached the nearest nun to ask if she knew of a campsite. She plucked a mobile phone from her habit and spoke into it rapidly before bidding me follow her past the church, down some steps, to a little door. This was opened to reveal a simple cell with whitewashed walls, gleaming icons and a bed. I could stay in there, she said, handing me the key.

No sooner had she vanished than another nun appeared, asking something about *masă*. I thought it might be connected with 'mass' so responded enthusiastically, but instead of taking me to church she led me to the dining room, where despite my unconvincing protests the table was heaped with macaroni, vegetable soup and hardboiled eggs. Then she vanished too, and another nun arrived – because of their identical garb I couldn't tell them apart from a distance – who wanted to know, in careful English, if I'd been to the Orthodox church in Essex, which she had heard much about. The table was cleared and coffee delivered. Another nun came to greet me. I was clearly on display, but, as homemade biscuits arrived along with cherries fresh from the trees, it seemed a very reasonable exchange.

The sky grew muddled with clouds and a gentle breeze from Serbia ruffled the leaves of the walnut trees in the garden. A path led through allotments and brightly painted beehives, where I stood watching stars emerge over the distant shore, listening to cuckoo song as darkness claimed the Balkans. From the church came the murmuration of the liturgy, the high, sweet singing of the women over the sombre intonations of the priest. Through the half-open door came a dark blaze of gold, candlelight gleaming on burnished icons. Later the cuckoo stopped singing; nightingales took its place.

Feelings of sweetness and sombreness remained with me the next morning, as I left my little cell and descended to Orşova to enquire about a boat. Before catching a steamer down the Danube, skirting the Serbian shore to the Bulgarian port of Lom, Paddy had taken a trip upriver to the legendary Kazan, where rock walls channelled the river into a deep and perilous gorge along which Roman armies once marched to wage war on the Dacians. The wonders of this region didn't end there. He had also stayed a night downriver on the island of Ada Kaleh, an ancient Turkish enclave left behind after the Ottomans withdrew – oddly marooned in time and place – where old men in fezzes and voluminous trousers smoked narghiles and sipped coffee, stuck in the perpetual twilight of the nineteenth century. I wondered if the backgammon game those drunks had been fighting over was a remnant of that Turkish culture.

If so, it was one of the only remnants left. Since my predecessor sailed from the quay on an August day in 1934 – the point at which *Between the Woods and the Water* ends – everything from Ada Kaleh to the Kazan, the legendary region of the Iron Gates that divided Romania from the Balkans, had undergone a change so complete it was hard to apprehend. In the 1970s and 1980s the Romanian and

Yugoslavian governments constructed two hydroelectric dams – the unimaginatively named Iron Gates Dam I and Iron Gates Dam II – that flooded the valley for hundreds of miles to transform one of the wildest stretches of the Danube into the gigantic pond I was looking at now. There had been no protests here in the style of those at Visegrád or the Donau-Auen; the water level had climbed fifty metres, displacing thousands of people from villages along both banks, submerging Orşova's old centre and wiping the island of Ada Kaleh – and all trace of Turkishness – out of existence.

No steamers sailed from Orşova's quay now, but along the promenade jostled rows of canopied tour boats; it was hard to envisage that beneath their hulls lay the flooded alleyways of an older town. A broad, suntanned man called Martin agreed to take me to the Kazan, or what was left of it, and soon we were rattling over the waves, tracing the border between the two countries. Martin was just old enough to remember the river before the dams: 'It used to be narrow at this point, the currents were extremely dangerous. Many sailors drowned here. Now a child could sail it.' When he told me how the dams had blocked the migrational routes of salmon, which no longer spawned here, I thought irresistibly of the Persenbeug polymath; he had been speaking of a different dam, but his words proved true here also. Yet enormous catfish, Martin said, proliferated in these calmer depths – 'fish weighing two hundred kilos. Fish as big as this boat. Monsters!' – and these words allowed me to feel a tweak of compensatory magic.

'See those platforms?' he said, pointing at a series of pontoons lining the Romanian bank. 'That's where soldiers used to stand to shoot people swimming over the river, trying to escape the regime. The Yugoslav soldiers wouldn't shoot, so if you got out of range of our guns you were safe. But many people didn't.' I wondered how many bullet-riddled corpses had sunk to the riverbed below, and whether they had anything to do with the profusion of bloated catfish.

We crossed into Serbian waters to see the Tabula Traian, an ancient inscription marking the passage of the Roman legions on their way to annihilate Dacia. In order to save it from the flooding it had been cut from its former place and cemented higher up; given the scale of destruction elsewhere, for hundreds of miles up- and downriver, this single gesture of reclamation struck me as quite pointless. Around the next bend, back in Romania, towered a rock-hewn head depicting Decebal, Dacia's last king, staring rather gormlessly at the opposing shore. The colossus – the tallest rock sculpture in Europe – was carved in 2004 yet already managed to give an impression of Ozymandian collapse: his nose and moustache had fallen off and been patched with cement.

Fragments of ancient Rome and Dacia, the vanished Turks of Ada Kaleh, the firing positions of Cold War snipers: as the boat guzzled upriver, towards the protruding clifftops of the Kazan, I had the sense of being in a vast and disconnected museum, a repository of missing pieces, relics from a broken history. The apocalyptic flooding of the valley had done more than drown a landscape: it had submerged thousands of years of accumulated memory, and the parts I was seeing now no longer formed a whole. 'Myths, lost voices, history and hearsay have all been put to rout, leaving nothing but this valley of the shadow.' Those were the last words of Paddy's book.

Martin swung the boat around; we had reached the crags that marked what had once been the Kazan gorge before the artificially raised water cut it off at the knees. Hillocks were all that were left of mountains, rocky clumps of clifftops. Again, a visitor to this place who had no knowledge of what was here before, of how much had been drowned, would still be impressed by the sheer walls, the hilltops densely packed with trees, and the smooth flow of the Danube passing in between. But the shadow of that knowledge dimmed the beauty that remained. 'Let us hope,' Paddy wrote, 'that the power generated by the dam has spread well-being on either bank and lit up Rumanian and Yugoslav towns brighter than ever before because, in everything but economics, the damage is irreparable. Perhaps, with time and fading memories, people will forget the extent of their loss.'

The sunlight gleamed on the river and the wind licked up small waves. If the parched Haţeg valley was once a sub-tropical island, then this change was not so huge. Cultures and dwarf dinosaurs both vanish. Perhaps, after all, it was better not to remember.

We made the return journey in silence, the boat sliding on the current. The sunlight waned, clouds rolled from the south and raindrops stubbled the river. Back in Orşova, I wandered out to an artificial island off the waterfront and stood facing the distant Balkan shore. Somewhere below, in a twilight murk – tangled by weeds, prowled by catfish, quietly rotting and barely remembered – lay the sunken quayside of the old town, from which my predecessor had embarked to unknown Bulgaria.

Standing here, I had arrived at the final page of the book I'd followed since crossing the bridge to Esztergom hundreds of miles upriver. The third and final book of Paddy's travels, posthumously published as *The Broken Road*, wasn't yet in existence – it would come out a year later, edited together from the scrawled notes he'd left behind – so this was a solemn moment: from now until the end of my walk, I wouldn't have his words to guide me.

His voice would be lost, like so many others, in this valley of the shadow.

There was only one way to mark the departure. I took my battered copy of *Between the Woods and the Water* and, without much ceremony, tossed it into the Danube. It drifted reluctantly towards the main river and passed out of sight. Perhaps it reached the Iron Gates Dam, or perhaps it went under long before then; perhaps it even made its way below to Ada Kaleh, to be nibbled by fish or disintegrate among the alleyways and bazaars that Paddy had once walked down.

The rain stopped. I returned to the nunnery, where a column of ants was marching down the wall and over my bed. I swept them away with a broom.

My bag felt lighter without the book. It was part sadness and part exhilaration, a simultaneous loss of a friend and a liberation.

The next morning, on my way out, I paused to look into the church. The interior glowed like a honeycomb, and beside the door was a pile of loaves left as offerings, each with a beeswax candle stuck into its crust. I bought a candle for half a lei and left it burning there.

Ileana, Count Teleki's great-granddaughter, picked me up that afternoon for a last Romanian adventure, driving deep into the Banat mountains to find Lacul Dracului, the Devil's Lake. In this place, the devil had challenged a shepherd to fry a fish without it bending; the shepherd agreed, but only if the devil could roast a goat without it smiling. The shepherd put his fish on a spear so it stayed straight over the fire, while the skin of the roasting goat peeled back to reveal grinning teeth. The devil was so furious at losing that he jumped into the lake and disappeared. It was a final fairytale to see me on my way.

We camped beneath a stand of willows, sharing a bottle of wine under an umbrella in the rain. The meadows were full of buttercups, lady's mantle and shepherd's purse, knee-high wild grasses, poppies dazzlingly red; it felt as if Romania's beauty was putting on a last display. In the morning Ileana navigated her tiny car down roads so potholed she claimed we could see the centre of the earth. In one village we came to a zigzagging trench that even she baulked at. A wedding party was in full swing, besuited men and beribboned women parading to the solemn dirge of saxophone and clarinet, and a ţuică-drunk wedding guest came to our aid, expertly piloting the car uphill. After gaining smoother roads we sped through the mountains and back to the Danube, tracing the drowned Kazan past the stone head of Decebal I'd seen from the boat two days earlier.

We zipped past the Iron Gates Dam, a pleated wall of reinforced concrete holding back millions of tonnes of water, keeping Paddy's submerged world submerged, through forests of pylons humming with energy tapped from the conquered river. In the golden evening light we bowled through the farmlands of Oltenia, mile upon mile of wheat fanning out to a level horizon, through slumbering villages with children playing and old people nodding on doorsteps, rolling into the port of Calafat with only minutes to spare. I just had time to dig out my passport and hug Ileana goodbye before the last ferry to Bulgaria pulled away.

SOUTH

The Broken Road

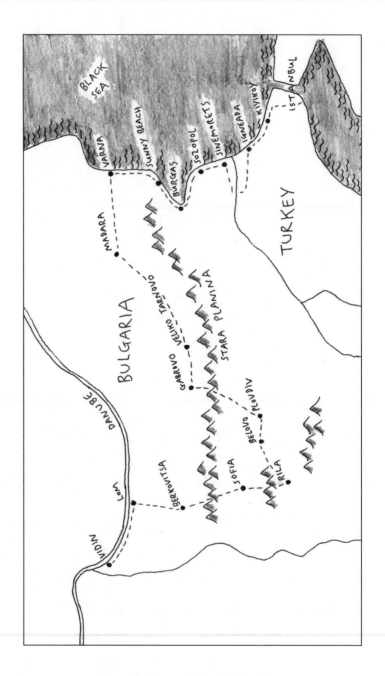

From Bulgaria to the Golden Horn

9

South of the River

Bulgaria

So recently had the yoke of Turkey been shaken off that Bulgaria seemed less the south-easternmost corner of Europe than the north-westernmost limit of a world that stretched away to the Taurus mountains, the deserts of Arabia and the Asian steppes. It was the Orient, and clues to the recent centuries under the Ottoman Turks lay thick and plentiful on every side.

The Broken Road

Now Ileana's waving figure, and the Romanian part of my journey, shrank swiftly behind me. The ferry was loaded with trucks shuttling between the two countries, and from the drivers swapping cigarettes on deck I heard Slavic sounds, half-familiar and half-strange, for the first time since leaving the yellow fields of Slovakia. Upriver, the pilings of a half-constructed bridge – intended to connect the two countries but years behind schedule – stuck up from the Danube. As I was soon to learn, a bridge that no one could be bothered to finish was a fairly accurate representation of Bulgaria's general attitude towards its Latinate neighbour. The ferry turned in midstream, anticipating the approaching quay, the sun went down like a molten ball, and by the time we reached the Balkan shore the land on both sides of the river had sunk into uniform blackness.

Arriving under cover of night only added to the sense that I was entering unmapped territory. Of all the lands of this great trudge, Bulgaria was the most unknown, and I had few preconceptions of its culture, climate or topography. From Artemis Cooper I had a rough route sketched out for the next few weeks – a path running south, north and south, like a low-frequency sound wave, from the Danube border to the Black Sea coast – but without Paddy's words to lead the way it would be a process of working backwards, imagining where he might have been, what landscapes, architectural oddities and cultural quirks might have caught his eye.

The town of Vidin lay several miles on and the authorities at the port were reluctant to let me walk. Before I knew what was happening, a taxi driver had been summoned, a grizzled man in a sagging vest, who rattled me jauntily into town, past tower blocks, under traffic signs adorned with blocky Cyrillic script, to deposit me at the train station. Policemen, children, station attendants, passengers and dogs were waiting with identically bored expressions. The streets were yellow with sodium lamps, and the loudest sound was the buzz of air-conditioners.

I was met by Lidia, a tall girl with a catlike face, who'd offered shelter for the night in the flat she shared with her mother Sashka. They sat me down on a chintz sofa and served me cool cherry compote, speckled with archipelagos of yoghurt, followed by bean stew. Sashka passed me a chicken leg and, seeing me fumble with knife and fork, reassured me with the phrase 'Chicken, fish and women you can catch with your hands', which set them both off giggling. Mother and daughter bombarded me with questions that had an innocent, phrase-book quality – 'Have you ever spent the night sleeping out beneath the stars?' 'Do you often go to disco-clubs to dance the night away?' 'What do you think are the advantages and disadvantages of living in a big city?' – and when I could answer no more, drowsy from food and heat, they made me up a bed on the sofa. As I drifted to sleep my head was full of Slavic sounds, but my body was bouncing down a potholed road in the Banat mountains.

By daylight, Vidin revealed itself as a town of boulevards and locust trees, ending at a riverside park blooming with pink roses. There was a holiday feeling in the air and the centre was full of people eating ice cream and drinking Italian coffee. I meandered in a daze, letting the Cyrillic lettering work itself into my brain, quietly stunned, once again, by the immediacy of difference. Grandmothers sold walnuts and herbs from plastic bags along the kerb, and the market stalls were heaped with machine parts and fake designer handbags. People looked darker and beefier, with a certain upper-arm meatiness that set them apart from Romanians, and a few unmistakably Tartar faces – slanted eyes, feathery moustaches and copper-coloured skin – mingled in the crowd.

'Rough-hewn and tough, shod and swaddled in the same cowhide footgear as the Rumanians, they padded the dusty cobbles like bears,' was Paddy's first impression of Bulgarians in *The Broken Road*, although I wasn't to read this until after my own journey was done. They were clad in 'big loose trousers, crossed waistcoats, a short jacket and the waist enveloped in thick scarlet sashes a foot wide in which knives were sometimes stuck'. No sashes or knives were on display now, but asking for directions I discovered that people shook their heads to mean 'yes', a sure indication I'd crossed a certain cultural fault-line.

In this last stage of my journey, I'd finally stepped beyond the domains of the old Hapsburg Empire and into lands the Turks had ruled for five hundred years. I was in the historical orbit not of Vienna or Budapest, but of Istanbul, and the clues to this gravitational shift were everywhere apparent. A reminder came in the form of a minaret jutting near the river, the remains of a combined mosque, synagogue and church, topped not by a crescent moon but an upturned heart like the ace of spades to symbolise peace between the religions. Nearby stood the angular fortress of Baba Vida, the stronghold of Ottoman pashas as well as Bulgarian tsars, and further on the shell of a synagogue, its roof and ceiling long since collapsed, its floor a jungle of flowers. Graffiti on its walls proclaimed allegiance variously to Nazism, Communism and Led Zeppelin, as if to add to the cultural confusion.

A chance comment of Lidia's later, as we strolled by the river, demonstrated the great divide I'd traversed the day before. We were gazing across the Danube, towards the darkly wooded and suddenly ominous opposite bank, and I asked if she often went there.

'To Romania?' she said, surprised. 'Of course not! I've never been there.'

'But it's only half an hour away. Don't you want to see what it's like?'

'I have no curiosity,' she replied, squinting across the water. 'The Romanians are not like us. They are different people.'

This was an attitude I'd find again and again among Bulgarians: not so much a hostility towards their northern, non-Slavic neighbour, but rather a profound lack of interest. Culturally and spiritually, Bulgarians looked south to the Balkans, east to Russia, or even – though they would hate to admit it – to their old imperial oppressors on the Bosphorus.

I left Vidin through a derelict industrial zone, past factories gutted or for sale. The shattered tarmac was stippled red with poppies, marking the death of economic progress. Beyond the outskirts the land grew green – a different green, indefinably, from that of Romania – and the roads were lined with wildflowers in yellow, purple, pink and blue, unknown stalks densely clustered with buds, and thickets of wild cannabis.

I followed the Danube all day, through a broad river valley muted by drizzle. An old man on a donkey cart saluted me as he passed; donkeys, rather than horses, were now the preferred beasts of burden. In the riverside village of Simeonovo the cottages were unkempt but the gardens blazed with marigolds; a woman was washing pots and pans in a sink beneath a cherry tree and stacking the dishes to dry in the branches. I kept coming across trees covered in what looked like elongated blackberries, and tentatively tried a few. They had a deliciously sweet, creamy taste. It was the first time I'd eaten mulberries.

Despite the plenty of the land, the fields past which I walked were fallow, growing only weeds. Sashka had told me that under Communism the region exported produce to Russia, Romania, Greece, the Balkans, even to Arab countries, but state-subsidised agriculture, like state-subsidised industry, had imploded after 1989. Now the farmland lay abandoned. Only once did I come across any sign of new investment: a fluorescent-lit concrete barn, inside which hundreds of cows were penned under ceiling fans. The EU flag fluttered outside; I had a vision of future historians pointing it out, alongside Soviet tower blocks, Ottoman mosques and Roman remains, as a relic of another past administrative sphere of influence. My mind went back to Transylvania, to cowbells and communal herds, with an unexpected pang of longing.

Just when it seemed that the drizzle had cleared, I looked around to see swollen clouds gathering behind me, like a child's painting of a coming storm. It overtook me soon enough. Lightning cracked across the sky and the roadside trees flashed into negative, then thunder ripped apart the air, and within seconds I was drenched. There were no buildings in sight, so I took cover beneath a tree and waited for the downpour to end. The thunder grumbled cathartically on and lightning spasmodically leapt from one horizon to the other, while I squatted under wet leaves with a waterfall running off my hat, inevitably probing its way towards my driest places. Before long I was shivering, so I clambered from the undergrowth and continued down the streaming road.

The light was dying and I was far from any village, so I began vainly searching for a sheltered spot to camp. I resigned myself to pitching my tent in the pouring rain, then decided to walk on for another fifteen minutes. After ten, I rounded a corner and came upon a guesthouse, the only one I'd seen all day, with woodsmoke twisting from the chimney. 'Come in! You can take a hot shower, dry your clothes and then come down to drink a glass of *rakiya* with me,' said the owner when I tramped inside, leaving a trail like a slug's. They were the finest words I could imagine.

The rakiya was deadly strong and knocked the chill straight out of my bones. The manager spoke of the virtues of Bulgaria in the same way Paul and Alexandra had spoken of Romania, extolling its wildness, its lack of repressive – or enforced – regulation, the greater day-to-day liberty that existed in the East. But when I mentioned Romania, he looked perturbed. 'I don't know anything about that. I have not been there. In Eastern Europe we are all Slav countries, all similar cultures and languages, apart from those two – Hungary and Romania. They do not fit in.'

His words recalled an ancient grudge: I had spent the last ten weeks crossing the linguistic wedge that Hungary and Romania – united in this, if nothing else – drive through the heart of the Slavic world, separating the West Slavic speakers of Poland, the Czech Republic and Slovakia from their southern cousins. There was something amusing in the way Bulgarians lumped them together, those implacable opponents, into one 'non-Slavic' whole, reducing their jealously guarded differences to insignificance.

Lom, which I reached before noon the next day, was Bulgaria's second-biggest Danube port, but apart from a few desultory cranes there was no sense of industry. A vagrant with a greasy beard ambled along the quay, a knotted bag swinging on the end of a stick, a cartoon image of a tramp. Debating whether or not to walk on, to abandon the Danube at last and strike south towards Sofia, I paused for a dose of caffeine by the river. The next table was occupied by a group of rough-looking men, and when they saw me switch from coffee to beer, a look passed between them.

Vesco, a ferrety fellow with the permanent squint of eyes adapted to a never-ending stream of cigarette smoke, pulled his chair up to my table. He spoke good English – he'd picked it up from British ex-pats moving into the area – and, without much preamble, invited me to a party in his village. 'There's a spare room. You can stay a few days. Stay as long as you want.'

I did a quick mental evaluation. The man looked like a total scoundrel, but I decided he was the kind of scoundrel I could trust. So within minutes I found myself being driven round Lom in someone else's car as he picked up essential supplies – meat, vegetables, fresh goat's cheese, radishes, beer, rakiya, homemade wine, bread, more meat, potatoes, more beer – and soon we were on our way east to his village.

The house was a ramshackle lean-to built by his grandfather, adjoined by various outhouses in an advanced state of dereliction. Grapevine trailed above tangled allotments, and a black dog leapt at the end of its chain, overjoyed at

company. Vesco set to work fixing the broken pump in the
well, while I and his friend Itso, a bristly hog of a man,
heaped the table with chopped vegetables. More friends
arrived, Petar and Georgi, bearing jars of wine. They swept
out the little tin pagoda, unused since last year's party, and
salad and rakiya were served – in Bulgaria these things
always went together – followed by chicken soup with the
feet still floating in it. Itso sucked down bowl after bowl
with groans of rapture. Vesco hopped around the garden
tending to simultaneous barbecues, grilling meat, frying
potatoes, wringing water out of what looked like a long
white dishcloth.

'Guts,' he replied when I asked, flinging a flailing wet
lump to the waiting dog. 'We will fry them later.'

It seemed the guest list was complete. I asked if any
women were coming, but Vesco only cackled. 'This is a
drinkers' party, Nikolai! Women just talk and get in the
way. I do have a number I could call later, a very nice local
girl. You know the kind of girl...'

'Drink slowly,' Petar said as another bottle of rakiya was
opened. 'The first bottle was for kids and ladies. This one is
for normal people. There's another bottle later, and that's
for professionals only.'

I prepared for a long night. Round of eating followed
round of drinking, like bouts in a wrestling match. A
Turkish-style narghile pipe went round the table, filling the
air with apple-flavoured smoke, followed by joints of local
grass. Somewhere in the midst of this, Petar approached
me with two long nets. 'Take one of these, Nikolai, I'll
show you something. I've been waiting for weeks for these
little bastards, and now, after the rain, they've come out.
We're going to catch them and eat them.'

The little bastards turned out to be snails, working
their way through the vegetable patch. Georgi already had

a whole sack. So we hunted snails by torchlight, climbing into neighbours' gardens to scour their allotments too, though I felt sorry for the little bastards and let most get away.

Significantly later and significantly drunker, after the third and professional bottle of rakiya had appeared as threatened, everything spiralled predictably downhill. Georgi had passed out in a flowerbed, and Itso was stuffing his face with fried guts, the smell of which made me gag. 'In the past, every year was a party like this,' said Vesco in a rare moment of lucidity. 'All doors were open, there was food and drink, there were beds to sleep in if you needed, so friends were always able to return. But that was thirty, forty years ago. Everyone has left. The villages are empty now. Now it's just us, drinking.'

A maudlin look had come into his eyes, but the moment didn't last. Soon he was dancing in shuffling steps around the pagoda, howling with laughter, which descended into a hacking smoker's cough. They were telling jokes about the folk hero Krali Marko, translated through sobs of mirth, with most of the punchlines centring on the size of the great man's penis. Vesco was still howling and choking by the time I collapsed in the nearest bed.

There had been something desperate about the night, and I felt sick and empty when I woke the next day. Survivors surfaced after noon, shambling around for coffee, picking through the detritus of empty bottles and half-consumed kebabs. The air was sticky, the sky glaring with unpleasant whiteness. I had the sense it was imperative to move – things would only get worse if I stayed – so after making a cursory attempt to clear the stack of dirty dishes I splashed my face with water and left, despite Vesco's protests. I knew he was disappointed I was going after only one night, and Petar complained in a hurt tone that I wasn't even staying for snails. I sloped away with bleary eyes, a pounding head and a sense of guilt, hoping I hadn't offended them too much.

'The way lay south through the roll of the Danubian hills and plains,' wrote Paddy in *The Broken Road*. 'Let us stride across this riparian region in seven-league boots and up into the Great Balkan range. This immense sweep – the Stara Planina, as it is called in Bulgarian, the Old Mountain – climbs and coils and leapfrogs clean across northern Bulgaria from Serbia to the Black Sea, a great lion-coloured barrier of lofty, rounded convexities, with seldom a spike or chasm...' These were the mountains I was making for now, but my boots were less seven-league than second-rate, and I was certainly in no fit state to stride. Instead, I staggered nauseously past lurid fields of rape, under clouds that throbbed with heat, sweating horribly under my clothes; after walking for half an hour I realised I was massively hungover, probably still drunk. My organs sloshed woozily, my heart thumped an irregular beat, and my steps dragged slower and slower until they stopped altogether.

Just as I was contemplating crawling into a ditch to sleep, a car skidded up and the driver gestured me in. It was a lifesaving offer. He was a gendarme, complete with handgun at his side and chevrons on his sleeve, and after I'd croaked something about the mountains I found myself flying down the road as he gestured wildly at the landscape, apparently pointing out local sights, once avoiding a head-on collision with a van by a matter of inches, until, in an absurdly short time, he flung the door open and let me out at the ugly little town of Montana.

From here the road climbed through trees into breezier foothills. The sweltering fields of the Danube Valley, and my underlying guilt at having fled Vesco's hospitality, fell away below. The hangover shifted with altitude, loosening its grip as I climbed, and the cooler and cleaner the air became, the better I started feeling. I walked long into the evening, running on the momentum of exhaustion, and it was night by the time I came to the mountain town of Berkovitsa.

This was a neat and self-possessed place with a definite whiff of wealth in the air – it was a ski resort in the winter – with roses growing along its streets and a plaza dominated by a mural of Marx and Lenin above a line of unstereotypically camp-looking workers. Convoys of recent high-school leavers were parading noisily, leaning out of car windows blasting whistles and air horns. I hurried to the sanctuary of a cheap hotel, dragged myself out for a plate of kebab, then returned for a shower and merciful collapse.

Twelve hours later, I awoke to the ominous drumming of rain. The bloated skies had returned, and the mountains above the town were swaddled in cloud. Groggy with sleep and aching all over, I pulled on my inadequate waterproofs and plastic-bagged my feet, knowing it would make no difference in a downpour like this. Feelings of deep anxiety had settled in the night, somehow linked to the lingering sense I'd given offence with my premature departure; I caught myself muttering out loud as I crossed the rain-washed square, suddenly feeling old and battered, my sense of adventure depleted. The only cure for this was walking.

My muscles took a long time to get going. The rain hammered ceaselessly and the water from overflowing drains lapped around my leaky boots, effortlessly seeping through my plastic-bag defences. But as I left Berkovitsa behind, switchbacking with the road through oak, beech and pine, past cascading brown rivers, up to the crest of the Old Mountain, my mind emptied and the pains in my body withdrew. Walking, as so often before, became less a means to an end than an end in itself. Like an act of meditation, it answered its own question.

It was two days' walk to Sofia, and the rain never faltered. Cloud suffocated the valleys, water bucketed from the trees, and my boots went up and down in slapping two-tone rhythm while thunder lazily rolled beyond the mountains. Pairs of cuckoos answered each other from dripping wood to dripping wood, and water buffalo swung their heads to watch me pass, amphibious beasts with snuffing nostrils, regarding me curiously from under crescent horns. The first night I camped in the woods on a carpet of wet leaves, and by the evening of the second day the Stara Planina was behind me; I was a few hours' walk from Sofia.

The thought of wandering the streets of a capital city after dark, as sodden and footsore as I was, was even less appealing than another night camping in the rain. Just as I was trying to decide what to do, there appeared a tin sign announcing the monastery of Архангел Михаил, Archangel Michael – the Cyrillic letters clumsily resolving themselves in my brain – and I followed a path to a tiny church, hoping Bulgarian monks would be as friendly as Romanian nuns. No one answered my knocks on the door, but a glimpse through the window of lined-up slippers convinced me that someone lived there. I sat down to wait, and after a while a man puttered up on a motorbike. His name was Ivo, and he was a caretaker for the absent monks; a small, tough man with a humorous face, who showed remarkably little surprise to see me loitering there. After I'd explained myself with a couple of carefully memorised phrases, he showed me into an empty room where I could stay the night. But first he insisted, in what was emerging as true Bulgarian style, on taking me to eat and drink in his village.

Sheltered under a plastic awning from another mon-
soonal drenching, a table was laid with stuffed peppers and
salad leaves pulled fresh from the garden. His family and
neighbours gathered round, and the neighbour's daughter
was summoned to handle the translations. The monastery, I was proudly informed, was where the patriotic hero
Vasil Levski had hidden from the Ottomans, though later
I was to discover that many Bulgarian monasteries made
an identical claim. Ivo pointed at me and said something
that made everyone laugh. The neighbour's daughter translated: 'When he saw you outside the monastery, with that
beard, he thought you were one of the monks!' My glass
was filled for the third or fourth time. A nightingale sang
in the rain. It was dark by the time he dropped me back,
and early next morning, under clear skies, I was on the
road towards Bulgaria's capital.

From a distance, Sofia's suburbs soared into view
monolithically, a windowed wall of tower blocks rising
from nothingness. The scrappy fields in the city's orbit
quickly gave up being fields as the urban clutter began,
bleeding into industrial lots, factories and auto-repair
shops, the post-industrial mycelium spreading through
every part of modern Europe. Once I'd passed through the
edgelands, the nowhere regions ringing the core, I found
myself inside the city with bewildering suddenness: there
were trams and fast-food stalls, kiosks and mobile phone
shops, people waiting in line for buses, commuters and
baby supply stores, Sofians going about their lives unre-
markably all around me. Soon I was barrelling through
the earth on a metro among city people with their private
faces and non-muddy clothes. I'd been around country
people so long I'd forgotten what they were like: a preponderance of shiny jackets, primary colours and stone-
washed jeans. The sensation was deeply familiar as well as

being acutely strange. I had the most peculiar feeling I had returned home.

I got off at Vasil Levski Stadium without quite knowing why, and then remembered the hero of the previous night's monastery. Two-storied buildings surrounded me, pigeons and trees and statued squares, social-realist effigies of wheat-clutching socialist mothers. Along Graf Ignatiev Street the market was heaped with apricots, and tramlines gleamed in the sun. From a vendor I bought a tub of sweet-corn dusted in parmesan cheese, and watched the long coats of women and men swish flappingly by.

'The aspect and atmosphere of the little capital is rather captivating,' wrote Paddy. 'The light, airy ambience of a plateau town reigns here, and above it all rises the bright pyramid of Mount Vitosha, throwing the sunlight back from its many facets, a feature as noble and inescapable as Fujiyama.' I could see the mountain from the room I stayed in, on the fifth floor of a weather-scabbed tenement block in the centre of town, hosted by a melancholy woman called Katlem who warned me about the thugs and prostitutes teeming the streets these days. Assuming the dual role of tour guide and guardian, she took me on a meandering walk around the same sights Paddy had seen – the parliament building, the state theatre, the crouching mass of the golden-domed St Alexander Nevsky cathedral – delivering a tragic history of the country on the way.

It was a litany of displacement, a palimpsest of five thousand years of migrations and colonisations. The ancient Celts were conquered by the Thracians – the southern cousins of Romania's Dacians – the Thracians by the Romans, who later became the Byzantines, and the Byzantines by the Bulgars, a Central Asian warrior tribe led by the magnificently named Khan Krum. The victorious Bulgars mixed with the Slavs filtering in from the north, and this melting pot produced the Bulgarian nation.

In medieval times Bulgaria was the heart of the Slavic world, an empire that touched three seas – Aegean, Adriatic and Black – the cradle of the Orthodox faith and the birth-place of the Cyrillic alphabet. But it also endured brutal conflict with Byzantine Constantinople, and at the end of the fourteenth century the region fell to a new superpower, spending the next five hundred years under Ottoman rule. By the time the Ottomans pulled out in 1878, after the Russian liberation prompted by Vasil Levski's uprising, Sofia was thoroughly Islamised, with over fifty mosques. Precious few were left today: according to local legend the Communists mined the minarets and dynamited them all one night, under cover of a thunderstorm. But later the Communists, in turn, witnessed the destruction of their own holy relics: in 2001, Lenin's statue in the former Lenin Square was replaced by a golden statue of Sophia, the clas-sical goddess of wisdom, itself opposed by the Orthodox, who condemned it as paganism. For thousands of years col-onising regimes had been tearing down each other's sym-bols and replacing them with new ones, trying to stamp their own mark on Bulgaria's soul.

Katlem's narrative went some way towards explaining the discombobulation I'd felt since leaving Romania; the feeling of not quite knowing where I was in the world. Every time I attempted to resolve this country in my mind – to compartmentalise what I saw as Eastern, Southern, Slavic, Balkan, ex-Soviet, ex-Ottoman – it would slip its definition and surprise me with something new.

My understanding got flipped once again the night before I departed the city, when her daughter Antonia took me to her favourite bar. The place was arty and Western-feeling, full of poets and students talking earnestly about truth and beauty – a disarmingly familiar scene that could have been found in any major city on the continent – but just when I'd got comfortable, a bizarre throbbing emanated from a smaller chamber. Before an enraptured audience, two young men were playing goatskin bags with pipes that protruded like broken limbs. One maintained an ominous drone while the other undulated on a weird scale, half Celtic reel and half Arab wail, filling the room with the sound of fucked-up trumpets and nameless dread, accompanied by ragged handclaps and whoops of joy. This was my first encounter with the *gaida*, bagpipes from the Rodopi mountains where, according to myth, Orpheus was born. It was unmistakably mountain music, a lonely keening that could never originate in any field or farm; it stayed with me as I journeyed on, a premonition of further mountains to come.

~~~

They came soon enough. By early afternoon the next day I was in the green shadow of Rila, the highest mountain range of the Balkans, which rises like an island from the flatlands south of Sofia. Paddy had taken a side trip here to visit the famous monastery, and I travelled the sixty miles by bus, believing he had done the same; later I found out he had walked, and felt a small ache of regret. My initial impression of the place differed little from his – 'a fortress-like building, almost a small towered city, embedded in fold after fold of beech trees and pine' – but history had almost ordained otherwise: the Communists intended to flood this valley to create yet another hydroelectric dam, a plan abandoned only months before the regime fell.

A quadrant of four-tiered cloisters, carved wooden galleries striped in red, white and black, surrounded a domed Orthodox church painted with phantasmagoric scenes of beak-faced demons herding sinners into rivers of fire; with the mountains jagging on all sides it had an oddly Himalayan look, as if it should have been populated not by black-bearded priests but by lamas in saffron robes. 'With its clattering hooves and constant arrivals and departures and the cheerful expansiveness of the monks, life was more like that of a castle in the Middle Ages,' wrote Paddy. The monastery may have been saved from drowning, but the throngs of pilgrims he had seen were replaced by tourists now; luxury coaches jostled for position in the overspilling car park, and the frescoes on the walls were strobe lit by camera flashes.

I'd vaguely planned to seek accommodation here, as he had done, but the crowds dissuaded me. Instead, I struck out uphill, making up for my laziness on transport earlier; instead of returning to Sofia, my plan was to cross the range northeast and pick up Paddy's path on the far side of the mountains. It was late in the day to start the ascent, and I barely allowed myself pause for breath, passing swiftly through the pines and emerging after an hour's steep climb into wild-flowered alpine meadows.

The meadows gave way to broken rock, and the rock yielded in turn to unexpected snow, a silent and secretive mountainscape hidden from below. The trail was marked by metal poles that ran like acupuncture needles along the smooth back of the ridge, and as the snow turned blue with twilight I reached what I'd been hoping to find: a hiking lodge with stout stone walls, where ice-hardened washing hung from a line, snowshoes were propped outside the door, and a bearded, weather-beaten man ushered me in to sit beside the fire.

The monastery below was dedicated to the hermit Ivan Rilski, and this could have been his reincarnation. The man served lentil soup and bread, and I supplemented the meal with my own meagre rations – spaghetti, cheese and sardines – which sent him into raptures of delight. I was his first guest for weeks, and he had the manner of someone estranged from human interaction: quiet or talkative as the mood took him, when he talked he talked too much, as if he found the balance hard to gauge. I wanted to learn about the mountain and its stories, but shyness overcame him when I asked. We finished our dinner in mutually understood silence.

After dark we stepped outside to see the sky ludicrous with stars, the full moon turning the slopes of the mountains bright as tin. Even though he lived up here for solitary months on end, my host seemed as awed as me at this vision of frozen beauty. He gestured, tried to say something, and couldn't find the words. He tried again, screwing up his face, and eventually simply spread his hands and whispered: 'Everything.' My predecessor, with all his verbosity, could not have expressed it better.

The next day's trail wound down Rila's northern slope, past the famous Seven Lakes, skirting the whale-backed peaks of Damga and Zeleni Kamak. After that the snow became patchy and soon vanished altogether. Tiny villages and roads took shape in the valley below, and to pass through the lower pines was to make a transition between the mountains and the human world, a limbo separating one reality from the next. I camped beside the Cherni Iskar river, and a footsore hike along roads the next day brought me to the town of Belovo, where I had an invitation to stay with a couple called Veny and Gary – a Bulgarian and a Bristolian – in the guest apartment underneath their house.

My first glimpse of Belovo wasn't promising: the town was dominated by the chimneys of a paper mill, the road lined with stalls selling discount toilet paper. But wooded hills surrounded it, the Maritsa river gurgled through, and my hosts had a garden full of geese, a cherry tree outside their gate and a little girl waving from the window; it was every welcome a traveller desires. Soon after I hobbled in we were toasting my arrival with rakiya, followed by bowls of bean stew flavoured with mint from the garden.

I stayed with them for several days. Karavansarays was the name of their guesthouse, after the regular caravan halts that dotted the Ottoman Empire; I later discovered Paddy had stayed in a 'caravanserais' in nearby Pazardjik, Veny's home town, one of those morphic resonances that now and then deepened the journey.

Gary was a lanky, ponytailed man with one silver tooth, Veny was tattooed and stout, and their little daughter Ellie clomped happily around in a pair of orthopaedic boots; her feet were partially paralysed from a brush with Lyme disease. Veny had grown up in the area, and possessed an encyclopaedic knowledge of local plants and flowers. During long walks in the hills, the pages of my notebook filled with forageable medicinal recipes: linden flower tea cured colds, wild garlic soothed wasp stings, the powder from puffballs could staunch a wound, and hay fever could be alleviated by patting an ants' nest and rubbing your face, as the mixture of pine needles and ant acid stopped the sneezing. She had an avaricious eye for mulberries and porcini mushrooms. My sojourn was full of leisurely meals and picnics in the mountains; it was a time to rest and fatten up, before the three-hundred-mile haul to the Black Sea coast.

It was the beginning of June and true summer had come. The schizophrenic weather of the weeks before ended in one last dramatic deluge, a lightning storm, and an earthquake that rattled the walls one evening as we were sitting down to eat – it felt like a train going through the house

– and after that I was hardly to see a cloud for the rest of my journey. Sunshine came to define Bulgaria as rain had defined the Rhine, and snow and ice the bitter nights of the Wachau Valley. People spoke of a coming great heat, just as in Bavaria they'd spoken of a coming great cold; imagining the dehydration ahead, I found myself, if anything, more nervous.

One afternoon, driving back from a picnic on nearby Belmeken Mountain, we stopped to buy honey in a village in the Rila foothills. The women at the stalls wore headscarves and long skirts, the men were somehow leaner and darker, and I thought they were Roma until I saw a minaret in place of an Orthodox dome. They were Pomaks, Bulgarian Muslims whose ancestors had converted to Islam centuries before. Paddy had seen them 'hatted with grey or white felt skullcaps that came to a point like an Arabian dome in miniature, or a Saracen's helmet stripped of its chain mail', and even without the fantastical headgear it was impressive they were still here, tenaciously clinging to their difference, considering the persecution they'd since endured. The Communist regime of Todor Zhivkov had attempted to wipe them out, forcing them to change their names from Turkish to Slavic – and murdering many who refused – which prompted the flight of thousands over the southern border. But thousands more had stubbornly outlasted state campaigns of ethnic cleansing, and their villages were still scattered across the Rila and Rodopi mountains; unlike the island of Ada Kaleh, these remnants of the Ottoman Empire had never been washed away.

Not so the thriving Turkish population Paddy had seen in Plovdiv, forty miles further east. Here my predecessor had encountered not only Bulgarian Muslims but Bulgarian Turks, still inhabiting the lost provinces of their collapsed empire. 'They were sashed with red like the

Bulgars, but they wore baggy black trousers and slippers and scarlet fezzes, often faded or discoloured by sweat and use to a mulberry hue around which ragged turbans, some of them patterned with stripes or spots ... were loosely bound. They sat cross-legged, with amber beads in their hands, eyelids lowered over the quiet intermittent gurgle of their nargilehs.' As with the Hunnish whips of Magyar drovers, or the cowhide moccasins of peasants in Transylvania, the flair and dash of sartorial cultural individualism had altogether disappeared, along with much of the diversity that had once defined the city: Turks and Pomaks mingling with Greeks, Sephardic Jews, Albanians, Armenians, Vlachs, a patchwork of ethnic differences that had, since 1945, largely been replaced by a monoculture.

The Maritsa valley trapped the heat, and Plovdiv sweltered. From one of its seven hills, green and rubbly humps that rose like islands from a sea of tiles, I could make out the pale folds of the Stara Planina to the north; between me and that faraway range was only yellow haze. In the merciful cool of evening I nosed along the alleyways – the 'undulating rose-coloured tiles, the radiating gullies of the lanes' prettified but little changed – the paving stones were polished smooth, the air gaggy with the smell of linden. Traditional houses from the Revival, which marked the bloom of nationalism in the dying days of Ottoman rule, crowded on either side: lilting wooden-framed townhouses with overhanging upper floors that made me feel I was far from Europe.

In the centre of the city the fourteenth-century Dzhumaya mosque hunkered over the ruins of an ancient Roman stadium, a cross-sectional diagram of successive colonisations. In a plaza nearby, watching a circle of water-sippers stooping around the trembling column of a drinking fountain – it had the look of a religious rite – I got into conversation with a young couple called Georgi and Elitsa. He was a soft-eyed, intelligent man with American-accented English, she was a slender woman as elegant as a gazelle, and together they made me an invitation: they were on the way to the mountains to sleep by a waterfall called Rai, Paradise, and I was welcome to join them. It was exactly on my route. Early next morning they picked me up in Georgi's gleaming Skoda, and soon we were speeding through dusty villages, out of the stifling heat of the valley, towards the projecting wedge of the Central Balkan Range.

We left the car in Karlovo, a foothill town where Paddy had encountered more turbaned and fez-hatted Turks, and been invited by an elderly *hodja* into the sanctuary of a mosque. The mosque was still intact, but there was little evidence of a Turkish presence; instead, hikers in light-weight sportswear packed the cobbled streets. The expedition to Paradise consisted of a dozen of Georgi and Elitsa's friends, strung out in a caravan loaded with home-cooked food and beer, and several hours' conversational climb brought us to our destination: a hiking lodge on a grassy plateau where the waterfall tumbled from a high rock lip, fed by the stump of a snowcap, widening as it fell.

It was Saturday night and the site was crowded with other groups; after dark the campfires grew rowdy with songs and rakiya. A folklore group danced the *hora*, a shuffling circle dance of hops and complicated foot rotations; accordions and guitars appeared, a gaida whined like a trapped mosquito, and bouts of Dionysian caterwauling ensued. They began with patriotic anthems to anti-Turkish uprisings and the mythical Krali Marko, he of the enormous penis, and degenerated into bawdy singalongs, the words of which, I was assured, were absolutely filthy.

Georgi wasn't joining in but spectating with a look of sad amusement. It turned out that he and Elitsa were soon to leave Bulgaria, emigrating to California to start a new life. I asked why he wanted to leave. Watching people sing and dance on a clear night under the moon, with the Paradise waterfall snaking into a mist of spray, life in Bulgaria looked quite idyllic. But he saw another side, the one that no foreigner could.

'Everyone is selfish here, obsessed with money. Under Communism we were taught to obey, to let the clever people in the Party make decisions for us, not to have opinions of our own. Fifty years of being told to be stupid and small-minded made us stupid and small-minded. So now we have democracy, but no civil society. It's called post-Communist apathy.'

Like Paul and Alexandra back in Arad, Georgi was of the generation who witnessed the dying days of Communism, the mafia free-for-all that ensued when Communism fell, and the old Communist leaders reinventing themselves as capitalists. 'They weren't stupid. They saw the transition coming and moved all the money to foreign banks until the fuss died down. Then they started bringing it back into the country as private investment. They were magicians, our politicians – they turned public money into private money. They put it in the hands of the *mutri*.'

The mutri, 'mugs', were nouveau-riche gangsters of the shiny-suited, big-necked type, the shock troops of free-market capitalism, and in the 1990s they had practically ruled the country. A popular anecdote told how they liked to park in the middle of the road, causing chaotic traffic jams, and sit back sipping cappuccinos, just to show they could. 'When people saw the mutri getting away with things like this, they tried to copy them. This attitude trickled down through society. No one cares about anyone else, as long as they get what they want. It's selfishness like this that makes me want to leave.'

I'd originally planned to return to Karlovo with my friends the next day, then skirt the Stara Planina east towards the Shipka Pass. But now it occurred to me that I was halfway over the mountains. There was no sense in losing height; from Paradise I could follow the ridge for days without meeting a road, and pick up Paddy's trail on the northern side of the range. So after a lazy morning drinking coffee in the sun, I scribbled a rudimentary map, stowed as much leftover food as I could, and said farewell, yet again, to newly made friends. 'Goodbyes like these were the only sad aspect of the journey,' wrote Paddy of a similar parting not far from here. 'There was something intrinsically melancholy, a sudden sharp intimation, like a warning tap on the shoulder, of the fleetingness of everything, in bidding goodbye to people who had been kind, as nearly everyone was, and knowing that, in all likelihood, I would never see them again.'

With a feeling much like this inside me, I zigzagged up towards Botev, the highest peak in the range, past the remains of the snowcap emptying into the cataract below. Shadowed valleys raced away to the south, back in the direction of Plovdiv. I stopped to drink from a stream that tasted of cold tin, then continued over the curve of the mountain.

For the next three days I walked on top of the range that divided Bulgaria, the north and the south of the country rolling away to my left and my right, suspended in the balance between two worlds; committed to neither, biding my time before the inevitable plunge back down. There was great serenity to be found at these heights. Unlike the rocky upthrust of Rila, jagging dramatically into the sky, the peaks of the Stara Planina were scuffed, eroded humps, chewed down by time. The tussocky grass sprang under my feet and the sloping moorland plunged into broken canyons below, architectures of lichen-spotted stone; here and there the green skin that covered the mountain had pulled away, as if tugged back by giant fingers, and jumbled rock burst out like sausage meat. Long-legged foals were attempting their first skittish gallops on the slopes, and a herd of horses followed me nose to tail for half a mile, part thuggish and part shy, until at last I reeled around and sent them cantering away.

I camped one night outside a cabin inhabited by a pitbull-faced man who spent his time anxiously scanning the peaks with binoculars; the next was spent under pines as lightning pulsed on the horizon. From there the moorland dropped into the beech forests of Bulgarka National Park, and on the third afternoon I wound down towards the villages once again. A drinking fountain gurgled in every square – one of the sweeter legacies of Ottoman culture – and the houses were top-heavy like the ones in Plovdiv, wood framed and wattle walled, with marigolds in flowerpots and trellises of grapevine.

Gabrovo, at the foot of the range, had the dubious distinction of being the longest city in Bulgaria, and carried as its municipal symbol a cat with a chopped-off tail. This, I discovered, was a local joke: Gabrovans were notoriously stingy, and were said to cut the tails off their cats to save heat when closing the door in winter. They were also known for fitting taps to their eggs, to draw no more than the yolk required, and making their donkeys wear green sunglasses to fool them into eating woodchips instead of grass. When I read *The Broken Road*, I was delighted to discover that this reputation for meanness went back to my predecessor's time: it was on the road to Gabrovo that Paddy, limping from the pain of an errant hobnail, was twice refused lifts by peasants driving empty carts, conduct 'unprecedented on any of the roads of Europe ... This passion to make money out of chance trivialities, like giving a pedestrian a lift in an empty cart, is a phenomenon I met several times in Bulgaria, but nowhere else in Europe, before or afterwards.'

I didn't linger in that city of scrooges, but pressed on for another ten miles in the furnace heat of the afternoon to the Dryanovo monastery, a steepled church huddled under cliffs and slabs of rock improbably slanting from the forest. There was a campsite by the river, run by a sweet old lady who seemed more entertained than disgusted at the volume of sweat pouring off me, and here I pitched my tent to a chorus of cackling frogs.

The monastery was made famous when the rebel battalion of Bacho Kiro, one of Vasil Levski's men, was massacred here by Ottoman troops in the 1876 uprising. Icons in the church – torched by the soldiers, but later rebuilt – depicted Archangel Michael stamping on a defeated Turk, while another angel did the same to a chained black man, from whose lips flared one last diabolical twist of fire. The mercilessness of the image alluded to hundreds of years of hate; wars that had been fought for so long their violence had become holy.

Beyond the monastery lay the entrance to the Bacho Kiro caves, a subterranean labyrinth riddling the gorge. In the system's deeper tunnels Neanderthal skeletons had been found, one of the earliest traces of human habitation in Europe. I rose before the heat the next day to stoop through stalactite-encrusted halls, working my way through intestinal corridors of dripping rock, and came back out to see white butterflies dancing over the cascades, the sun climbing once again in a cloudless sky. I set out, like an emerging caveman, to explore another new world.

After half an hour of walking, the water in my bottle was as warm as soup. The air was dense with pollen and the blossom reeked so sweetly it was quite unpleasant. I filled my hat with cherries and plums, spitting a trail of stones, and wandered the morning in a daze, stupefied with heat.

Blisters were becoming a problem for the first time on my walk. Hastened by the rubbing of sweat and the gradual collapse of my boots, they ballooned on my heels and toes, and my supply of blister packs – carefully hoarded since the Hook of Holland and hardly touched until now – was rapidly depleted. The soles of my boots had worn thin enough that I could feel the texture of the road; I bought a pair of secondhand shoes to cannibalise for soles, and superglued rubber patches over the holes as they appeared.

In the centre of Veliko Tarnovo, after a long highway tramp sucking in dust and diesel fumes, I practically collapsed outside an expensive café. My head was pounding with heat stroke and my chest flared with prickly heat, like thousands of red-hot filaments needling into the skin. A waiter took pity on me, served me glass after glass of water, and led me down a ramshackle flight of steps to a hostel clinging to the side of the hill. There was a cool bed by a window, and a balcony overlooking terracotta rooftops tumbling steeply down to the Yantra river.

'The airy town jutted with oriental balconies craning on diagonal beams above the gulf, and hundreds of window-panes threw back the evening sun in tiers of square flaming sequins, as though fires were raging within,' wrote Paddy; from my window this vision unfolded much the same. At night the city resembled a fossil, an ammonite blazing with tiny lights. I rested there for several days, gently wandering the lanes and discovering hidden alleyways, cockeyed timber-framed houses and shaded gardens where cats squinted evilly from their hiding places. In medieval times

Veliko Tarnovo was the capital of the Second Bulgarian Empire, and nearby lay the ruins of Tsarevets, a battlemented fortress seemingly squeezed from the natural rock. This fairytale City of the Tsars symbolised a lost golden age, a vision of the nation's glory before the Ottoman conquest.

After leaving Veliko Tarnovo, Paddy had struck north across the Danube and the Wallachian Plain, back into Romania to sample the high life of Bucharest, before catching a train south to the Black Sea port of Varna. Ignorant of his route, I kept slogging east towards the sea. Even had I known of this diversion – a round trip of three hundred miles – the idea of plunging deeper inland, away from the promise of the coast, would have been violently unappealing; increasingly dishevelled, daily encrusted with grime, my clothes discoloured from the endless cycle of sweating, drying off and sweating again, the thought of reaching the sea was starting to obsess me.

I had a companion for the first few days of this hinterland trudge. Veny had taken time off work, left Gary with Ellie and the geese, packed a tent and change of clothes, and caught the train to join me. My visit to Belovo, it seemed, had given her itchy feet, made her nostalgic for the carefree days before work and motherhood, when she used to embark on similar wanderings; she arrived sleep deprived with excitement at the prospect of adventure.

It wasn't quite the happy-go-lucky saunter she might have envisaged. Out of practice at walking, Veny became dehydrated after an hour, and by the end of the first afternoon her feet were raw with blisters. We camped at the edge of a cornfield, downwind from a stagnant lake that smelt unpleasantly of dog food, and her suffering lessened with the cool of the evening. But the second day was even hotter than the first, and by noon she said she had black dots dancing before her eyes; our pace slowed to a crawl, staggering from one patch of shade to the next like a couple of vampires fearful of the sunlight. We managed to reach the Yantra to pitch our tents beneath a weeping willow, spending the afternoon eating fruit and wallowing in the shallows. Then after an hour's walk the next morning her blisters burst again and we had to abandon the adventure completely, hitching a lift on a Gypsy cart as far as the next village.

Here we waited out the day in the shadow of a walnut tree, and in the morning Veny caught the train back to Belovo. I hoped she hadn't suffered too drastically on our short excursion. But later she wrote to say that she was already planning a hike to the mountains, and that Ellie remembered me and sometimes asked when I'd come back. 'When I grow up I want to be a traveller,' the little girl had said, 'so I can go and find him.'

As the temperature soared, my walking pattern changed. I started packing my tent before dawn, walking until the sun was high, and then retreating under the trees until it was cool enough to emerge. The weather elasticated the days: while at the beginning of my journey it had been night by five o'clock, in the summer of the south the light was slow to leach from the sky, and there was a special sense of freedom to seeing my shadow lope ahead as the sun went down at my back, a feeling that the night belonged to me alone. With the dying of the heat each day, the land and all the living things in it breathed an almost audible sigh of relief. I avoided cities and large towns, skirting their peripheries in favour of dusty country roads; I camped one night in a field of wheat like an advert for a breakfast cereal, the air alive with mites and motes, and the next in a dried-up gulley with fireflies pulsing between the trees. On another occasion I fell asleep to a sound disturbingly like babies crying, the yapping lament – I discovered later – of Caucasian jackals.

A few miles east of the city of Shumen, a plateau of yellowish limestone sprouted from the blandness of the plain, dominating the landscape for miles in every direction. Veny had told me about this place and I reached its foot as the cliffs turned Arizona red in the sunset, each contorted rock formation casting a deformed shadow. It was clearly a site of significance, and as I wound my way uphill I had the feeling of approaching a temple; which, long ago, was perhaps what it was. A flight of stone steps led up to the Madara Rider.

The ancient Bulgars had carved it there, though some believed it was centuries older, and depicted a Thracian god: a simple relief of a mounted hunter – the horse's hindquarters now severed by a vertical crack in the rock – with a hunting dog loping behind and a lion at the horse's hooves, ground down in symbolic defeat. No other carvings surrounded it, no dedications or commemorations, as if those figures said everything the carver wanted them to say. There was something familiar in the angle of the rider's spear, the lion's misery under the hooves, and it took me a moment to recognise what: if the lion was replaced by a lizard, the image was identical to St George and the dragon. When I later discovered that St Georgi was Bulgaria's patron saint, a clear line leapt back to ancient Bulgarian culture.

I pitched my tent at a campsite nearby, in the company of a boss-eyed mongrel and a Pekinese with an underbite; the quality of hounds had clearly gone down since ancient times. I spent the evening killing mosquitoes, and discovered in the morning a place of even stranger magic: the Sanctuary of the Nymphs, a sacred place for the pagan Thracians, a vast depression in the rock like a bowl standing up on end. The wall flexed inwards in such a way it was hard to tell how big it was, or how far back it went, and sometimes it fooled the eye into thinking it wasn't concave but convex, bulging outwards like a great stone bubble; too huge to take in as a whole, the effect was similar to an IMAX cinema screen. I felt sure the unknown carver, whether Bulgar or Thracian, must have stood in this exact spot, craning back their neck in the same way I was doing now.

East of Madara the countryside grew increasingly parched, beaten down by sun. The jungle green had disappeared and swathes of the land were yellow – yellow with wheat, yellow with rape, yellow with sunflowers – and marched across by pylons snaking power towards the coast. People were less friendly here, less inclined to wave or smile, and subsequently I found myself feeling more suspicious. It was a tougher, poorer region; there was a sense of violence in the land, and no shade on the road.

On a road through sunflower fields I was overtaken by a man with no legs, trundling in a cloud of dust on an electric wheelchair. Past the village of Zhitnitsa a car pulled up containing four Roma boys, none looking older than sixteen, with broken teeth and chests already covered in homemade tattoos. They asked where I was going. I told them Padina, the next village, and they beckoned me in. It was the least advisable lift I'd been offered yet and I have no idea why I accepted – the words 'ah, fuck it' ran through my head – and seconds later we were going at ninety miles an hour down the road, Balkan music pumping from the speakers, while they whooped and threw cigarettes at each other and the driver kept turning round to grin, as if driving was the least important thing he was doing at that moment. An hour's walk evaporated in a few terrifying minutes, and we just had time to exchange names before the car screeched to a halt, exactly where I'd asked to be dropped. After a round of handshakes they were gone, and I was alone again in another cloud of dust.

I'd been making for Padina because my map showed
a lake behind the village, and I envisaged my last night
inland camping on its shore. But the lake turned out to
be a retention pond containing the poison-blue effluence
of a PVC factory, ringed by lights and service roads, and it
was another two hours before I reached safely wooded hills
above Razdelna. Smokestacks dominated the horizon, and
fields of sickly looking crops grew alongside canals filled
with water the colour of detergent, run-off from the chemical reservoir; the landscape was confused between industry
and agriculture, as if, the closer it got to the sea, the less
it knew what to do with itself. Even so, the woods were
real woods, dappled with evening sunlight. Mysterious
pathways through the trees gleamed with cobwebs of enormous tensile strength, stretching like elastic as I shouldered
through them. I wandered in where I wouldn't be found
and gathered sticks for a fire. It was the night of the summer solstice and I felt savagely glad. The next day I would
reach the Black Sea.

I'd pictured the arrival over and over in ambulatory
daydreams: a lonely coastline, a final rise dropping to a
deserted beach, the unimaginable pleasure of cool, rolling
water. But in the manner of many arrivals, my first sight
of the sea fell flat. Industry had wrecked the prettiness of
the Varna estuary, where a trapezoid mountain of chalk
erupted dust into the sky, and processing plants and load-
ing bays blocked my view of water. A brief vision of blue
opened up and then was whisked away by hills. The E5
road corkscrewed into the sky and I found myself on a four-
lane highway on a concrete bridge soaring above the estuary, from where the sea was only a hazy band beyond the
cranes.

The vision of water vanished again as the flyover
plunged me into Varna, the biggest city on Bulgaria's coast.

I paced like a madman through the outskirts, determined not to let the sea get away, hurrying without much interest past a golden-domed cathedral, dwarf palm trees in pots, a maze of pedestrianised shopping streets, mobile phone shops and ice-cream stands, dodging a pair of baby-faced Mormon missionaries, past a row of stone columns, Greek or Roman, I didn't care which, until at last I crunched onto sand, threw off my rucksack and my clothes, and collapsed into the waves.

'Everything.' I thought of the hermit in the Rila mountain lodge. That was the only word to describe how good it felt.

It was a crowded city beach splayed with the tanned and beautiful, the topless and the should-be topless, with lines of parasols you had to pay to sit underneath. I was the whitest and hairiest person in sight, pale legs chicken-poxed with mosquito damage; I felt like a northern barbarian stumbled into paradise. Waiting out the afternoon, watching the topography of bodies change as groups came and went, a feeling of peculiar melancholy grew as evening gathered. Roma wrestled in the shallows, hurling their children into the air – dressed noticeably more modestly than the Bulgarians, who flaunted everything – and it made me feel dislocated, far removed from beach life. Reaching the sea after all these months had something of anticlimax and something of loneliness. Mostly, though, it was simply the sadness of arrival.

At night the city came to life and that sadness faded. Coloured lights lit the pillars and palms, and fire jugglers and street musicians drew ice-cream-eating crowds. In the murmur of bars and the pulse of music, the men handing out flyers for strip shows outside clubs and casinos, Varna made sense of itself: a pleasantly seedy Black Sea port, with all the quiet sins and amusements of any seaside city.

I stayed with an archaeologist called Vassil, a connection that had come about in such a convoluted way – a friend of a friend of a friend – that I wasn't even sure how it had happened. He put me up in an attic room with a view over tiled roofs to the sea, where I woke to the raucousness of gulls. Eating fried fish later with archaeologist friends on the beach, he elaborated on the country's history, how Bulgarians were pulled down by the weight of their conquered past. 'On national holidays it all seems wonderful. People think "we had a great empire." Yes, but that was ten centuries ago. I think people feel like they're living at the end of history, that everything is behind them. All they have to do is live a little longer and get it over with.'

'Deep in our soul we are part of Europe,' said his companion, a black-bearded man who'd been introduced as Big Ivan. 'In medieval times we were one of the most powerful countries in Europe, the heart of the Orthodox world. But then the Turks made us part of an oriental empire for five centuries, a culture totally foreign to us. Then we got dragged away again by fifty years of Soviet rule, another eastern empire. When the EU accepted us in 2006 there was national celebration. Finally we had made it home to the European community, after centuries of separation. There was such hope for the future! And now the EU's falling apart. All that hope has disappeared. That's Bulgarian luck.'

He took a forkful of fish and another swig of beer. 'Can you imagine how it feels, after waiting six hundred years, to arrive just as the train leaves the station?'

The next day Vassil drove me and a carload of friends to swim at Shkorpilovtsi, a beach twenty miles south, and left me there to continue on foot along the coast. It was late afternoon; I shumped down the sand away from the few struggling bars, until there were no more manmade things, and pitched my tent between the dunes. Here, free from sunbathing crowds, Balkan techno and the roar of cars, I could hear the waves for the first time.

I sat there all evening, sand between my toes. Darkness spread from the east, drawing the sea and sky together into a single stain. A flight of birds in V formation whistled northwards up the coast, too high to identify, perhaps on their way to the Danube delta in faraway Romania, and the lonely light of a ship on the horizon slipped south towards Burgas or Turkey. Varna had been a false arrival. It wasn't until that night, rolled to sleep by the slow boom of waves against an empty shore, that I really reached the sea.

10

The Concrete Coastline
The Black Sea

Attuned for nearly a year to nothing but hinterland pros-
pects of plain and mountain, my eyes, alighting now like a
stranger's on the stepped woods and the shore below, found
something so improbable and extreme in the beauty of this
interlock of vegetation and sea that it appeared an illusion.

The Broken Road

THE SUN CAME UP LIKE A BLOODY BUBBLE. EVERYTHING SHONE
with a bright translucence, a light that was indefinably different to any that would fall inland. For a few moments,
squinting at the beachgrass shivering in the wind, I was
back at the Hook of Holland. But this was a different sea.

I swam, letting the smack of the waves knock all sleep
from my body. After so many sweat-slathered weeks the
pleasure of being clean was addictive, and from this point I
would stop to swim more frequently than I ate. By the time I
returned to my tent, a lizard had taken up residence inside.
Along the tideline sprawled a sun-dried fish almost as long
as my body, blunt snouted, stubby toothed, a misfit from
the depths. Other leavings from the sea littered the sand
towards Cherniya Nos, the Black Cape: the raggy carcasses
of gulls, assorted polycarbonates, ubiquitous flip-flops.

My walk became very simple now: due south, keeping
the sea to my left, hugging the coastline all the way to the
Turkish border. It was easier to go barefoot, though with
the burden of my bag walking on sand could be as exhausting as walking in snow – the same soft collapsing rhythm,

one step forward and a half-step back – and I learnt to walk below the tideline where the sand was densely packed. My feet were deeply cracked in places, raw where blisters hadn't healed, and sand worked its way into the wounds; but this was a minor discomfort compared with the wreck of my boots.

At the end of that first cape a yellow cliff dropped to the waves below, and I rebooted myself to struggle through aggressive undergrowth, spiked, scratched, entangled and stung until, after a bitter fight, emerging at another beach. There were huddles of tents and caravans half-hidden in the woods, glimpses of the deckchair existence of beach-dwelling summer tribes. Outside a boarded-up shack two boys were doggedly filing through the chain around a beer fridge; they grinned when they saw me coming, then resumed their work. With such initiative, they would doubtless make fine mutri one day.

Dunes turned into hills, and the hills became Bialiya Nos, the White Cape, beyond which, down chalky roads, lay the resort of Byala. The town was suffering the development disease, multistoried with cancerous outcrops of sea-facing apartments, and concrete frames jutted from the outskirts like the promise of an uglier future. I swam, ate ice cream, and pressed on. Obzor rose ahead, on the far side of a no-man's land of half-constructed holiday homes populated by permatanned Russians – the new masters of this coastline – who helped me find my way down newly metalled roads. I wanted to swim, but the sea was as crowded as a rush-hour tube.

Beyond Obzor lay a stretch of merciful emptiness, either too cliffy to build on or granted a temporary reprieve by the economic crisis. Once I'd cleared the last hotels, the bars pumping sweaty beats, the last of the construction sites – a billboard showed a proposed 'Club Resort' the size of another small town – the sand segued into rocks and the coast was again unmanned. The elongated hump ahead was the last vestige of the Stara Planina, the range I'd crossed twice already, before the Old Mountain plunged underwater, barrelling under the waves towards Russia. I walked beneath cliffs over rubble and rocks, aurally balanced between the slosh of waves and the chirrup of insects, encountering no one but fishermen and isolated communities of nudists politely nodding hello.

Irakli beach had attained phase one of despoilment – the developers had got as far as a chill-out bar, complete with potted palms – but construction had tentatively halted there for now. The other end was inhabited by hippies peering shyly from the woods, surrounded by driftwood totem poles like charms against further encroachment. Here, Vassil had given me instructions to find the path leading up through the forest beside the fisherman's stone cottage. There was the cottage, complete with fisherman – who looked like a fat Ernest Hemingway – there was the path winding into the trees, and after half an hour's climb I was on top of Emine cape, overlooking the glittering endlessness of the sea.

Vassil's directions led me along the dirt road to Emona, where a friend of his lived in the second house past the church. There was the church, and there was the second house, and there, sure enough, was Burya, a blue-eyed woman in her sixties waving from the garden. 'You have arrived at the perfect time,' was the first thing she said. 'We are eating fish and drinking wine.' Minutes later, so was I.

The fish was *popche*, 'little priest', named for the cross-shaped bone in its body. The wine was from a local vineyard and had the tang of retsina. Burya, her husband and their neighbour Hristo had moved here decades ago to found an artist colony, and it was inaccessible enough, and high enough above the sea, to have escaped the construction craze that had flattened the individuality of villages up the coast. They showed me to a spare room underneath a shaded terrace, a stone chamber full of light and air, lizards creeping up the wall. From the terrace, on clear days, you could see the mountains of Turkey. Thick darkness swallowed the bay and stillness fell on the land. It didn't quite get dark, however: light pollution from the west, where the coastline would take me the following day, made the sky smoulder white, the all-inclusive resort hotels blazing into the night. Fireworks burst above the sea, silent and unreal from this distance.

Hristo and his daughter Maria walked with me the next morning, picking out a secret pathway back to the sea through the coastal hills. The slopes were scattered with broken stone, and the electric fizz of cicadas and the pungency of thyme put me in mind of Greece or Spain; suddenly I became aware I had entered a mediterranean climate, baked and barren, with an impression of deep antiquity. We swam under crumbling cliffs in an uninhabited cove, the only other occupants a herd of cows swishing flies beneath the trees.

'It was, and is, hard to capture the charm of the journey along this almost deserted coast, and its pervading atmosphere of peaceful seclusion and consolation,' wrote Paddy. These few-and-far-between stretches of overlooked, undeveloped beach were a glimpse of the coastline he'd walked down, when the region – apart from a few large ports – was a peripheral fringe, the wildest and outermost edge of the continent. Somewhere not too far from here, he came across an encampment of Sarakatsani, 'the only true nomads of the Balkans', transhumant Greek-speaking shepherds who grazed their flocks in the mountains in summer, driving them down to the lowlands when winter came. The vision he had of them was like something from the Dark Ages: 'The place reeked of horses and goats and curds and woodsmoke. Everything was made of twisted branches, thorns, reeds and timber; all was pegged, plaited, woven and lashed with thongs ... these black-hooded and cloaked figures, these black and white zigzagged women, these conical huts and their teeming tintinnabulation of flocks through the rainy woods of Rumelia comprised the most mysterious community I had ever seen.'

The Greek population of the coast, like the Turks of the hinterland, had practically disappeared now, destroyed by the homogenising trends of nationalism, Communism and economic advancement. It was hard to imagine stumbling, as my predecessor did, over the rocks one night into a cave of carousing Bulgarian and Greek fishermen, who danced mad as dervishes to the music of gaida and bouzouki. Before publication of *The Broken Road* this account appeared as a separate story called 'A Cave on the Black Sea', and for years travel literature enthusiasts – geekier souls than I – had tried to pinpoint the cave's whereabouts, combing the text for geological evidence. It was generally agreed that it must have been somewhere in this region, south of Varna and north of Burgas, but no one had ever identified a convincing location. Either the coast had shifted since then, the sea had risen or the cliff had fallen; or – as Artemis Cooper suggests – the cave was another of Paddy's confabulations, a literary composite melded together from disparate elements. From what I'd seen of the coast so far, I had another theory: it wasn't inconceivable that someone had slapped a hotel on top. His tattooed Greek fishermen had been replaced by tattooed English tourists, and the bouzouki music he'd heard lived on in Ibiza techno.

As if to support my fantasy, there came a roar of engines. A convoy of 4×4s thundered from the woods and ground to a halt on the beach, disgorging a score of brightly clad tourists to take photographs of each other, an allotted ten-minute break in their 'off-road safari'. My friends ignored their presence with zen-like serenity, and after the intruders had smoked their cigarettes, gazing disinterestedly at the sea, they clambered back into their vehicles and rumbled away again.

'Too close to the concrete coastline,' said Maria. The cows reassembled under the trees. Hristo took off all his clothes and resumed his swim.

The concrete coastline began after that last lonely cape. First, a hotel the size of a cruise ship. Then another, slightly larger. Then hotel followed hotel as far as my eye could see along the grand sweep of the bay, the conjoined resorts of Elenite, Robinson, Sveti Vlas, Sunny Beach and Ravda sprawling ten miles down the shore. Sunny Beach had been the first – an unremarkable fishing village developed by the Communists as a resort for holidaying Eastern Europeans – but after 1989 mutri money flooded in, and in the construction boom of the 2000s the area had been transformed into a summer metropolis, a glass and concrete monument to capitalist excess.

The architecture of the temple complex seemed to have inspired the hotels along the beach: colossal stepped ziggurats shimmering with balconies, surrounded by landscaped lawns and lurid turquoise swimming pools, while the sand itself could hardly be seen for the sun worshippers who covered it, sizzling on loungers and anointing themselves with oil. Glistening faces scowled defensively as I lumbered past; I scowled defensively back, feeling peculiarly exposed in this tourist paradise. Inadvertently I wandered into an all-inclusive resort – everyone apart from me was wearing coloured wristbands to demonstrate their allegiance to a particular package deal, like a form of indentured servitude

– and stood in horrified fascination watching fifty people perform a synchronised dance routine led by a whooping girl in Lycra, until a security guard arrived to escort me off the premises. I wasn't sure if he'd noticed my bare wrists, or simply recognised, correctly enough, that I didn't belong.

Behind the first tier of mega-hotels, the main drag of Sunny Beach was lined with condominiums, casinos, sports bars, bingo halls, themed restaurants, nightclubs, strip clubs, amusement arcades, crazy golf courses, Irish pubs and all-day English breakfasts. Tourists browsed the beachwear shops in flip-flops and Hawaiian shorts, ate fish and chips under palm-frond roofs, while hip-hop videos pumped and dazzled from flatscreen televisions. This was not Bulgaria, but an international zone with signage in a dozen languages, and the colonising flags of Britain, Russia, Germany, Australia and the USA gave the impression of a frenetic collision of nationalities; adverts for endless pleasures and distractions demanded attention on every side. The walk became a purgatory of identically repeating scenes, scrolling past mechanically while my feet stamped up and down on the ice-cream-splattered pavement.

Marooned in the middle of all this, at the point where Sunny Beach merged into its neighbouring resort – the separate villages of the bay having long since been sub-sumed into one contiguous sprawl – a causeway ran into the sea towards a little isthmus. I followed it, hoping for respite: this was the ancient Greek port of Mesembria, now rechristened Nesebar, to which Paddy had been drawn with romantic inevitability. 'A strange, rather sad, rather beguiling spell haunted the cobbled lanes,' he wrote. 'In the few winding streets and the coffee house, it was Greek rather than Bulgarian that I heard spoken, and Greek too among the little fleet of beached fishing boats and the rus-set festoons of looped net. For it was an amphibian place.

The water lapped at the end of the streets, hulls and masts broke up the skyline, there was even something of the ship-wright's trade about the jutting timbered upper storeys of the old houses, which confronted each other across the lanes like the poops of galleons anchored stern to stern. So muted, ambiguous, watery, with the dimness of the after-glow contending with lighting-up time, the town might have been at the bottom of the sea.'

There was nothing muted or ambiguous about the Nesebar of today. Its proximity to Sunny Beach had turned it into another theme park, an archaeological Disneyland, to which a steady stream of tourists was channelled on a miniature train, frowning as if they didn't quite know how they had ended up there. Pizzerias and souvenir shops out-numbered the Byzantine churches, and the ancient stone walls were a backdrop for posing Russian blondes. At least with Sunny Beach there was no hint of what had existed before; here, remnants of the past served only to emphasise the crassness of what had replaced it.

Retracing my steps to the mainland, I resumed my escape attempt from the concrete. Hopeful signs of green-ery appeared between half-built hotels, empty plots sur-rounded by fences and 'For Sale' signs, and then the roll of hills gave shape to the land once more. At last, feet stinging from the incessant pounding of the road, I came to a halt at a village called Aheloy. I hadn't quite out-walked the sprawl, but had succeeded in getting myself to the least fashionable part of it: an odd little campsite on a silted beach, where a line of rusting aluminium pods – some once-futuristic Soviet concept of novelty accommodation – mouldered by the sea. No one else was in residence but an elderly man in a straw hat and Y-fronts, and I was soothed to hear the hiss of waves on sand again. When I went to sleep that night, visions of hotel balconies reeled behind my eyelids.

The worst was behind me now. To the south, wetlands and deltas guarded against further epic construction; the next morning, without looking back, I followed a narrow thread of sand between saline lakes and the sea, meeting no one but a group of bathers glistening head to toe with black mud, renowned for its restorative properties. A sign informed that the lakes were home to the wonderful-sounding glasswort and herbaceous seepweed, smotherweed and lesser sea spurrey; protected under EU law, these slimy succulents had halted development where everything else had failed.

That night I camped again a few miles outside Burgas. This was a large industrial port, confident enough to hold its own against absorption into the holiday coast, and tankers and naval vessels lurked offshore. The underwhelming plaza in the centre was fronted by weather-cracked apartment blocks, and the streets had a reassuring air of lazy normality. The sea was a lovely bottle-green, darkening towards the horizon, and the waves formed perfect triangles in the evening wind.

I didn't know it at the time, but this was where the final chapter of *The Broken Road* breaks off mid-sentence: the narrative of Paddy's great trudge ending, somewhat cryptically, with 'this little multiracial port in which many of the races of the Balkans were represented; and yet, in another sense, although', before leaping two hundred miles to his first scattered impressions of Istanbul. My time in Burgas was similarly abbreviated; instinct told me to keep moving, and my glimpse of the city was as brief as my predecessor's own.

Protected wetlands to the south forced me to veer inland and I spent a weary day tramping the verge of a highway. The exhaustion was worth it: at the end of a dusty, dirty afternoon, I reached the refuge of Sozopol.

The town lay on its own little cape, and from a distance looked like a cluster of barnacles on a rock. Its houses leaned towards one another in gossipy togetherness, their upper storeys overhanging to shade the alleyways below. With their clinker-built walls, bleached by salt and sun, they looked like houses made by boat-builders, and probably they were. This was another ancient port town founded by seafaring Greeks, part of a wave of Hellenic settlement around the Black Sea, a tantalising vision of what Nesebar must once have been. Also like Nesebar it depended on the tourist industry, but it lay far enough south to have escaped overdevelopment; it harboured an artist population of the watercolours-of-boats variety, producing an atmosphere a bit like a Bulgarian St Ives. It was the kind of town that only makes sense when you get lost, safe in the knowledge that a certain number of twists and turns will inevitably lead to a sheet of coruscating blue between the buildings. There were tiny chapels with trembling candles, washing flapping from balconies, huddles of old men and women doing their evening sit. Grandmothers sold green fig jam, and bearded gentlemen snorkelled offshore trailing nets full of edible molluscs.

The Greeks had called the town Apollonia, after a temple to Apollo, and I found a cheap hotel on a street of that name. But sleep, for some reason, was beyond me, so after midnight I left my room and picked my way under blackened cliffs above the dark slop of the waves, energised by the spreading silence of the sea. It was almost dawn by the time I got to bed. Sleep deprivation gave the next day's walk a pleasant unreality – secluded bays where cormorants stretched their wings on guano-covered rocks, an impassable river delta that forced me miles inland – and in a kind of rambling dream I arrived at Kiten beach, on the afternoon of June 30, to meet a man called Nikolay for the festival of July Morning.

We'd met briefly in Sofia, in the bar in which I'd heard the gaida for the first time. He was a writer and spent his summers living in a tent on the coast; a sandy-haired man with a broad, smiling face, older than I remembered from our smoky encounter in the bar, and accompanied by his red-haired wife Maria. 'Here you will feel *kef*,' he said as he showed me to their home: a forest village of tents and caravans a hundred metres from the sea, where a bear-like man with a black moustache was cooking stew over a fire. They came to this place every year, 'the last free beach on the shore', where they could live for months without being disturbed. It had the feel of a settlement of castaways after a shipwreck.

Kef was one of the many Turkish words that had drifted into Bulgarian during Ottoman occupation. 'It means good, but it's better than good. It's the biggest good you can feel.' Another Turkish-origin word soon entered my vocabulary: 'You are Nicholas, I am Nikolay. If someone shares a name with you, that means they are your *adash*. You are my adash – we are name-twins.'

Bulgarians had been telling me about July Morning since I'd crossed the border. 'You know the band Uriah Heep?' they asked when I told them where I was from, 'you know the song "July Morning"?' People seemed slightly shocked that I didn't. When it was explained that July Morning was a festival, at which people gathered on the coast to watch the sun rise in the east, I'd assumed the festival had come first – an ancient Bulgarian custom, perhaps pagan in origin – and Uriah Heep had sung about it; though why a British rock group from the 1970s had written a song about an obscure Bulgarian folk tradition was unclear.

From my adash I learnt it was the opposite way round. The 1971 hit, with its generic rock lyrics about the power of freedom and love, became a counter-cultural anthem in

Communist times. In the early 1980s a group of friends had gathered in Varna to sing this song as a subtle act of defiance against Soviet rule. To their surprise – and doubtless to the astonishment of Uriah Heep – the idea took on a life of its own: the final years of Communism had seen hundreds, then thousands of people flocking to the beaches on the last night of June, and after the Iron Curtain fell it remained an annual fixture. Now tens of thousands joined in, there were DJ sets and all-night raves, and – as with any genuine tradition – the younger revellers had mostly forgotten the festival's origins.

At sunset the dwellers of the forest village heated an iron griddle and cooked flatbread smothered in melted sheep's cheese, washed down with wine. There was no big party on the beach, but people huddled in blankets on the tideline and the sand was scattered with isolated fires, pools of music drifting and merging, each group absorbed in its private meanings. I slept a few hours in Nikolay's hammock and woke to see the sky already reddening over the sea, so I hurried down to the only bar to grab a beer and join the others in their quiet waiting.

The sun popped up surprisingly, as things do when you wait for them long enough to forget what you're waiting for. It cleared the horizon in seconds, drenching the waves blood-red. People leapt from their blankets and ran into the sea, dogs splashing after them, as the song blasted from the speakers: 'Here I was on a July morning/ I was looking for love/ With the strength of a new day dawning/ And the beautiful sun/ At the sound of the first bird singing/ I was leaving for home/ With the storm and the night behind me/ And the road of my own...' In many ways it was an unlikely choice for an anthem, with no chorus and five minutes of rambling psychedelic organ riffs, but perhaps this represented the freedom people had been yearning for, a reaction against the straitjacket of totalitarian culture. It left me nonplussed at first, but as the guitars and organs wailed on, as people leapt in the shallows or stood quietly alone, contemplating the brightening sky, my eyes flooded with unexpected tears.

The tears were partly for the song, for what it must have meant. They were partly for my sleeplessness, and for beer first thing in the morning. But they were also for my walk; the realisation hit me now that July was the month I would reach Istanbul.

But not quite yet. Days went by. I slipped all too easily into life on the last free beach, spending mornings in the sea, afternoons outside the bar, evenings around the fire eating charred fish and potatoes, discussing books with Nikolay and various friends who came and went, assembling and dismantling tents and wandering naked between the trees, and nights in the hammock. I kept planning to leave, but it never took much for Nikolay to dissuade me. 'Hey adash, what's the rush? You can stay as long as you like. Stay a month, why not?'

Yet the Strandzha mountains rose to the south, and beyond those mountains was Turkey. When I stopped to focus on it the proximity of my destination caused a near-constant flutter of nerves, butterflies not in my stomach but in my feet, my lower legs, my shoulders, below my collarbones; the parts of my body most affected by walking. It was like being on the verge of meeting a legendary character whose existence I had always known of, but never entirely believed in. Under the laziness of those days ran a current of excitement, of fear, of curiosity, and when the time was right I allowed it to dislodge me. I went for a final swim, said goodbye to my adash, and left the forest village on another cloudless morning. The current gently picked me up and carried me away.

Soon I would have to turn inland. At last I was leaving EU jurisdiction, and the border could only be crossed at designated points: the Rezovo river and a Turkish military zone lay due south, neither of which was passable. But first was a journey along some of the loveliest coastline I'd seen, and I determined not to let the sea out of sight.

This obstinacy almost killed me on the first morning. An unwise decision led me up cliffs I could climb neither up nor down: every piece of rock I grabbed at broke away in my hand, landslides of scree skittered under my boots, and the weight of my rucksack pulled my body off balance. I sent the bag crashing to the beach below and inched down to start again; attempting an easier-looking route, I somehow managed to get myself in an even worse position. Toeholds crumbled under my feet, handholds flaked at the slightest touch, and for one horrible, disbelieving second I felt myself peel away from the wall, dragged towards empty space, before lurching for a thorn-covered stalk I trusted blindly would hold my weight. Using this, I hauled myself to solid ground. My fingers were bloody, my arms scraped raw and my legs too wobbly to walk. When I finally carried on I felt chastened by the land, as if I'd overstepped a line and received a strongly worded admonition.

I became humbler after that, and the coastline followed suit. The next two days were beaches of sand, beaches of stone and beaches of shells, alternated between bare feet and barely functional boots. I followed cliff-top paths, secret shores of rockpooled rocks, and when forced to use the road I was happy to find it potholed, less cared for than before, petering out as it trickled towards the border.

Sinemorets, on the far side of the green Veleka river, was my last halt on the Bulgarian coast. Between two widely spaced rock humps arced a perfect fingernail of sand, the forest spilling jungle-green down the slopes behind. At the northernmost end of the beach the river gurgled into the sea, its current pushing back the waves, and wading across this confluence of waters brought me to a tent-sized spit of sand squeezed between rocks and river. The water hopped with tiny frogs skirting the boundary of salt and fresh; river fish held themselves in the current, pulling against its flow. I let my body drift downriver and be carried into the sea, over smooth stones, flat-bodied on the sandbar, into clearer, cooler depths with the wavering shadows of rocks below. The moon came up red, then orange, yellowing as it climbed, cooling to a soft eggy shade and finally white as bone.

The moment the sea was out of sight, the temperature rocketed. On a path parallel to the river I sweltered westwards into the verdant swathes of the Strandzha National Park, windscreen-wiping sweat off my face, out of my eyes. There were locust trees and waist-high wild grasses, subtropical humidity, an unfamiliar ecology of beeches densely hung with vines, forests of enormous ferns and prehistoric-looking tendrils on stalks. The air swarmed with hornets as sinister as Chinook helicopters, and iridescent insects that weren't dragonflies and looked like flying silverfish, which appeared to move only horizontally. The path became overgrown and I lost all sense of direction. By the time I had found the Veleka again it was covered in dark and slightly nightmarish lily pads; the water had a hallucinatory quality and – was it my imagination? – seemed to be flowing the wrong way from the sea.

It was an alien and threatening new environment. I hated it there, and it seemed to hate me back in equal measure. The track divided, looped back on itself, inexplicably vanished. Under a tin roof in the woods I found an old man asleep, a shepherd without his sheep, and woke him up apologetically to ask for directions. He seemed only too happy to help, but the track he pointed out went the same way as the first, melting away like an illusion, and I had to retrace my steps and wake him up again. This time he walked me deep into the forest, explaining something very slowly and precisely in Bulgarian, saying goodbye when we reached what looked like a confident path. Five minutes after he'd gone, the path disappeared again. I gave up, set my compass west, and plunged into the brush.

For the rest of the day I battled through woodland, mosquitoes hanging off my arms, a walking waterfall of sweat. The rising, plunging hills made going west impossible, so I struck south until I regained the Veleka. It had lost its nightmarish aspect, bubbling clear with deep emerald pools, and I dragged off my sodden clothes and lay in it for a long time, trying to wash the Strandzha off my body.

In the indolent village of Kosti I found kebab, salad and beer. In lazy loops around the plaza cycled a little girl reading from a book balanced on the handlebars, and the old man who shared my table had eyebrows merging into his sideburns, while one hand took the form of a fleshy pincer with two muscular thumbs instead of fingers. The evening road led from there into dense beech forest, winding ever up and on, into the border mountains. I walked surrounded by tiny flies that hovered inches in front of my eyes, as if trying to see in, behaviour that was absolutely maddening. The unvarying tunnel of trees gave me no reason to stop in one place more than any other, so I carried on until exhaustion forced me off the road.

My penultimate night in Bulgaria was marked by a visitation: a creature I had been waiting to see – half with hope and half with fear – since my wanderings in the Carpathian foothills. Lying in my tent at dusk, I heard a crunch of branches that I supposed to be a deer, but as the sound got louder and closer I realised that deer didn't move like that, didn't have that physicality at all. The steps were ponderous, deliberate and accompanied by a noise horribly like heavy breathing. In all my time camping in the wild, I'd never got over the primal fear of hearing something approach my tent, its species and intentions unknown, and that fear gripped me now. It was worse to stay inside and imagine what might be coming, so I crept from my flimsy shelter to peer into the dimness of the forest.

Leaves cracked, sticks bowed and snapped beneath the weight of the thing. The huff of laboured breath increased. A black shape loomed into view and for a second I saw a dog, some brute of a Doberman, but it was bigger than that. It stopped. An ear swung like a fan. Then my eyes pulled into focus and I was looking at the thrusting snout and tushes of a wild boar, like a monster from a fairytale, standing square and facing me head on.

It was utterly unlike a pig; that was my first observation. I could see the coarse hairs on its nape, the muscle of its shoulders. I couldn't believe how large it was: it seemed the size of a small horse. It took a couple more weighted steps, stopped again, considered. We regarded one another. I ran through various options. There was a knife in my bag, but the thought was ludicrous. Probably I should climb a tree, but there were no trees that could be climbed. Perhaps I should throw rocks at it, startle it away. That scenario played out in my mind, and I thought of the many ways that aggression was bound to go wrong; more than anything it seemed rude, in the same way that throwing rocks at a stranger in the street was rude. The idea was almost embarrassing. I understood that if it wanted to attack me – if it had piglets to protect or was simply in a rotten mood – there was absolutely nothing I could do.

In a way that was a relief; the social obligation was on the boar, and all I could do was respond in whatever way seemed appropriate. Its ear swung back. It made a noise like it was clearing its throat. Then it turned away, as if pretending we had not seen each other, and picked another route through the trees.

When I was sure it was gone I armed myself with stick and knife – defences that were patently useless – and hung what little food I had in a tree as far away as I dared. Later that night I heard it again, snuffling and shouldering, but it seemed to be keeping its distance. Unless it was creeping, I thought, half-asleep. Could pigs creep? It seemed unlikely. At least the tent was a symbolic barrier. Did pigs understand symbolic barriers? That seemed unlikely too.

'Every year he kills someone in forest. He is very dangerous,' said the owner of the guesthouse I stayed at in Malko Tarnovo. He had seen me studying the boar's head mounted on the wall: its frozen snarl and protruding tusks were horrific, but the expression of rage was nothing like the look on my boar's face. It was anti-boar propaganda. The use of the personal pronoun, however, put my boar in a different light, and for a second my memory added a murderous gleam to his eye.

I had reached Malko Tarnovo – Small Tarnovo, the diminutive cousin of Veliko Tarnovo, Great Tarnovo, which I had left three weeks before – after a journey of dust and trees, enveloped every step of the way in a halo of face-flies. Unusually for a border town – though the border was some miles distant – it was a pretty and tranquil place, with streets of traditional Revival-era houses, winding steps overgrown with weeds, gardens of pear trees. In the square Roma women were beating the dust with rush brooms, managing somehow to transform menial labour into an act of ownership. Later the Strandza's humidity broke. Rain washed over the mountains, bringing forth a deep green smell and a feeling of relief, as if something had finally been decided.

Mountains and forests rose on all sides, rolling away to Turkey. Not long ago, much of this region was a forbidden military zone; greater perils than wild boars lurked in the trees. Until 1989 the Strandzha was the no-man's land between the Warsaw Pact and NATO, another point where East met West – ideologically and geographically – and anyone entering those forests was likely to end up like the bullet-riddled corpses sinking to the riverbed between the Iron Gates. Even locals, said the guesthouse owner, had needed permits to work here. 'And still it is dangerous. Now illegal immigrants come – North Africans, Afghans, Kurds. Wolves too. Wolves from the mountains...' He gazed wistfully at the wall, as if imagining a mounted wolf's head to accompany his boar, and maybe a couple of immigrants to go with them.

Talk of illegal border crossings made me anxious the next day, on the ten-mile stretch towards the checkpoint, not knowing how the Turkish authorities would react to me walking. There was no particular reason why crossing on foot should be a problem – there was nothing illegal about it – but it seemed to be one of those things that conjured darkly suspicious feelings in many officials. Somewhat anticlimactically, no one looked at me twice. I paid €15 for a visa from a man who looked as Turkish as the Turks in every East London corner shop, got it checked by a pretty young woman who seemed to live her life constantly laughing, passed the sign that read TÜRKİYE, and strolled into my eighth and final country.

The vision of a new flag had instant power. After a continent of tricolours, that white star and crescent moon on a field of red was a statement of altogether different intent, proudly and unmistakably un-European. That, and the portraits of Mustafa Kemal Atatürk – glowering under a tall wool hat, eyebrows flared like a B-movie vampire – shifted everything into a different reality.

Half an hour from the checkpoint, though, I'd almost forgotten I was in another country. Apart from a better-maintained road than any I'd seen in Bulgaria, so wide and so empty of cars it felt almost agoraphobic, nothing in the landscape was different to how it had been for the last three days. The mountains were the same mountains, the rolling forests of oak and beech were the same rolling forests of oak and beech, the birds sung the same songs, and my head had accumulated an identical cloud of face-flies. The highway unspooled down the mountain towards yellow lands beyond, but I struck east down a smaller road, from where I could start to work my way back towards the sea.

A village lay some way ahead: Dereköy, said the sign. Its outskirts appeared the same as any Bulgarian village – whitewashed houses with tiled roofs, chickens pecking in rubbly yards – and the only immediate variation was the white minaret. Women in hijabs and floral skirts were making their way towards the centre, and I followed in their wake. There the change was so abrupt and startling it was like waking up on a film set. Suddenly, I was in a truly different world.

11

Among Tea-Sippers
Turkey

How odd, I thought, as I set off, that the relics of the Turks in Europe, to which, after all, they had brought nothing but calamity, should be distinguished by so much charm and grace: the architecture of houses, the carved wooden ceilings, the baroque plaster work, the wells and fountains, the pillared loggias and above all, these globes and these elegantly ascending pinnacles that ennoble the skyline of the meanest hamlet.

The Broken Road

CURTAINS OF DUST SWOOPED IN THE BREEZE, PARTING TO REVEAL a vision steeped in gradations of beige and brown, saturated in the glare of mid-afternoon sunlight. The air was jaundiced with diesel fumes, a fleet of grimy minivans spluttered up and down the road, and rows of men were sitting under ragged awnings on plastic stools, tinkling spoons in tiny glasses of copper-coloured tea. There were people everywhere, but no sense of movement. Although no one reacted to my appearance I still felt I must be on show, standing there with a baffled expression and sweat dripping off my nose, so I took the obvious course of action and sat down in a chair.

Faces swivelled to take me in, pale eyes peered from under cloth caps, heads nodded in brief assent and turned away again. I offered cigarettes and had cigarettes offered in return, always a shortcut to belonging, and I knew I had reached a certain level of acceptance when a glass of tea appeared at my elbow. Almost at once I found myself imitating the watchers around me, languidly swatting flies away and squinting at the light, stirring sugar cubes to fill the air with the same pleasing chime as the spoon twirled round the glass. Handshakes, I discovered, were followed by the solemn, graceful gesture of touching the palm of your hand to your chest, as if taking the greeting to heart. It was a fresh set of rituals to be learnt.

'A journey is good for the health, physical and mental. These are the words of the Prophet Mohammed, peace be upon him.' The young man who took a seat at my table told me he was a *haji*, one who had taken the pilgrimage to Mecca, so he understood what it meant to be a stranger in a foreign land. He helped me with my first Turkish words – *ben gidiyorum*, 'I'm going', *yürüyerek*, 'on foot' – and after the symbolic third glass of tea my assimilation was almost complete. When I tried to pay, he shrugged the suggestion aside. 'You don't need to say thank you. Even if you are in our village for only half an hour, you are our guest – it is our duty to look after you. For us it is a great honour you are here. The way we see it, you have walked all this way just to meet *us*.'

The sepia tones were gone and colour flooded into the picture as the blue hills of Rumelia – European Balkan Turkey – rolled before me. I plodded east through tended land on a straight path back towards the sea, past willow groves and unknown crops bunched lushly on the slopes, trees flapping in a cooling wind. Every car and motorbike hooted at me as it passed, and I caught glimpses of curious faces and hands raised in greeting.

Another minaret announced the village of Karadere. At once I was back among tea-sippers, tinkling the spoon in my glass under a grapevine-shaded porch, sharing a bench with assorted elders in cardigans and shirtsleeves. I'd eaten nothing since breakfast in Bulgaria, so I used my few clumsy words of Turkish to ask where I could buy food.

Immediately someone went off and returned with a loaf of bread, and someone else was dispatched to fetch a lump of rubbery white cheese, along with a picture of a cow to reassure me of its origin. 'Ne kadar?' 'How much?' I asked. Solemnly they shook their heads and spread their hands out: nothing. As I left the village, another man stopped me and gave me a bar of halva.

The tea was powerful stuff: it fuelled me through a valley of beech trees, up ever-climbing bends, to another identical village of tiled roofs around a pale minaret. Here the tarmac ended and a dirt road continued southeast, parallel to the border. So far I'd only encountered men, and it was a relief when two elderly women in headscarves and bright billowing trousers called me over to ask where I was going. They showed me the road with strident gestures – the right-hand road, the right-hand road – the left, they darkly warned, led to 'Bulgaristan'.

I walked myself to a standstill a few miles past Şükrüpaşa. Buoyed by my delight at the generosity of this land, I must have walked twenty-five miles that day without knowing it. In a tree-shaded meadow I pitched my tent and unwrapped my gifts; the bread was much better than Bulgarian bread, the cheese more rubbery, a cross between feta and cheddar. There was no sound but cicadas, and later the cries of owls.

It was the same in Armutveren, the first village of the morning: tea that no one let me pay for, prayer beads clicking through work-gnarled fingers, faces that somehow managed to scowl and smile at the same time. The old men looked older in Turkey, more bleached and dried and salted. Young boys sat drinking tea in the same way, watching and listening to the adults as if quietly studying to be men. I bought halva bars in a dim shop stacked with cardboard boxes, and as if upset to see me pay, the owner dropped a free pack of biscuits and an orange in my bag.

The heat rippled the road ahead, but there was a sense of water bubbling underneath the land. The roadside fountains were lovingly cared for, each inscribed with the name of the dutiful Muslim who had paid for its construction, and sometimes Koranic verses in flowing Arabic script; either that, or the ubiquitous Atatürk portrait. The significance of his handsome and rather devilish countenance was lost on me in those first few days. I knew he had founded the Turkish republic, in its modern secular form, after the Ottoman Empire dissolved in 1922, but I thought the iconography was simply a nod to the country's history, like a statue of an old war leader in a village square. I had no idea of the extent to which he still divided the nation. The cult of Atatürk lay along the very fault-line of Turkish identity, between Islamic and secular values, orient and occident; those roadside fountains were a place where the two came together.

The village of Sarpdere was deserted; a pile of shoes outside the mosque explained the empty streets. The next village was another tea stop, another congregation of old men, as Turkish wrestling took place on a flickering television. The roads grew tacky with melted tar, the steady build-up of which started to have the effect of resurfacing my boots, actually holding the split soles together, and I made a point of taking a route through the stickiest patches. By the end of the day, descending into the town of Demirköy, I was walking on an inch-thick crust of reconstituted road.

Demirköy was a country town, with almost no sense of division between cows and farmland one moment and banks and internet cafés the next. The call to prayer was belting out from minaret-mounted speakers, and boy waiters in crimson jackets circulated with silver trays of tea in the plaza. In the first restaurant I saw I feasted on delicate dishes of fava beans, chicken, rice, roasted peppers, okra in oily tomato sauce. The flavour spectrum shifted away from

Europe and into the Near East: Ottoman culinary imperi-
alism from the borders of Persia to Greece and the Balkans,
with a hint of Arabia somewhere in between. After weeks
of meals that were mostly variations on a theme – meat and
bread, salad and cheese – it was a revelation.

Buying a SIM card for my phone brought Asia closer
again. I'd purchased local cards in most countries on my
walk – the ease of communication was one of the subtlest
yet profoundest differences between mine and Paddy's
journeys – and had been delighted by how the process reinforced cultural themes. In Germany and Austria, it had
been a simple, slick transaction. In Slovakia, it had involved
queuing for a numbered ticket while gloomy sales assistants
ignored me with Soviet contempt. Here, it took an hour
of drinking tea on a leather sofa in a small, sweaty shop,
while chain-smoking men did something inexplicably complicated involving numerous phone calls; I got the feeling
there was something vaguely illegal going on. Finally they
produced my card, and we all had to have another glass of
tea to cement the transaction. I slept the night in a cheap
hotel, where the muezzin woke me in the morning.

Hours further down the road, a flash of blue appeared
ahead between pine-stubbled hills. After that five-day
inland loop, I had made my way back to the Black Sea.

While it was the same sea, it was a very different coast.
İğneada was a seaside resort, but was emphatically unlike
anything north of the border. Apart from the gleaming
tower of a single luxury hotel, everything was reassuringly
scrappy, with market stalls along the shore selling inflata-
ble toys and flip-flops, fake designer sunglasses, and chaste
swimming garments for Muslim women, a sort of all-in-one
gown with attached hijab. On the beach the Islamic and
secular divide was apparent: half the women were in bikinis
and half enveloped in these gowns, which floated around

them as they bathed with jellyfish-like grace, clinging and billowing with the waves. The sight produced a mirror-world feeling, a sense of altered reality; but the cultural dissonance really struck when I encountered my first Turkish campsite.

My initial impression was of entering a refugee camp, a holiday shanty town sprawled along the shore. People appeared to have packed the entire contents of their homes into cars and caravans and reassembled it here. Spilling from voluminous tents, extended with the addition of tarpaulins strung between the trees, were dining tables, cushioned chairs, carpets laid on the grass, ornate samovar-like teapots bubbling on gas stoves. Women were pounding washing in tubs, hanging clothes to dry on lines, preparing elaborate meals, while men hammered stakes into the ground and erected barricades of plastic sheets in aggressive territorial expansion. There was a sense of furious energy, as if people were digging in for a long campaign. With the crescent-moon flags and Atatürk portraits fluttering above the tents, it looked like the coastal encampment of some nomadic army.

My neighbours regarded my own small tent with scarcely concealed pity. They brought me a table, a chair and a watermelon, and stood around watching as I ate; they clearly didn't understand why anyone would want to go camping without at least a dozen family members. Later I joined them for coffee, shockingly sweet and strong, while they bombarded me with questions I didn't understand. When I said I was walking to Istanbul, it sounded plausible for the first time.

South of İğneada lay the impenetrable swampland of the Longoz, one of Europe's last floodplain forests, a muddle of tributaries, deltas and salt lakes my neighbours warned – I understood from their impassioned gestures – I'd get hopelessly lost in if I attempted to cross. In the morning I took their advice and followed the beach instead, an arc of sand stretching eight miles south, past the coastal salt lakes of Mert Gölü and Saka Gölü, balanced on the bridge of sand between lakes and sea. Away from villages and roads the coast was almost entirely deserted; I encountered no one but a woman in a black abaya chasing a giant yellow beach ball wearily down the tideline. The beach became a desiccated boneyard of washed-up trunks like petrified limbs, littered with the carapaces of brown beetles, and broken shells stabbed my feet, making it easier to wade along the shallows.

Ahead of me, a herd of cows lowed belly deep in the waves. Suddenly they erupted with fear; the air tore apart with a horrifying thunder, a directionless scream that filled the sky, and I stared wildly at the sea, believing something terrible was about to come out of it, poised to drop my bag and run. It was a pair of fighter planes swooping along the coast, banking steeply away at the Bulgarian border. I'd fully expected monsters.

A cowherd was sheltering under a canopy of trees. I asked if I was close to Paniyr, and he bellowed '*sahil, sahil!*' 'beach, beach!' through a mouthful of blood-coloured teeth. Shepherds, cowherds and goatherds invariably shouted at top volume, habituated to yelling at reluctant beasts. His finger pointed dead ahead towards an outcrop of rocks, and sure enough, beyond the next cape, was the campsite I'd been seeking: another holidaying horde in occupation of the shore, defiantly hoisting Atatürk flags against the emptiness of the sea.

South of Paniyr, the beach petered out and the coast became woodier and wilder. Cliffs forced me inland the next day into a forest of coastal oaks, orange dust billowing from the road and coating my legs and feet; the way became less and less certain of itself, growing waist high with weeds, frequently threatening to fade from existence. Wild tortoises pebbled the ground, the baby ones no bigger than eggs, and when I got too close their armoured faces slipped inside their shells with a hiss like an airlock door. The dawdling trails brought me down eventually to a beach between the cliffs, where the waves thunderclapped on the rocks, foaming white as they broke, and the water shone so blue it hurt my eyes. I could stay there for the rest of my life, or not at all. Any compromise would be too painful.

By afternoon I was limping again, my feet torn ragged from sand and shells, and I must have looked a sorry sight as I hobbled through the stone archway into Kıyıköy. The call to prayer sounded triumphantly and the wall was sur-mounted by a giant Atatürk portrait, as if he'd just taken the town in battle. Actually, the image of conquest wasn't far off: the town had formerly been populated by Greeks and Bulgarians expelled in the genocidal population exchanges of the 1920s, as the Turkish nation lurched painfully into existence. It still had the feel of a Greek port village, with its somnambulant air and a sense of precariousness on the edge of the sea, and its overhanging houses, cracked timbers and disintegrating walls gave the impression of a more decrepit Sozopol. The streets were scattered with tiny restaurants where men – always men – sat doing nothing in a way that made it look supremely important, folding and unfolding newspapers and blowing smoke at the ceiling.

At dusk the alleyways bubbled to life, the lanes filling with strolling couples and families parading together, from crookbacked grandmothers in black shawls down to the smallest children. Here was another Turkish ritual – it was a variation of the *corso*, the 'universal evening promenade' Paddy had observed in Hungary, a practice stretching 'all the way from Portugal to the Great Wall of China' – but it was a ritual of community, and one I couldn't be part of. From my hotel balcony, I watched as women dragged tubs from their houses and used their feet to wash clothes, stamping ankle deep in foam. Elderly men clacked backgammon pieces on the benches of Atatürk Park, and a street sweeper was jokingly cleaning a policeman's uniform, straightening his collar and brushing down his epaulettes. People slowly drifted inside as darkness fell. The only things that moved at night were dogs and cats and the shadows of dogs and cats, floating plastic bags and the shadows of floating plastic bags. In the morning the smell of fresh-baked bread filled the narrow lanes, and as I passed beneath the arch, back into the dusty world, I felt as if I'd witnessed the town's entire lifecycle.

That day was a parched and airless journey through a terrain of canyon walls, valleys gulleyed with dry canals, past a mostly evaporated lake where buffalo wallowed up to their chests in the one remaining pool. Jagged cliffs prevented me from hugging the coast as I desired, and for hours I stumbled on broken rocks down an interminable backwoods road, aching for water in the heat, at one point having to climb steeply down and up again where the road had collapsed into a ravine. At Cilingoz sprawled another campsite, this one less like a nomads' encampment and more like a low-density slum, and I was too exhausted to contemplate going any further. As I pitched my tent, two sunburnt twin girls regarded me with expressions of horror, a dripping man covered in hair; I smiled '*merhaba*', 'hello' to them, and they fled.

A violent wind sent white-topped waves crashing into the shore. I joined a few intrepid families fooling around in the surf, but it was too bruising to swim, so I repaired to a shabby bar a little way down the beach. The man who brought my Efes beer turned out to be from Kazakhstan, a student in Istanbul, and he reacted with surprise when I asked if he'd struggled learning Turkish. 'Kazakhstan is a Turkic country. If I go to Uzbekistan, Kyrgyzstan, Turkmenistan, even Uighur region in China, I can understand the people, almost everything they say. We are one family.'

I felt my cultural preconceptions go yawing to the east: suddenly I was no longer on the eastern fringe of Europe, but on the western extremity of a vast, unknown Turkic world. The people chatting at tables around me were, as Paddy observed, 'the westernmost remnants, the last descendants of those shamanist tribes of Central Asia, kinsmen of the all-destroying Mongols, who had surged westwards, turned Muslim ... and finally, by capturing Constantinople, inflicted the greatest disaster on Europe since the sack of Rome.'

Twenty miles further down the coast, after another sweltering day of hills, low forest and the crunch of dust, I was hailed by an imam outside the mosque at Karacaköy. A plump, jolly man resplendent in skullcap and immaculate smock, trousers so baggy they filled like sails in the wind, he sat me down to drink cups of Nescafé and answer questions about where I was from, clumsily translated by assembled witnesses. Did it rain in England? Did people eat rice or bread? Were there any Muslims?

'*Evet, çok,*' I said, 'yes, many.' The imam was overjoyed at the news, his opinion of my country much improved. He was a man in love with smell: from a pocket in his long grey waistcoat he produced a phial and splashed my wrists with perfume that smelt like caramel, chuckling happily all the while, and every so often brushed his fingers over a basil plant on the table, inhaling with great delight. Before I left he donated me a string of plastic prayer beads and showed me how to intone 'Allah' at every breath. He asked where I was going now.

'Istanbul,' I said.

'*Inshallah,*' he smiled, and pressed his hand to his heart.

The Black Sea was at its greenest when I came to it again, scintillating with reflected sun out towards the darker depths, and under eroded cliffs Ormanlı beach swooped away to the village of Karaburun silhouetted on a distant headland. There was a sadness to the sight: tomorrow would be my last coastal walk before turning inland and heading south, cutting the end off the Balkan peninsula to avoid the giant stone quarries blocking the way further east. The sea had accompanied me, on and off, for the last three weeks, and the thought of leaving it for good was quietly appalling.

These feelings didn't last long. A white-moustached man called Rafiq noticed me standing alone, and seemed to feel duty bound as a Turk to interrupt my solitude; within minutes I had joined him outside a corrugated shack on the cliff, where roguish friends were drinking *rakı* and grilling fish over a fire. By now I was well accustomed to these chance invitations, but the delight of such open-hearted encounters never lost its magic. Rakı was liberally dispensed, clouding milky white with water, and I sat with them long into the night while they translated jokes, each punchline ending in uproar and a breathless 'Allah-la-la!' The man to my right laughed so hard he snapped the leg of his plastic chair and toppled into me; the leg of my chair snapped as well and both of us rolled, clutching at each other, almost off the cliff. Rafiq helped us up with howls of laughter and refilled our glasses.

There was a serious side to Rafiq, and even a serious side to the act of drinking. Atatürk, he said gravely, had been a famous drinker. But now the Islamist government of Recep Tayyip Erdoğan wanted to destroy Atatürk's secular legacy, to make Turkey into an Islamic police state. The country was becoming less tolerant, more religiously right-wing. Alcohol was being restricted, drinking banned at public events; the sale of beer had even been prohibited at a recent beer festival.

The jolly imam and drunken Rafiq stood on opposite sides of a widening fault-line. It was the same divide Paddy had glimpsed eight decades before among Turks in Bulgaria: pious Muslims considered Atatürk 'little better than an infidel. The shift to Latin characters from the sacred script of the Koran, strong drink, the dissolution of the dervishes, prayers in the vernacular, the proscription of the fez and the unveiling of women – all this was Satan's work.' This cultural war was raging still, possibly fiercer than before, fuelled by the modern resurgence of political Islam. The Atatürk flags weren't just Atatürk flags, and drinking rakı wasn't just drinking rakı: they were powerful emblems of what kind of country Turkey wanted itself to be.

At sunrise I woke beneath the cliffs, where I'd staked my tent on the sand with lengths of hammered driftwood. The beach was scattered with plastic bottles that glowed like precious stones in the dawn, the tideline deposited with scraps from the Black Sea's many shores. As I walked, I kept coming across foil pouches with lettering in Cyrillic and English containing 'Emergency Drinking Water, Approved by Russian Maritime Register of Shipping'. It wasn't an emergency, but I drank them anyway. It must have been a perilous coast, for what I took to be an island lying a little way offshore turned out to be the rusted hull of a shipwreck, from which divers were sawing away chunks of steel that a salvage team were reeling in with a generator-powered winch. Sinewy, suntanned and tattooed, the men stopped work when they saw me coming and sat me down for homemade lentil soup. At times, the generosity of Turks verged on the ridiculous.

The beach narrowed and widened again, suddenly became thronged with sunbathing hordes of holiday-makers – Istanbulis, I gathered, escaping the metropolis on this sweltering summer weekend – and then a long wooden stairway switchbacked up the cliffs: this was my departure point from the sea. I swam one last time, reluctantly pulled my boots on again, and followed a crowd of men in shorts, women in abayas and women in bikinis up the steps towards the village of Karaburun above.

At the top, Turkish hospitality struck again. I'd just finished plodding up an interminable hill, sweat sodden and hungry, when an expensive car stopped beside me containing a slightly wild-eyed bald man yelling, 'Hello! I can help you!' When I said I didn't need help, he looked even wilder. 'Yes! Food! A place to stay! Please, I can help, I can help!' Eventually I submitted and got into his car. To my intense irritation he did a U-turn and sped back down the hill I'd just climbed, but seconds later the journey ended at a ranch-like house, where a trestle table was being laid under a grapevine-shaded trellis. A barbecue was lit, meat grilled, and assorted grandmothers and cousins took my arrival in their stride, as if the man – his name was Yusuf – came home with strays like me on a regular basis.

During the course of the meal I could never work out how many people were at the table: there must have been fifteen or twenty, but they moved around so rapidly to attack the food from different angles it was impossible to count. There were uncles and aunts, two identical hook-nosed widows with plump hands folded across their bellies, grandchildren and the friends of grandchildren, heaping their plates with food in an organised frenzy. The food was being digested in minutes, and tea and halva followed.

For all his kindness, Yusuf turned out to be a bit of a religious nut. As he sipped his tea, he advanced a theory that was so absurd it was quite impressive: the Taliban were secretly Jewish, as well as being alcoholics, and were part of a complex conspiracy involving the Kurdish Workers' Party, the Zionists and the Rockefeller family. Someone else at the table sighed and rolled her eyes. Her name was Sevim, a slender women in her early twenties, a feminist and an atheist, who represented perfectly Turkey's secular face. She claimed she couldn't live without beer, and that several of her friends were in jail for drugs or politics. She kept the tattoos on her arms covered with long sleeves at the table, just as she concealed from her family the fact that her boyfriend shared her flat. Later, as Yusuf and the grandmothers were talking, she sighed even louder. I asked what the conversation was about. 'Oh, they're just wondering who will go to Paradise. I'm not on the list.'

It wasn't only a generational thing: she had inherited her views from her late grandfather, a lifelong secularist in the Atatürk mould. 'My granddad believed in freedom of thought, modernisation, equality of women. He brought me up always to believe in myself, be strong and speak my mind. Now everything he believed in is being destroyed. Erdoğan's government has declared war on people like me. They hate us, and it's getting worse. In a few years' time, it won't be possible for me to live in this country. I will leave, and I won't come back again.'

At the time I had no way of knowing how much of this was idealism, how much paranoia – there was a sense of desperation, even of tragedy, to Sevim – but her words resonated with those of Rafiq the night before; the undercurrent of frustration clearly ran deep. I would only realise just how deep when anti-government uprisings exploded eleven months later, seemingly bringing the country to the verge of civil war.

A bed was found for me that night. Sevim departed early next morning on a bus to Istanbul, inviting me to come with her. Yusuf offered a lift too – it would only take an hour, he insisted – and it was hard to make them understand how impossible it was for me to accept. Sevim's brother walked me to the road and pointed me in the right direction. As a parting gift, he gave me something to remember his family by. It was a pair of his grandfather's cufflinks.

I had no cuffs to link, or I'd have worn them proudly.

12

To the Golden Horn

Istanbul

The long intervals of silence were like the spreading of rings across a pool; the last vibrations must die away and the surface of the sky be still again before the next phrase, of which each word is a pebble dropped into the void, can launch its new sequence of circles. The muezzin was shifting along his little walled platform to another point of the compass ... The last hoop of prayer had expanded to infinity.

The Broken Road

ISTANBUL LAY THIRTY MILES SOUTH. THE SEA WAS BEHIND ME now. My last glimpse of electric blue was snatched away behind hills, and ahead glowered yellow scrub, lakes that looked almost solid in the heat, bleached minarets lancing on the skyline. The sky was baked void of colour, the greenery dull with heat. On a road of smoking dust three water buffalo stood their ground defiantly until I was upon them, then wheeled away with a twirl of horns. Stone quarries cratered the earth and much of the land was fenced, with plots of unhappy-looking forest corralled into pens. The only option through these enclosures was along the motorway – empty apart from trucks ferrying heaps of rock – and I traced the hard shoulder to a tarmac horizon undulating in the morning glare.

It seemed as if all the blisters that hadn't afflicted me in seven months chose this penultimate day to attack, as if sensing the imminence of my destination. They burst with a burning pain and the skin rubbed raw. My feet were coated in thick grey dust, which had mixed to form mud with the sweat; my toes looked like artefacts from a volcanic eruption. There wasn't much to be done, just as there wasn't much to be done about my chafing collarbones, my aching back and shoulders. My face, neck and arms were deep brown, the rest of my body grub white. My beard was ridiculous. My clothes looked like I had stolen them from a corpse. I must have resembled a scarecrow lurching along the verge.

I found shade and an ice-cold drink in a truckers' cafe off the road, a tarpaulin stretched from an old VW camper over plastic chairs. Thick-armed men offered lifts, and when I declined they looked perplexed, but the owner gave me a free packet of biscuits as I left. The trucks shuttled back and forth all afternoon on the motorway, and the truckers waved and blasted horns as they thundered past. It was a victory parade, but I kept getting left behind.

A few miles on, my eyes reached Istanbul.

Somehow, I hadn't expected skyscrapers; tower blocks maybe, but not skyscrapers. Nevertheless, there they were, a cluster of abstracted rectangles so far off they almost vanished if I looked at them too hard; it had been the same with mountain ranges. For a moment I thought perhaps it might be some other city, but there was no other city. It was difficult to know what to do in this situation.

I felt something should be attempted. I threw back my head and whooped, but the sound quickly faded. I didn't particularly feel like whooping. I didn't feel like doing anything – I didn't know how to do anything – except walk on in the silence of the road. When the skyscrapers dipped behind the landscape, it was almost a relief.

An afternoon's limp brought me into Göktürk, an affluent satellite town within a commuter's morning drive of the metropolis proper. Nothing about the place was real:

not the stacked apartments with glass balconies, not the sprinkled artificial lawns, not the signs advertising valet parking, and especially not the garden of the Caffè Nero in which I awkwardly unwrapped the mud-caked sock from my mud-caked foot to apply my last plaster, which kept slipping off in the sweat. The customers were young professionals with shiny hair and BlackBerrys; conspicuously, no one here offered to buy me tea.

In an air-conditioned supermarket a security guard tailed me through the aisles as I filled my basket with fizzy drinks and fruit. Past gated communities, country clubs, stores selling kitchenware and ceramics, I left the town through the arches of an ancient aqueduct and didn't stop until Kemerburgaz, where there was another. It was a functionally elegant, elegantly functional construction, spanning the road across a forested valley, and I climbed to its second tier of arches and walked until I found a path into oaks and pines. In my tent I collapsed to the lullaby of engines.

When I opened my eyes, I felt more used than I'd ever felt before. My bones ached, my organs ached, my feet were bloody and they had dirt in the wounds. Thirty weeks of walking had waited till now to catch up with me, accumulated punishment for every mile I'd travelled. A dog wandering in the woods barked at my tent and fled in fright as I emerged, almost sick with exhaustion, for my last eleven miles.

At walking speed, arrival is a process that happens only gradually, and bits of me staggered in at different times. My eyes had got there the day before with that glimpse of skyscrapers, but that arrival was no more real than an abstract thought. My mind would reach its destination in synaptic fits and starts over the next few days, as my brain slowly caught up with the fact that my feet had stopped. As

for my body itself, it was difficult to know. At some indefinable point the patches of woodland petered out, and
the shapeless spillage of industrial parks, cement factories
and auto-repair shops began to coalesce into what felt like
outermost suburbs. There were mountains of gravel and
tyres behind razor-wire fences, chained hounds gnashing
their teeth in yards, then stucco walls, television studios,
traffic signs, apartment blocks clumped on a hill. Under
the concrete legs of a flyover bigger than any aqueduct, I
pushed my way into the refrigerated cool of a petrol station
café. I ordered coffee and sat by the window, watching the
traffic lanes and the trees. A cement mixer waited at a red
light. There was a pneumatic drill. Mostly, I felt like crying.

A businessman paused by my table. 'Hello! What are
you doing? I saw you walking by the road.'

'I've walked here from Holland.'

'Oh,' he said.

As an epitaph for a walk, I kind of liked it.

~~~~~

'Strangely, even in his diary, he recounts nothing of the
leftover Byzantine glories of the old capital,' writes Artemis
Cooper of Paddy's arrival on the first day of 1935. 'Perhaps
the end of his journey was weighing on him with the
traveller's bewilderment of at last reaching his goal.' The
entries published in *The Broken Road* read like hasty postcard scrawls: 'A lovely day, the sun shining on the Golden
Horn, and the town full of a hundred sounds ... Went to
Stambul bazaar, fascinating, look at thousands of carpets,
swords and yataghans etc. I bought a cigarette holder with
amber mouthpiece ... wandered round again by docks; what
quantities of cats!' These fleeting and disconnected impressions capture that bewilderment, suggesting less a journey's
conclusion than its confused fragmentation. In that petrol

station café I experienced the same: not so much a feeling of triumph as profound perplexity.

But my journey hadn't finished yet: I couldn't take off my broken boots until I'd reached that legendary, impossibly romantically named waterway leading to the continent's end. So I drained my coffee and walked on; it was up to me to fill in the gaps that Paddy had left.

There was no symbolic arch, no gate through which to pass. Constantinople's ancient walls were broken by its conquerors in 1453 – the momentous arrival of the Turks – and every car pouring into the city was a fresh reinvasion. At the end of my predecessor's journey Istanbul wasn't much bigger than the Byzantine capital of five centuries before, and its population only numbered in the hundreds of thousands. Now it was a megalopolis of over thirteen million souls, one of a new breed of global super-cities. Indescribably vaster and more complex, its architecture had long been tumbling outwards from its ancient core, replicating and expanding; as I walked, it multiplied around me like a pathogenic growth. There were merciless concrete walls, biscuit-dry under the sun, and functional modern minarets that looked like telecommunications infrastructure. Pedestrians strolled head-on into seething roadways and the traffic had a way of resolving itself around them. Girls in Beşiktaş football shirts smoked and texted as they walked; there were women in sunglasses and chadors, women in sunglasses and miniskirts. Air-conditioners rattled and wept outside fluorescent-lit cafés.

Having breached the architectural outlands, the first and second circles of the city, I saw the buildings grow grander while keeping their crumminess intact. A helicopter roared overhead, swooping low over satellite dishes and alighting fussily on a hotel. In a shop-lined boulevard I swerved into a clothing store and came out wearing a pair

of new jeans, dumping the trousers I'd worn for months –
since the snow-covered summit of Mount Retezat – uncere-
moniously in a bin. They would become part of Istanbul's
landfill, another layer in the sediment of the city.

Soon came an older, seedier district, its buildings gutted
and vandalised, with flashes of rubble-filled rooms sweet
with the pungency of piss, old prostitutes gazing from doorways with expressions of worked-in anguish. There were
Greek Orthodox churches, a half-demolished house front,
a tree growing inside a room; then pretty sunlit and shaded
streets, bougainvillea cascading down walls, visions of cool
courtyards where men in clean shirts clacked backgammon
pieces as rapidly as prayer beads. The air smelt of mint and
hot plastic.

The labyrinthine lanes that followed were a hubbub of
conversation, a warren of outdoor cafés and bars, live with
the rattle of drums and the tremble of bouzoukis. Vats of
ayran sloshed and churned. Vendors sold fresh mussels
from carts, and the ornate copper stands of shoeshine men
gleamed like Ottoman treasure caskets. The city's past was
peeling back a decade or two with every mile; layer by layer
I approached the core at which Paddy had arrived.

On Istiklal, the city's great commercial street, an antiquated German streetcar slid through the pedestrian
throng like a ship parting the sea. Fez-hatted vendors
twirled Turkish ice cream on long silver scoops, and window displays of Turkish delight were garishly illuminated.
The rangy African men hawking fake designer wallets were
the same rangy African men to be found in cities from here
to Lisbon, working their way ever northwards into richer
climates. Down one side street came a glimpse of a water-
cannon-mounted armoured truck, and riot police with
teargas guns waited, bored and businesslike, while a noisy
demonstration catalysed nearby. It was an image beamed

back from the future: in a year these streets would be the scene of running battles between police and protestors, and the paving stones on which I walked would be broken up for missiles.

The sky ahead was lightening. There was a sense of expanding space. And then between buildings came a flash of blue, a glitter of bright water. Tumbling down the final hill, past the fairytale turret of Galata Tower – scooters rumbling down slabbed streets, overloaded carts clattering up them, heaved by dripping men in vests – only trams and traffic lanes now lay between me and my arrival. White ferryboats churned their way. As if on cue, the sky flourished with gulls.

There was a brief, dramatic intervention. The traffic stopped, policemen moved to block the crowds, and a motorcade of black limousines slid past in a strobing of lights, flanked by motorcycle outriders, professional tough guys leaning from windows with submachine guns at the ready. 'Erdoğan,' said a woman next to me when I asked what was going on: the prime minister himself, probably making for his office near Dolmabahçe Palace. With unreal speed the convoy was gone, a missed beat in the city's pulse; the policemen moved aside and the crowds flooded over the road, carrying me with them.

Over the last seven months I'd reached this point many times, my imagination outpacing my body, flowing ahead through mysterious landscapes that existed only in Paddy's words, and stopping abruptly at a postcard image of minarets, domes and water. Now that image became real. In three-pronged convergence my mind, body and imagination arrived at their destination together, gaining the same place at the same time, triangulating my position precisely on the map.

There was the clutter of the old town – the Constantinople that Paddy, with typical romantic perversity, had always insisted was his goal – across whose skyline Ottoman mosques seemed to crawl like gigantic scarabs. Huger and stranger than I'd envisaged, too big to look remotely real, they rose in a dividing and subdividing propagation of domes, bubbles popping out of bubbles, minarets that had the appearance of antennae or insect legs; a bizarrely arachnid, crustacean architecture that told me, more than anything else, that I'd arrived at a wholly different place from where I'd started.

And there, at last, was the Golden Horn, a radiant waterway flecked with sun, fishermen reeling in scores of silver fish from Galata Bridge. At the inlet's mouth lay the Bosphorus, the strait between two continents, high over which the Bosphorus Bridge soared into the sky. Beyond that, in a haze of sea mist, sparkled the Asian shore. There was nothing left of Europe.

It was July 16. I'd been walking for two hundred and twenty-one days. With the twists and turns the road had taken it was impossible to say how far; two and a half thousand miles was my rough calculation. I'd passed through eight countries and three seasons, followed two major rivers and dozens of minor ones, and crossed three mountain ranges, one of them twice. I'd picked up fragments of seven languages, and met more people than I could remember. I'd walked through three books: two real, one imagined. I'd worn one pair of boots.

With great satisfaction now, I saw that these boots had fallen apart, self-destructing on that final schlepp with almost suicidal intent. Supergluing patches of rubber over the cracks had worked for weeks, but the cracks had lengthened now, branched, run together. The bituminous coating of melted road was stuck with gravel and flaking away. There were holes in both the soles, and every stone and piece of grit jabbed the balls of my feet, bringing them into intimate contact with the landscape. The boots were no longer waterproof, no longer dustproof, no longer road-proof; they were barely even boots any more, and taking them off – as I did now, sloughing the foul tubes of my socks – was like taking off a particularly disgusting part of my own body.

A ship's horn sounded one long blast and a freighter grumbled down the strait from the direction of the Black Sea, heading towards the Sea of Marmara and the Mediterranean. The mosques lit up like gentle grubs as the sun went down over Europe. In gathering blueness the hard lines and edges imperceptibly faded, melting into the air, as if already retreating into memory. The cry of gulls was joined by the cry of minarets, the sound swelling hugely over the city, merging the continents.

The smell of engine grease and brine. The slop of oily water. The tarmac warm under my feet. In perfect contentment, with nowhere to go, I stopped. I simply stopped.

Walking the Unbroken Road

PADDY'S INTENTION WAS TO TRAVEL LIKE 'A TRAMP, A PILGRIM OR a wandering scholar', and in many ways my walk went along similar lines. Sleeping rough and general dishevelment were testaments to trampiness, and while I wouldn't call myself a scholar, those seven months on foot were an education in culture, language, landscape, history and other people's lives. As for being a pilgrim, the journey involved physical hardship, occasionally mental hardship, the retracing of a route laid down by long-departed feet, and a dialogue with a somewhat ghostly presence; one occasionally glimpsed or guessed at, but mostly existing somewhere between fact and imagination.

I had set out in search of change, but perhaps the most striking revelations were the deep continuities between our times. Suburban sprawl, motorways and hydroelectric dams may have irrevocably altered landscapes, and – as suggested early in my journey – silence was often compromised by the roar of cars and planes, but Europe's wilder edge seldom felt far away. Even in the most urban and industrialised countries of my walk, it only took a touch of snow to revive a sense of fairytale magic, and I discovered wonder in the most unexpected places. Due to the effects of urbanisation, rural areas often seemed emptier than in my predecessor's age; deer, polecats, beavers and boars all made their appearances and, in the Carpathians, wolves and bears lurked close enough. At least one wild population – the Caucasian jackals I heard in Bulgaria – have enjoyed a population boom in the last fifty years, and didn't exist in anything like current numbers in Paddy's time.

Similarly in human terms, everything and nothing had changed. The liquidation of the aristocracy throughout

Eastern Europe, the erosion of Roma culture, the ethnic cleansing of Bulgarian Turks and the horrific fate of Jewish communities everywhere were indeed momentous changes; yet beyond these larger tragedies, people's lives, with their everyday quibbles and concerns, hadn't greatly altered. Attitudes had remained fixed, especially in the countries of the East, where Communism hadn't destroyed them but sent them into hibernation – and, in some cases, encouraged them – ready to burst out fifty years later as bellicose as before. This went for good as well as bad: in every country of my walk I encountered kindness and generosity that Paddy would have recognised, and, in Romania at least, a thriving peasant culture deeply rooted in tradition.

People often assumed that walking alone must have been dangerous, and never tired of warning me about the perils ahead. But apart from an isolated stone-throwing incident – negligible in the grand scheme of things – the worst treatment I ever received was indifference or mild suspicion. Not once did I feel threatened by another human being, though the same cannot be said for dogs. The general rule seemed to be that the further east I travelled, the people got nicer and the canines got nastier.

One question I was frequently asked is whether I got lonely or bored; the answer is a resounding 'no'. Though I often went for days without talking to anyone but myself – and, of course, with the shade of Paddy – it was an intensely social time, sometimes exhaustingly so. Between boundlessly generous hosts, friendships struck up on the road and incomprehensible conversations with drunks across the continent I never felt alone for long, and my times of true solitude – sleeping out beneath the stars or gazing down from snowcapped peaks – were ones to cherish.

As for boredom, even on the most monotonous stretches of the journey – the Great Hungarian Plain springs to mind

– gradual but continuous changes kept my mind on the move. With practice I learnt to become aware of a different order of fascinations, from incremental shifts in topography to the bodies of animals killed on the road, scraps of rubbish that hinted at local tastes in food and drink, the trees and plants along the verge, the insects at my feet. Increasingly, walking itself became a source of happiness, something to be enjoyed in its own right, bringing an intensity of experience and a sensual awareness of surroundings that grew more addictive by the mile. On the few occasions I resorted to lifts or public transport I felt I had cheated myself, missed out on some small but significant wonder I would never have the chance to see again.

My strategy of setting out in deliberate naïvety of what lay ahead delivered more surprises than I ever could have wished for. Most of the revelations of this walk came about not through expectation – and certainly not through planning – but through unpredictable encounters, happenstance and good fortune, and if I'd departed from the Hook of Holland one day earlier or later it would have been another journey altogether, filled with different stories. To misquote Heraclitus, 'no man ever steps on the same road twice'; future wanderers on these trails will experience something else again. Maybe in another eight decades, another pair of boots will follow.

DEC " 2014

Acknowledgements

Special thanks must be given to Artemis Cooper, Andrew Hayward and Gary Pulsifer for encouragement and enthusiasm, Nicholas Brealey, Ruth Killick and Sally Lansdell for bringing this book into being, Michael Geoghegan, and Tom Sawford, who runs the blog at patrickleighfermor. wordpress.com. Also to Anna Ilsley, and all beloved friends and family who waved me goodbye and welcomed me home again.

Much of this journey was funded by the crowdfunding website WeDidThis. Generous financial support came from James Alpass, Dr Ali Alsam, Roger de Brantes, Paola Fanutza, Dot and Norman Heyman, Caroline Hunt, Jennifer Hunt, Ron and Alisa Hutchinson, Marga Mariño, Nicholas Robinson, Uwe Schober, Donna Simpson, Dr Tom Stafford, Colleen Toomey, Sue and Dudley Thomas and Ed Whiting. I'd also like to thank Joseph Hughes for unfailing technical support, the Globetrotters Club for buying me the boots I destroyed, and Dark Mountain and Ether Books for publishing my writing from the road.

Lastly, thank you to everyone – in Europe and beyond – who offers kindness and hospitality to wandering strangers.